ANCIENTS AND MODERNS

General Editor: Phiroze Vasunia, Reader in Classics, University of Reading

How can antiquity illuminate critical issues in the modern world? How does the ancient world help us address contemporary problems and issues? In what ways do modern insights and theories shed new light on the interpretation of ancient texts, monuments, artefacts and cultures? The central aim of this exciting new series is to show how antiquity is relevant to life today. The series also points towards the ways in which the modern and ancient worlds are mutually connected and interrelated. Lively, engaging, and historically informed, *Ancients and Moderns* examines key ideas and practices in context. It shows how societies and cultures have been shaped by ideas and debates that recur. With a strong appeal to students and teachers in a variety of disciplines, including classics and ancient history, each book is written for non-specialists in a clear and accessible manner.

BROOKE HOLMES is Assistant Professor of Classics at Princeton University. Her first book, *The Symptom and the Subject: The Emergence of the Physical Body in Ancient Greece*, was published in 2010. A co-edited volume, *Dynamic Reading: Studies in the Reception of Epicureanism*, was published by Oxford University Press in 2012. She has also written on Lucretius, the *Iliad*, Euripides' *Heracles*, Plato and Aelius Aristides' *Sacred Tales*.

ANCIENTS AND MODERNS

GENDER
ANTIQVITY AND ITS LEGACY

BROOKE HOLMES

OXFORD
UNIVERSITY PRESS

OXFORD
UNIVERSITY PRESS

Oxford University Press, Inc., publishes works that further Oxford University's objective of
excellence in research, scholarship, and education.

Oxford New York
Auckland   Cape Town   Dar es Salaam   Hong Kong   Karachi
Kuala Lumpur   Madrid   Melbourne   Mexico City   Nairobi
New Delhi   Shanghai   Taipei   Toronto

With offices in
Argentina   Austria   Brazil   Chile   Czech Republic   France   Greece
Guatemala   Hungary   Italy   Japan Poland   Portugal   Singapore
South Korea   Switzerland   Thailand   Turkey   Ukraine   Vietnam

First published by I.B.Tauris & Co. Ltd. in the United Kingdom

Published by Oxford University Press, Inc.
198 Madison Avenue, New York, New York 10016

www.oup.com

Oxford is a registered trademark of Oxford University Press

Library of Congress Cataloging-in-Publication Data

Holmes, Brooke, 1976-
Gender : antiquity and its legacy / Brooke Holmes.
p. cm. — (Ancients and moderns)
Includes bibliographical references and index.
ISBN 978-0-19-538082-8 (hardcover : alk. paper) — ISBN 978-0-19-538083-5 (pbk. : alk.
paper) 1. Sex role—Europe—History—To 1500. 2. Sex—Europe—History—To 1500. 3.
Civilization, Greco-Roman. 4. Rome—Civilization. 5. Greek literature, Hellenistic—History
and criticism. I. Title.
HQ1075.5.E85H55 2012
305.30938—dc233   2011031155

ISBN (HB): 978-0-19-538082-8
ISBN (PB): 978-0-19-538083-5

Typeset in Garamond Pro by Ellipsis Digital Limited, Glasgow
Printed and bound in Great Britain by CPI Group (UK) Ltd, Croydon, CR0 4YY

CONTENTS

ACKNOWLEDGEMENTS

This book has benefited enormously from the generosity of a number of friends and colleagues. I'm especially grateful to the two anonymous readers for their extremely thoughtful and useful remarks and criticisms. Violaine Sebillotte Cuchet, Joshua Katz, David Kaufman, Miriam Leonard, Phiroze Vasunia, Nancy Worman and Froma Zeitlin read an earlier version of the manuscript either in part or in full and the final product has been much improved by their comments. I am much indebted to Phiroze as well for all his guidance during the book's trajectory from proposal to published product. Josine Blok, Caroline Bynum and Helen King generously offered advice and bibliography at crucial points, for which I'm very grateful. Finally, I would like to thank the Fondation Hardt pour l'étude de l'Antiquité classique, the American Council of Learned Societies, and the Elias Boudinot Bicentennial Preceptorship for providing support during the writing and preparation of the manuscript.

FOREWORD

Ancients and Moderns comes to fruition at a propitious moment: 'reception studies' is flourishing, and the scholarship that has arisen around it is lively, rigorous, and historically informed; it makes us rethink our own understanding of the relationship between past and present. *Ancients and Moderns* aims to communicate to students and general readers the depth, energy, and excitement of the best work in the field. It seeks to engage, provoke, and stimulate, and to show how, for large parts of the world, Greco-Roman antiquity continues to be relevant to debates in culture, politics, and society.

The series does not merely accept notions such as 'reception' or 'tradition' without question; rather, it treats these concepts as contested categories and calls into question the illusion of an unmediated approach to the ancient world. We have encouraged our authors to take intellectual risks in the development of their ideas. By challenging the assumption of a direct line of continuity between antiquity and modernity, these books explore how discussions in such areas as gender, politics, race, sex, and slavery occur within particular contexts and histories; they demonstrate that no culture is monolithic, that claims to ownership of the past are never pure, and that East and West are often connected together in ways that continue to surprise and disturb many. Thus, *Ancients and Moderns* is intended to stir up debates about and within reception studies and to complicate some of the standard narratives about the 'legacy' of Greece and Rome.

All the books in *Ancients and Moderns* illustrate that *how* we think about the past bears a necessary relation to *who* we are in the present. At the same time, the series also seeks to persuade scholars of antiquity that their own pursuit is inextricably connected to what many generations have thought, said, and done about the ancient world.

Phiroze Vasunia

INTRODUCTION

Gender has become one of the defining terms of our era: endlessly talked about, analysed ad infinitum and hotly debated. It seems to show up everywhere you look, not just in college classrooms and academic journals but in CNN Entertainment updates on 'gender-bending celebs', dispatches from the genderqueer revolution, debates at the United Nations over how to talk about the status of women – the list goes on. The concept of gender has always been controversial. Throw in its rapid ascent, and it's no surprise that even early advocates have pushed back in recent years, complaining that gender's critical edge has grown dull. Like any star phenomenon, it's suffered from overexposure. But gender is now too deeply rooted in the cultural consciousness, at least in the English-speaking world, to be easily set aside. Whatever the uncertainties about its future, all the evidence points to its continued hold on who we imagine ourselves to be, even (maybe even especially) when we refuse to identify ourselves according to gender.

Gender: Antiquity and Its Legacy is based on the conviction that the debate about the future of gender needs to be based on an understanding of its past. The reader at this point, noticing that the book in his or her hands is part of a series called 'Ancients and Moderns', probably expects a rehearsal of the ancient Greek and Roman origins of gender. Things turn out to be a bit less straightforward. For as it turns out, what we call gender is a fairly recent concept. It's not that people in ancient Greece and Rome didn't talk and think and argue about the categories of male and female, masculine and feminine and the nature and extent of sexual difference.

1

They did, in ways both similar to and very different from our own. The problem is that they didn't have the concept of gender that has grown so influential in the humanities and the social sciences over the past four decades. What's more, just assuming that they did have it or something like it can make us blind to other, potentially troublesome, assumptions that dog our thinking about gender.

Nothing that I have just written prevents us from using the concept of gender as a tool of historical analysis. In fact, some of the most important work on classical antiquity has come out of the study of ancient Greek and Roman representations of men, women and sexual difference. The following pages couldn't have been written without this work. Over the course of the book I make regular forays into the ancient evidence to see what it might have to say about the issues that fall under the contemporary rubric 'gender'.

But this is not a book that sets out to apply the category of gender – and the related categories of 'sex' and 'sexuality' – to the past. Rather, it tracks some of the most consequential encounters between 'the ancients' – a tough term that I come back to at the end of this introduction – and discussions and debates about gender from the 1970s to the present. Why take such an approach? In recent years, a number of general overviews of gender have appeared in print. It's also become easy for non-specialists to find surveys of sex, gender and sexuality in ancient Greece and Rome. (Examples from both groups can be found in the 'Suggestions for Further Reading' section.) What has been missing is a book that examines how strategic engagements with classical antiquity have contributed to the conceptualisation of gender as a modern and postmodern category of analysis; that is to say, a book that follows the ways in which the ancients have been used over the past forty years to help us formulate the very *idea* of gender. If we can get a sense of the entanglement of the classical past in the field of gender studies, we might be able to gain some insight into how we can think differently not just about the history of gender but also about its future.

Of course, as I have already pointed out, we can hardly understand this history without at least some sense of the ancient material that lies at its heart. I have aimed, accordingly, to keep that material in the foreground as much as possible. It goes without saying that in a short book it's impossible to be comprehensive. I can't even begin to do justice to the evidence under discussion. Those looking for broader and more in-depth approaches to the ancient evidence should seek out the surveys that I just mentioned. My own highly selective interventions in the ancient material necessarily reflect choices that have already been made in the game-changing discussions of ancient Greek and (less often) Roman texts in feminist and gender theory. Still, they aren't simply dictated by these choices. When I do return to the original sources, I have tried to clarify why 'the ancients' have been interpreted in sometimes very different ways by teasing out something of the complexities in our sources, especially in cases where those complexities have failed to register in contemporary debates. My overarching goal has been to move away from narrow interpretations of 'the ancients' either as radically different from us *or* as the origin of everything Western to promote a more nuanced approach to the Greco-Roman past as a resource for thinking about gender in the twenty-first century.

The concept of gender, as I've just said, is recent. So what is it and where does it come from? Simone de Beauvoir famously wrote: 'one is not born, but rather becomes, woman'.[1] De Beauvoir's groundbreaking feminist text, *The Second Sex*, was first published in French in 1949 (and translated into English in 1952). But the term 'gender', which had long been associated with grammar, only started to move towards what she was describing in the later 1950s and 1960s. At first, 'gender' was used to differentiate 'psychological' sex or the 'sex of the mind' from 'biological' sex or the 'sex of the body', primarily in psychoanalytic and psychiatric circles. While the idea of a 'gender identity' didn't initially imply a theory of origins, over the course of the 1960s, especially in America, gender increasingly came to be understood as the result of environmental and cultural conditioning in early childhood in an echo of de Beauvoir: one is *made* into a girl or a boy. The assumption was that gender, at least in the early stages of life, is malleable, responsive to external cues. The consequences of such a situation were potentially dire. For if gender in childhood is unstable, there's room for unhappy deviations (the feminine boy, the masculine girl). By the same token, though, there's also room for correction. The 1960s thus witnessed the rise of 'gender identity' clinics designed to help waywardly gendered children reconcile their sense of identity with the sex of their body.

In the late 1960s and 1970s, the malleability of gender was enthusiastically taken up by feminism, undergoing a radical reconceptualisation in the process. In the hands of feminists, the character of gender became, as Kate Millett wrote in 1970, 'overwhelmingly *cultural*'.[2] What the charged word 'cultural' came to stand for was the range of ways we develop gender identities through socialisation: by being dressed in pink or blue, princess costumes or baseball caps; by the roles we assume at school, at home and in the workplace; by the idealised representations of men and women that saturate our environment; by the micro-adjustments we make when we walk down the street or look in the mirror, unselfconsciously conforming to the norms we see around us.

The feminist appropriation of gender didn't just extend the impact of gender as a concept. It transformed its implications. For millennia, cultures around the world have subordinated women to men. They've often done so in the name of nature, turning the 'raw material' of women's biological role in reproduction into a gendered social role through variations on what's been called the 'sex/gender system'. But as soon as feminist theorists recognised that the lived identities of men and women and the social roles that they have been made to play aren't determined by male and female bodies but, rather, by specific cultures of oppression, they opened the door to a realm of new possibilities. Change the ways that gender operates in a given society and you can change what it means to be a man or a woman and, indeed, what it feels like to identify as male or female. The idea of gender became synonymous with the possibility that women, as well as men, could be liberated from the constraints of gender norms. It was suddenly imaginable that the two sexes might even dissolve into multiple and fluid genders.

For someone dreaming of just such a world, are the ancient Greeks and Romans anything more than a ball and chain? Why *should* classical antiquity and its weighty humanist legacies matter to those committed to creating a future not only unsaddled by the past but also increasingly spoken of, at least in some theoretical circles, as posthuman? To better grasp the strategy that this book adopts to answer the question, it's worth taking a brief look at how the fates of gender studies and the study of ancient Greece and Rome have been intertwined over the years.

Before the early 1970s, the discussion of the sexes and sexual difference in Greco-Roman antiquity was, more properly, a discussion about ancient women, isolated from their male counterparts and excluded from mainstream historiography. The field was dominated by a debate that had been going on at least since the Enlightenment about the status of women in antiquity and especially in Athens. Were ancient women maltreated by a less civil society? Or was the Athenian attitude towards women – namely, that women are to be respected for the virtues specific to them but kept subordinate – much like our own 'civilised' view of the subject?

Everything changed with the rise of feminism within the academy. Women were legitimised as subjects of history 'properly' speaking. Encouraged by the new critical climate, classical scholars started to look for material and textual evidence that could offer a window onto the lives of ancient women. In 1973, the new research agenda got an airing at the first conference on the subject of women in antiquity, held at the State University of New York in Buffalo. The papers were published later that year in a landmark special issue of the journal *Arethusa*.[3] Sarah Pomeroy's breakthrough study, *Goddesses, Whores, Wives, and Slaves: Women in Classical Antiquity*, appeared two years later.[4]

The next three decades witnessed further transformations of the field. As the concept of gender gained traction in the humanities and social sciences through the 1980s and 1990s, ancient historians became increasingly interested in an evolving set of research topics: the construction of sexual difference in classical antiquity; the interaction between the category of gender and other culturally significant concepts; the ideals of masculinity; and the study of ancient sexuality. The ascent of gender was not universally embraced. For some feminist classicists, gender studies threatened the study of women in antiquity by focusing too much attention on *representations* of women in male-authored texts while pushing the real lives of ancient women back into the shadows. The arguments that research on gender is a distraction from the realities of ancient life haven't gone away. But neither have they blocked the onward march of gender in the field.

So gender studies can boast of impressive gains within the study of classical antiquity. Has antiquity, in turn, made a mark on the study of gender? One thing that ancient historians, especially those influenced by the methods of anthropology and cultural history, have brought to the table in recent years is a sharpened sense of the differences between ancient and contemporary ideas of masculinity, femininity, male and female and sexuality. Their work has helped strengthen the very viability of gender as a category of analysis. After all, it's in part by studying the past that we become more attuned to the contingency of our own gendered norms. Herodotus was already well aware in the fifth century BCE that ideas and practices stop looking natural when you put them next to those taken for granted by another culture. The classical past holds considerable power to decentre us by forcing us to acknowledge the historical specificity of our unspoken assumptions about sexual difference, sexuality, gender norms and the gendering of power.

But the ancients, for better or worse, have held more than anthropological interest for the moderns. They've also long played a pivotal role in grand narratives about the origins, structure and values of Western civilisation. When these stories have turned to constructions of gender in ancient Greece and Rome, they've rarely been uplifting. The earliest account in Greek of how the cosmos came into being, Hesiod's *Theogony* (c. eighth century BCE), systematically subordinates maternal generation to patriarchal order. The Athenian democracy, many feminists have argued, is built on – and perhaps even defined by – the exclusion of women, although recent work has complicated these claims. The men who competed in the high-stakes arenas of power in Republican and Imperial Rome were haunted by charges of effeminacy, the weapon of choice for rhetorical assassination.

Much of Greek philosophy, starting with Plato and Aristotle, is arguably founded on the denigration of a feminine principle identified with materiality, bodies and emotions in the name of a masculine principle residing in a rational soul in harmony with the cosmic order. From this perspective, we should care about the ancients not because they're alien but because we're still dealing with the 'seamier legacies' of antiquity, among which patriarchal bias and systemic misogyny rank high.[5]

But we can go further still in defining the relevance of classical antiquity to late twentieth- and early twenty-first-century debates about gender. 'The ancients', as I suggested above, have informed the very conceptualisation of gender in the past few decades. Again and again, philosophers and cultural historians interested in the genealogy of ideas about sexual difference and sexuality in the West have turned to Greek and Roman texts as starting points. There are problems with uncritically accepting the category of 'the ancients' (or 'the Greeks') handed down to us by canonical thinkers such as Hegel, Nietzsche and Heidegger. But we can't get around the fact that classical antiquity has operated as a privileged site for conceptualising sex, sexuality and gender in the present. And the ancients exercise a fascination that goes far beyond the at times arid theoretical debates about gender. Figures from Greek mythology like Demeter and Antigone are more popular than ever among novelists, playwrights, philosophers, poets, artists, literary critics, political theorists and filmmakers trying to represent, challenge and reimagine sexed and gendered identities today. The ancients are woven into the very fabric of 'gender' as we now understand the term.

The chapters that follow are organised around three main areas where classical antiquity has been productive for modern and postmodern concepts of gender and related concepts. The first chapter looks at how ancient authors understand what it means to be, *by nature*, a male or a female, and especially the role of the sexed body in establishing these categories as fixed identities. I start with the poems of Hesiod, whose narrations of the Pandora myth have often been taken as representative of early and classical Greek thought about the nature of sexual difference. I go on to fill in the background to the claim, most often associated with the cultural historian Thomas Laqueur, that the ancients hold views about gender and the sexed body that are diametrically opposed to those of the moderns, before suggesting grounds for a critical re-evaluation of that claim. In the last section of the chapter, I review influential feminist readings of Plato and Aristotle that have brought to light the gendering of nature, matter and the body as 'feminine' in these authors. These readings have gone a long way, as we'll see, towards inscribing classical Greek philosophy at the origins of some of the most tenacious assumptions about sexual difference in the Western tradition. They have thus made the engagement with 'the Greeks' a vital part of the critique of those assumptions.

In the second chapter, I shift from sexed bodies and the gendering of the body itself to 'masculine' and 'feminine' as labels applied to individuals regardless of whether they're identified as male or female. The question of what it meant to be a real man in ancient Greece and Rome has been a particularly productive and provocative area of study for several decades. A good deal of research has focused, in particular, on how sexual desires and behaviours were used to define who was and was not a man in antiquity. In fact, the debates about ancient same-sex erotic relationships have probably had more impact on contemporary issues than any other area of ancient history in recent memory. I chart a path through the so-called 'sexuality wars' that raged at the end of the last century after the publication of the first three volumes of Michel Foucault's *History of Sexuality*, before exploring some of the new avenues of research into practices of gender that emerged in the aftermath of these battles. I examine along the way the extent to which gender in both Greece and Rome is used to describe not simply individual subjects but roles and positions: to act or to do something to someone, especially in a sexual context, is to be masculine, while being acted on is to be feminine.

In the third chapter, I turn to Greek mythology and, more specifically, to female figures known for challenging male-dominated political and social hierarchies, such as Clytemnestra, Demeter and Antigone. I explore how such figures have informed modern and postmodern conversations about the relationship of women and 'the feminine' to an order described alternately as social, normative, public and political. I begin by surveying a range of strategies for bringing a feminist or gender-sensitive perspective to ancient myths, taking into account the ways in which the myths themselves invite competing perspectives. I then take a closer look at two myths in particular, starting with the myth of Demeter and Persephone. After having reviewed several feminist strategies for approaching the position of Demeter as a mother, I situate interpretations that claim greater historical significance for the story the myth tells in relationship to the broader fascination with theories of a prehistoric matriarchy. In the second half of the chapter, I focus on Antigone who, since the 1970s and increasingly in the last decade, has been an enormously influential and contested point of reference in debates about the relationship of women to the state; of femininity to marginality; and of outsiders and outcasts to ethical truth and political transformation. The current obsession with Antigone acutely demonstrates how classical antiquity has played and continues to play a central role in our attempts not only to understand how gender works in the political realm but also to probe the ways in which the idea of the political is gendered.

Before getting underway, I want to flag two complications worth keeping in mind over the course of this book. First of all, the word 'gender' has a range of meanings. For our purposes here, we can reduce the complexity of the semantic field to two main areas of analysis. On the one hand, gender is used to talk about culturally constructed identities, roles and traits correlated with the categories of 'male' and 'female'. The concept of gender in this sense relies largely on a corresponding notion of biological sex that is ostensibly grounded in the physical body. It primarily applies to men and women living in societies structured by sexual difference. On the other hand, gender has been analysed for the ways in which it structures symbolic systems and cultural networks of meaning beyond the relationships of individual men and women. The use of gender in this sense is particularly indebted to the work of Joan Wallach Scott. Scott, in her paradigm-shifting article 'Gender: A Useful Category of Historical Analysis', largely sets aside the categories of 'women' and 'men' to concentrate on how sexual difference is used to talk about relationships of power.[6] In adopting this approach, she roots gender more firmly in the practices of history and cultural analysis taken as a whole. Each of these aspects of gender will come into play in the chapters that follow.

But the moment we set out to talk about *any* aspect of gender in antiquity, we run into the problem that we started with, namely, what's the relationship between our ideas about gender and a corresponding category of ancient 'gender'? Part of the difficulty comes from the fact that, in English, the very language of the sex/gender binary reflects different strands of its classical inheritance. The Romans use the word *sexus* to refer to male and female in a very general sense. The word *genus* fulfils a similar function. Greek writers, by contrast, usually just talk about men (*andres*) and women (*gynaikes*), the male (*to arren*) and the female (*to thēlu*). Yet they also use the word *genos* of the two sexes, a practice that, given the broader meaning of *genos*, implies both common descent – Hesiod, for example, refers to a 'race' of women descended from Pandora – and a common class or type. The Greek grammarians also use *genos* to classify words as masculine or feminine, without the relationship with biological sex being entirely severed. This usage continues with the Latin *genus* and in some modern languages (e.g., English 'gender', French *genre* and Spanish *género*).

So the words 'sex' and 'gender' do have Greek and Latin antecedents. What isn't handed down to us in an easily recognisable form by the ancient languages is the *binary* between sex and gender, indebted to the binary between nature and culture. Again, this doesn't mean we can't use these terms when analysing the evidence from classical antiquity. We need some way, for example, of distinguishing between discussions of males and females (and the male and the female), on the one hand, and of 'masculine' and 'feminine' traits, on the other (which can be implied by various metaphorical terms in both languages, with the language of 'softness' doing considerable work to express femininity as a trait available to women and men). I have found it most expedient to use 'sex' in the former case, 'gender' in the latter. Still, we have to be wary of simply assuming that the ancients thought in terms of our conceptual system.

We have to be particularly careful about applying our own, deeply entrenched opposition between sex (nature) and gender (culture) as a tool for organising the ancient evidence.

The second complication concerns my use of the term 'the ancients'. So far, I've been treating this as if it were a transparent designation, albeit one that needs scare quotes. In truth, the term requires at least two caveats. Neither will succeed entirely in dispelling the problems that it raises.

First, when we talk in general terms about the difference between 'the ancients' and 'the moderns', we aren't just talking about the difference between the ancients and ourselves. In the Renaissance, people were already feeling a keen sense of rupture between the classical Greco-Roman past and their own present. In fact, the self-conscious awareness of being alienated from 'classical' Greek culture seems to have been felt as early as the Hellenistic period (third to first centuries BCE), becoming more and more entrenched in the first centuries CE. The idea of a 'quarrel' between the ancients and the moderns, however, comes out of the increasingly vexed debate about the value of the old versus the new in the early modern period, which came to a head in England and France at the end of the seventeenth century. The quarrel itself has long since passed, having been largely decided in favour of the moderns. Still, the idea of an epochal break between 'the ancients' and 'the moderns' continues to operate today, most notably within histories that segregate the premodern from the modern period.

The traditional periodisation, however, is *not* the one I use here, for the reason that gender, as we've seen, is in its present form a relatively recent concept, dating only to the 1960s and 1970s. Rather, I use the adjective 'modern' to designate the previous half-century, sometimes adding 'post-modern' to emphasise that the lifespan of gender extends over both those feminisms seen as late modern and those traditionally identified as postmodern.

The next caveat is more problematic. The blanket term 'the ancients' immediately raises the question of *which* ancients we're talking about. The world didn't begin, of course, with Greece and Rome, nor were they the only cultures active and flourishing two thousand or so years ago. Moreover, a term like 'the ancients' glosses over all kinds of other salient differences: those that divide the Greeks from the Romans, for example, or sixth-century BCE authors from authors writing in the early centuries CE, or the cultural norms of gender presented in a tragedy by Seneca from those reconstructed from the material traces of honorary statues and inscriptions in the same period. Indeed, one of the strengths of the field of sex and gender studies within ancient history has been the resistance, at least in principle, to totalising accounts, matched by a collective enthusiasm for pluralism, diversity and micro-histories. It seems counterproductive, then, to proceed with a sweeping term like 'the ancients'. For that term risks dooming us to a myopic view of the ancient Mediterranean that reduces it to its most canonical texts and the narrow chronological and geographical boundaries of classical (fifth- and fourth-century BCE) Athens and late Republican and early Imperial (first century BCE to first century CE) Rome. So why hold on to a term as misleading – even pernicious – as 'the ancients'?

This is a very tough question. I have decided to keep using the phrase for the reason that the focus of this book is on modern discussions of sex, gender and sexuality in ancient Greece and Rome that are self-consciously concerned with the present and define the past against – or at least in relationship to – the present. What's more, most of the material I treat here conforms to traditional constructions of the canon. There's certainly a risk in continuing to stack the deck in favour of male-authored canonical texts. But a project such as this one, which is not primarily a survey of sex and gender in the ancient world, has to acknowledge the ways in which those texts have been read, reread and appropriated by those who have most influentially *used* classical antiquity to theorise and historicise gender. The majority of the important battles on these fronts have been fought in the domain of the canon. My choice of material reflects this, as does the term 'the ancients'.

Nevertheless, I ask my readers to recognise in that term its incompleteness, which is to say its biases and omissions (for example, the preference for texts over material artifacts – with the exception of classical sculpture, as Michael Squire has shown in his book for this series – and for certain *kinds* of texts and authors).[7] At the same time, even if I have not got much beyond the limited parameters of 'the ancients' in the chapters that follow, I hope to have given some sense of the complexities and contradictions present even within the small body of texts that regularly do the work of representing the cultures – infinitely richer than we can ever know – that produced them.

But it's important to remember, above all, that these texts are not just the rarefied musings of an intellectual elite, far removed from the gritty realities of what it meant to live as a man or a woman in the past. Rather, the ideas they develop have had and *continue* to have consequences for lived experiences of gendered norms: legal battles surrounding homosexuality in Colorado, politically defiant performances of Greek tragedy in Johannesburg, New York and Buenos Aires, and debates about the future of sexual dimorphism are just a few examples where Greco-Roman antiquity exerts pressure on the present day. The concept of gender that has emerged in part from an engagement with the ancient Greeks and Romans operates in all kinds of less obvious but still consequential ways in our lives.

In writing this book, I have aimed to speak to both specialists and non-specialists, located both inside and outside the fields of gender studies and classical studies. If the book succeeds in encouraging readers who are not classicists to go directly to the ancient material and read it for themselves, if it spurs students of the ancient world to find places in contemporary debates about gender where they can make 'the ancients' speak to the present in provocative new ways, it will have achieved its goals.

CHAPTER I

THE NATURE OF GENDER, THE GENDER OF NATURE

Sliding Scales

The concept of gender defined in opposition to sex rests on the answer to the following question: What does it mean to have the body of a man or the body of a woman? Over the past few decades, the question has become less straightforward with the greater public awareness of complexly sexed identities, from post-operative transsexuals to cross-gender Second Life avatars to intersexed athletes. But the meaning of the sexed body is no less complex if we turn to the fourth-century BCE Greek medical treatise *Epidemics* VI, which has been transmitted to us as part of the Hippocratic Corpus:

> In Abdera, Phaëthusa, the wife of Pytheas, a woman who kept to the house, having given birth at an earlier time, stopped getting her period for a long time after her husband had been exiled. Later, pains in the joints and redness. After these things happened, her body was made male (*ēndrōthē*) and became hairy all over; she grew a beard, and her voice became harsh. Despite the fact we did everything possible to draw down the menses, they didn't come, but she died after surviving only a little while longer. The same thing happened as well to Nanno, the wife of Gorgippus, on Thasos. It was the opinion of all the physicians that I met that the sole hope of her becoming female (*gynaikōthēnai*) was if the menses would come. But with her, too, this wasn't possible, although we did everything, and she died without delay. ([Hippocrates] *Epidemics* VI 8.32, Littré 5.356)

In classical Greece, the attributes in question – body hair, a rough voice and, above all, the beard – would have identified an adult man in the public sphere and secured his social privilege. But when they appear on the body of a woman, as we see with Phaëthusa and Nanno, they become pathological signs. Both the author and his medical colleagues think that these women will survive only if their bodies 'become female' again, a process that seems to depend on the return of normal menstruation. Despite all their efforts to bring this about, though, they fail, and the women die.

What's going on here? Notice, first, that the transformations at stake take place at the level of the body, which is the subject of the verb 'to become male or masculine' in the case of Phaëthusa. The patients themselves don't seem to have anything to do with what's happening to them. The problem seems to be that the body's hold on femaleness is too loose to kept it from drifting towards maleness under certain conditions.

But if the sexed body seems surprisingly fluid, its fluidity is not absolute. These metamorphoses, after all, are ultimately unworkable. The bodies can neither survive their inclination towards maleness nor be compelled to return to their original condition. The difficulty, then, is not just that these bodies resist being 'refeminised'. Something in or about them also prevents them from becoming wholly male, something ineradicably female, at least in the eyes of our author (some later readers will see in the story of Phaëthusa a total sex change).[1] He doesn't just believe that resumed menstruation is the only way the patients will survive. He uses the feminine participle (*biōsasa*) to refer to Phaëthusa even at the moment of her death, suggesting that he sees her as a woman to the end. What we have, then, are nominally female bodies caught in a no man's land of sex.

The puzzling cases of Phaëthusa and Nanno show, at a glance, the challenges of mapping ancient Greek and Roman concepts of the sexed body – and the concept of the physical body more generally – onto contemporary ideas about sex, gender and the biological body. For it's hard to understand what happens to these women in terms of the standard formulation of the sex/gender binary. The binary dictates that the biological body is always already determined by nature and its aims, while gender, conversely, is susceptible to cultural notions and social practices. In the Hippocratic text, the physical body is, on the one hand, unstable; matter is slippery. Female turns male. If the author thinks the body has a sex, his understanding of sex is very different from our own. On the other hand, even after their transformations, Phaëthusa and Nanno are still identified as female. The physicians, accordingly, try to make their bodies behave in the way proper to their sex, seeing this as the only hope of saving their lives. Despite its plasticity, then, the physical body plays a role in fixing the patient's sex. In short, the stories of Phaëthusa and Nanno don't offer an inverted picture of our own ideas about sex and gender, a premodern mirror in which sex is fluid while gender is fixed. But neither are they entirely consistent with modern ideas. Rather, these case histories suggest an embodied gendered identity that is fluid *and* fixed, covering a continuum of traits ranging from the contingent to the essential.

In this chapter, I take up two interlocking sets of questions that have to do with how male and female 'natures' are represented in texts from early Greek poetry, Greco-Roman medicine and classical Greek philosophy. These questions matter deeply not only for a history of how different societies have represented sexual difference but also for an understanding of our own concepts of sex and gender.

I ask, first, how our ancient sources understand the concepts of male and female at the level of human beings and, in the medical and philosophical texts, at the level of the body. Do these sources see men and woman as having different 'natures'? If so, where is difference located? How is it explained? I explore, too, how our own assumptions about sexual difference, often organised by the split between sex and gender, have influenced the way we look at classical antiquity, as well as how the ancient evidence has been used to give the sex/gender binary a history.

The second set of questions has to do with the relevance of gender to the idea of nature – and related concepts like matter and the body – in early Greek medical and philosophical texts. Do these texts see nature as more feminine than masculine? And how have feminist critiques of gendered representations of nature and materiality in Greek philosophy helped define the contemporary debates about gender, matter and the body? Does the ancient material have anything new to offer these debates?

I start with sexual difference in the archaic poet Hesiod. One reason I begin with Hesiod is that he supplies us with two of our earliest and most canonical Greek accounts of the origins of the cosmos and the human condition. But reading Hesiod for what he says about men and women (and male and female) is also a useful introduction to what we might call the politics of interpretation. For as we'll see, it's impossible to isolate the stories that scholars have told about the 'origin' of gender ideology in the West from debates about the nature, history and social significance of sexual difference. I then turn to Greek and Roman medical and philosophical texts to examine how the concept of the physical body transforms Hesiod's idea that men and women constitute different 'races', before offering a critical reassessment of the influential claim that these texts lack a concept of the sexed body. Finally, I take up interpretations of classical philosophical texts by feminist philosophers who are interested in using the history of philosophy to rethink materiality as 'the site at which a certain drama of sexual difference plays itself out'.[2]

The Myth of Pandora: Woman as Other?

The word gender shares a root with 'genesis' and 'generation'. How and why did the Greeks think that men and women came into being? These questions are trickier than one might think. The best place to start looking for answers is the myth of Pandora, whose fateful opening of a jar – or, a box, as we find in the later Western tradition – is central to the long history of representations of Woman as a 'beautiful evil'. For the earliest versions of the myth we have to go back to Hesiod, who tells the story twice, once in the *Theogony* and once in the *Works and Days*. Hesiod's stories of Pandora do have something to say about the origins of humanity, or at least the human condition as we know it. But, in recent years, they've been read more for what they assume about the different origins of men and women, becoming the most important touchstones for debates about archaic and classical Greek representations of sexual difference. More specifically, Hesiod's description of the creation of a 'race of women' (*genos gynaikōn*) apart from men has often served as Exhibit A for the influential argument that, in the mythological imagination of early Greece, 'the feminine' functions as the 'Other' to the masculine norm. To understand this argument, we need to take a brief look at the primary material.

One of the curious features of Hesiod's poems is that they describe neither the creation nor the birth of mortal men: *Genesis* this is not. Rather, in both poems, we become aware of man's presence only at the moment he's about to leave the company of the immortals forever. In the *Theogony*, Hesiod sets the scene with a feast for the distribution of honours in the evolving cosmos. The Titan Prometheus, working on behalf of mortal men, tricks Zeus into accepting a lesser portion of meat – a sign of status – by wrapping it in glistening fat. Zeus retaliates by withholding fire, but Prometheus outwits him again, stealing the fire in a hollow fennel stalk. The price for the theft, Zeus determines, will be an evil thing for mankind: Pandora. The craftsman god Hephaestus fashions a figure from earth in the likeness of a *parthenos*, a young, unmarried woman, and the gods and goddesses outfit her with various adornments and attributes. Mortal men, seduced by Zeus's creation, take her into their midst and end up paying dearly for it. For Pandora stands at the head of the race of women, a race of drones that drain households of their wealth and sap men's strength. The story that Hesiod tells in the *Works and Days* follows roughly the same arc but begins with the theft of fire and ends with the release of troubles from the jar. Both versions make it clear that Pandora is created as a punishment for mortals. By receiving this poisoned gift, mankind becomes a race that has to struggle to survive, a race that never gets any good without an evil in return. The account of Pandora has to be read, then, as part of a larger story about the emergence of the human condition.

How should we understand this larger story? For nearly half a century, the most influential reading of the Prometheus myth has been that developed by Jean-Pierre Vernant, the French historian of antiquity best known for extending the structuralist anthropology of Claude Lévi-Strauss to the study of ancient Greece. Following the central principles of the structuralist interpretation of myth, Vernant breaks down the two versions in Hesiod into their component actions and identifies the recurring patterns. He then offers a schematic analysis of the correspondences that, he argues, constitute the underlying logic of the myth, which is to say 'its organisation of the mental space (with its classificatory categories, its way of organising and codifying reality and its delineation of the different semantic fields) within which these myths were produced'.[3] The myth of Prometheus, according to Vernant's analysis, offers a snapshot of the origins of the three institutions that define man in relationship to the gods and animals: sacrifice and the use of fire, agriculture and marriage. Each institution, as we've seen, develops within a web of deceptive exchanges, leading Vernant to conclude that the myth expresses the ambiguous nature of the mortal condition: for people, nothing good ever comes easy.

The centre of the myth's semantic network is, crucially, occupied by Pandora, 'the symbol of the ambiguity of human existence . . . combin[ing] all the tensions and ambivalences that characterise the status of man'.[4] In establishing Pandora as the lynchpin of the structuralist reading, Vernant builds on earlier work in which he had shown the significance of the binary masculine/feminine to the logic of Greek mythology. Yet he doesn't himself elaborate the implications of his reading of Pandora for the question of sexual difference. These implications have been developed instead in several Vernant-inspired readings of the myth that have become classics in their own right.

One of these readings is developed by Nicole Loraux, another French historian of antiquity who was closely associated with Vernant's Centre Louis Gernet in Paris (and who dedicates her reading to Vernant). For Loraux, the asymmetry of Hesiod's account, according to which only women are actually created, is the blueprint for a lopsided view of sexual difference that persists through archaic Greece and into the classical period. From this perspective, Woman is forever estranged from the collectivity of Man. Pandora enters the world, in fact, as the bearer of difference *tout court*. She not only separates mortals from immortals but also, by introducing sexuality, divides men from themselves. She arrives, moreover, as a crafted object. 'The first woman is everything but a natural being', Loraux observes.[5] She is, in essence, a pawn, expertly crafted by the master technician Hephaestus as part of Zeus's plan to enforce, once and for all, the hierarchy of gods and men. No wonder, then, that Pandora embodies the ambiguities that haunt mortal men. The beautiful exterior concealing a thievish nature recalls the deceptive gifts of the gods, while, as an insatiable belly (*gastēr*), 'the woman literally embodies the principle of corporeality, the fact of mortality', as Marilyn Arthur has written.[6] Zeus's ploy lies in making any man who wants progeny consort with this 'beautiful evil'. Even after the woman is taken into the house, she remains an alien being. Pandora gives rise to a band of outsiders.

The interpretation of Pandora as a sign of sexual difference is developed further in the reading of the myth offered by Froma Zeitlin, who builds on the work of Vernant and Loraux. Like Loraux, Zeitlin reads Hesiod's account of Pandora's creation through the lens of a radical asymmetry between the sexes.

> Logically, both male and female should come into existence at the same time as the human species is created. Each is the complement of the other, each indispensable to the other's identity. As a pair, they attest to the universal fact of gender in nature and assure reproduction of one's own kind. The mythic imagination does not view matters this way. More often than not, woman is an afterthought, created as a secondary category following the emergence of man. Her ontological status is therefore not a self-evident or spontaneous fact. To account for her supplementary presence requires a motive, a reason, a purpose – in short, a myth.[7]

For the Greeks, the myth is that of Pandora, which is:

> . . . conspicuous in creating woman as a separate and alien being, the first exemplar of a race or species, the *genos gunaikōn*, who as the

agent of separation between gods and mortal men remains estranged, never achieving a mediated partnership with man.[8]

For Zeitlin, the estrangement of the female race has to be read through Pandora's late arrival in the story that Hesiod tells of the formation of the cosmos. The genesis of the cosmos is structured around sexual reproduction from the moment that feminine (Gaia, 'Earth') and masculine (Ouranos, 'Sky') principles emerge from a primeval – and neuter – Chaos. But the complementarity of the sexes doesn't carry over to the realm of mortals. The birth of Pandora is situated *outside* the generative dynamics (parthenogenesis and sexual reproduction) that have governed the creation of the world and the gods to this point. Insofar as she is the invention of Zeus, 'she is far removed from femininity as an original category'.[9] Pandora's fundamental isolation from the natural order becomes the condition of her descendants: the race of women.

Hesiod reinforces the status of Woman as Other, Zeitlin argues, by downplaying her role in sexual reproduction. He doesn't deny the female reproductive capacity entirely. He acknowledges that a man has to take a wife if he wants children, and indeed, other scholars have seen Hesiod placing more weight on Pandora's fertility.[10] But on Zeitlin's reading, he primarily associates Pandora's belly with voracious appetites rather with than the fecundity of 'the feminine' as a natural, divine principle. Such an association is consistent with a larger story in the *Theogony* that unfolds at the level of the gods, one in which fathers – and above all Zeus – appropriate the generative capacities of Gaia. Consider, for example, the birth of Athena from Zeus's head after he swallows her mother Metis or the fact that goddesses who conceive on their own can produce only monsters. If we look at Pandora, we see something similar. The power to generate is located primarily in her creator, rather than in her creative capacities. By casting Pandora as a primarily destructive presence in the household, rather than as a source of fertility, Zeitlin concludes, Hesiod insists not simply on sexual difference but on a form of difference that denies women a proper place in both the natural order and the human community.

The difference between men and women in Hesiod mirrors the opposition between masculine and feminine at the cosmic level. Yet Loraux and Zeitlin bring front and centre the Otherness of the 'race of women' engendered by Pandora. The stories that Hesiod tells about Pandora emphasise asymmetry rather than complementarity. They represent women in terms of artifice, bestiality and, more distantly, the grim necessity of sexual reproduction. Having traced aspects of Hesiod's portrayal of women to other archaic and classical texts, both Loraux and Zeitlin argue that the idea of women as a separate race is an entrenched cultural preoccupation in early Greece. The otherness of the race of women operates, on their view, as the principal axiom in the archaic and classical Greek understanding of sexual difference.

The readings of Loraux and Zeitlin have become axiomatic themselves over the years. By inscribing the radical difference of women into some of the earliest texts of the Western tradition, they've helped shore up the equation of Woman and Other that has been integral to feminist critiques of this tradition, as we'll see further at the end of the chapter. But the sweeping applicability of their interpretations of Hesiod to Greek culture as a whole has been called into question in the intervening years by scholars hesitant to abandon both historical women and the concepts of 'the female' and 'the feminine' to the inert and shadowy space of the Other. The polarities that seem so sharp in Hesiod, these scholars have argued, can keep us from seeing the active and in some circumstances highly prestigious roles that women did play in various domestic and civic spaces. Instead of taking categories like Woman or women in Greece as monolithic and 'natural', we should interrogate how they intersect with other forms of difference such as age or status.

We can see how these critiques have played out more specifically by looking at Loraux's reading of the feminine Other in classical Athens. Loraux has argued extensively that the Athenian city-state (*polis*) was constituted by the exclusion of actual women.[11] The 'feminine', nevertheless, dominates the space of the political imaginary as a means of representing threats to the social cohesion of the city and the integrity (corporeal and ethical) of the (male) citizen. More than once, she points to the masculine gender of the Greek word for citizen (*politēs*) as metonymic of the entire Athenian political edifice.

Loraux's characterisation of Athenian citizenship in terms of the exclusion of women has recently been challenged by the ancient historian Josine Blok.[12] Blok doesn't deny that Athenian women lacked political decision-making power (that would be a hard argument to make). But she stresses the many different ways that women *were* integrated into the civic community, above all through their participation in public religious cults. The extent of women's participation in the life of the city leads Blok to defend a broader definition of citizenship than that adopted by Loraux. Blok's own definition embraces precisely what seems so strange in an age of the separation of Church and State: an understanding of civic life that includes religious cult alongside the mechanisms of deliberative democracy. Joan Connelly has also drawn attention to the strongly political nature of state cult and the roles assumed by priestesses in the ancient Greek and Roman worlds.[13] The calls of Blok, Connelly and others to enlarge the category of the political echoes what is happening in the study of other ancient societies. The archaeologist Rosemary Joyce, for example, has argued that the production of textiles in Classic Mayan societies, usually undertaken by women, should be seen as a form of political agency rather than as domestic labour.[14] She points out that textiles in such societies were luxury goods, circulated in order to build alliances between families and between communities, as is true, in fact, in archaic Greece. Rather than denying difference, then, these scholars have directed our attention to the *difference* of difference in societies where modern binaries like public and private or religious and secular function otherwise or not at all.

Historians of classical antiquity have also increasingly shied away from the universalising binaries of structuralist analysis, focusing instead on the differences built into concepts of 'Woman' or 'the feminine'. Kate Gilhuly, surveying rhetorical, dramatic and philosophical texts, has recast 'the feminine' in classical Athens as a spectrum incorporating a range of roles, most notably the prostitute, the wife and the priestess.[15] Focusing on canonical Greek literary texts, especially tragedy, Mark Griffith has protested that the term 'woman' is 'too clumsy an umbrella for too many separate categories (daughter, sister, virgin, bride, wife, mother, princess, captive, etc.)' in the ancient material.[16] Something of this clumsiness is present, in fact, in the translation of Pandora as the 'first woman', since the Greek word *gynē* really only takes on its meaning (something more like 'wife') in relationship to *parthenos*, which, as we saw above, describes a girl who's on the cusp of mature sexuality but has not yet married or given birth.

It's a natural outcome of these lines of reasoning to speculate on whether gender should even be privileged as a category of social differentiation in our analyses of ancient Greece and Rome. Is it possible that what we see when we look at the ancient evidence is overly determined by the preoccupations of late twentieth-century scholarship? For many years now, some feminists and critical theorists have argued that the concept of sexual difference has been formulated at the cost of repressing other kinds of difference, especially race, class and sexual orientation. Has the focus on sexual difference also led us to overlook historical and cultural difference? Depending on the type of evidence we use when we try to understand ancient Greek and Roman societies, gender doesn't always seem to be the most salient category of classification, as Violaine Sebillotte Cuchet has stressed.[17] What's more, it is always entangled in other categories such as age, as we've just seen with the terms *gynē* and *parthenos*. The category of social status is just as important. The Roman concept of a real man, *vir*, for example, is heavily dependent on status and, more specifically, on whether one is free or a slave. The sexual politics of Greek New Comedy make little sense without the knowledge that women in democratic Athens fell into at least two camps: those who could produce future citizens and those who could not. The affiliations created by gender are thus complicated and in some cases superseded by relationships and communities organised by other kinds of common ground.

These critiques of the Woman-as-Other model have raised or reintroduced difficult but important questions. For one thing, how should we reconcile different kinds of evidence from the ancient world? The majority

of our textual evidence was produced by male elites. Whatever the importance of gender in the societies of these authors, they themselves often use
gender in ideologically charged ways to describe social and political order
and perceived threats to order, as well as to judge each other as legitimate
social and political actors. Loraux's work has shed a good deal of light on
the ways in which gender is used in these canonical texts to define the
boundaries of the city and elite masculinity. Indeed, one of the break-
throughs of scholars working in the last decades of the twentieth century
has been to recognise that gendered terms are often mobilised in both ancient
Greece and Rome to express relations of power, regardless of whether actual
men and women are involved – even numbers can be organised by gender.

And yet, Loraux's account isn't the whole story. Her interest in totalising accounts sometimes leads her to pay too little attention to the specificities of the evidence that she's considering. More generally, 'the feminine'
can be a category that hides as much as it reveals, especially as we move
beyond the sometimes reductive and polemical categories embedded in the
canonical texts. 'Archaeological materialities', Joyce writes, have the capacity
to 'resist reduction, break through overly simple models, and force us to
confront our own least interrogated assumptions'.[18]

What we need, then, is a picture of gender in ancient Greece and Rome
that acknowledges its own fragmentation, representing not just the gaps in
our sources but a spectrum of meanings and the genuine plurality of experiences in a range of societies over centuries, not just for different individuals (say, a citizen and a slave) but also at different points within individual
lives. Yet at the same time, we shouldn't lose sight of the fact that gender
seems to have operated in highly reductive ways in ancient texts and lives,
reinforcing polarities of thought and laying constraints on how individuals
expressed their interests, talents, desires, fears and hopes, as well as how
they saw each other.

If that sounds like a lot to hold together at once, it is. Every intervention in the writing of history has to navigate its own path between the past
and the present, neither of which are monolithic domains. Even the most
rigorous and sensitive students of the past make choices that are motivated

in some way by the conversations they're engaged in in the present. For a prehistoric archaeologist, it might make sense to draw attention to the socio-political status of 'women's work' in ancient communities to combat entrenched narratives that place women in the home from the dawn of time. A contemporary political theorist might be interested in precisely the narrower, more conventional sense of the political in order to probe the potential of a figure like Antigone to help us think about challenges to the state, perhaps against the backdrop of the historical reception of Sophocles' *Antigone*. Both the archaeologist and the political theorist might find it useful to shift attention from gender to some other category. These decisions emerge not only in relationship to the ancient evidence but also in the crucible of contemporary debates about gender, *including* debates about whether gender should take centre stage as a category of analysis.

In fact, we can see the influence of our own ways of thinking on the question I posed at the beginning of this chapter about the *nature* of sexual difference in ancient Greece. For us, the slide from nature in this context to biology is almost too easy to notice. So, too, are the assumptions that biology is the most stable of realms and that the division into two 'opposite' sexes is a natural given. Indeed, the traditional formulation of the sex/gender binary turns on a contrast between the fuzziness of gender and the crispness of biological sex. But what do we mean when we talk about nature in ancient Greece and Rome? If we turn to the ancient biological writers, do they share our sense that the natures of men and women are grounded in the body? Do they think male and female natures are radically different?

In his 1990 book *Making Sex: Body and Gender from the Greeks to Freud*, the cultural historian Thomas Laqueur answers these last two questions in the negative, arguing that before the eighteenth century, men and women were thought to share the same basic body.[19] While the moderns hold the biological body to be the bedrock of sexual difference, the ancients – here understood broadly as the premodern West – look for stability in an order that's both metaphysical and social: the space of 'gender'. Laqueur's claim, in other words, is that the sharp polarity between male and female that we find in Hesiod's account of cosmic creation ('metaphysical') and the human condition ('social') disappears when we look at how the bodies of men and women were actually understood. The premodern view of sex and gender, Laqueur concludes, is the inverse of our own.

Laqueur's account of the premodern period, twenty years after the publication of *Making Sex*, continues to exercise a powerful influence on how contemporary ideas about sex and gender are mapped onto – and authenticated through – the past. It's worth turning, then, to the ancient evidence in order to examine more closely the extent to which early Greek and Roman medical and biological writers stabilise sex as an attribute of the body. We will then return to Laqueur's arguments, their own historical and intellectual context and some of the problems they run into.

One thing to keep in mind, however, is that the very attraction of these texts – and, indeed, our interest in nature itself – is partly due to the fact that medicine and biology have played such a significant role in the understanding and representation of sex and gender over the past several hundred years. That's not to say there wasn't widespread interest from the late fifth century BCE among elites in medicine and biological theory. There was, to an extent often not acknowledged by scholars of ancient Greece and Rome. But we can't assume that ancient medical and biological texts played the same role in their societies that their modern counterparts do in our own. It is in large part because these texts have had such an impact on the contemporary conversation about gender and its relationship to sex that I use them to explore the following question. How relevant was the biological body to ancient medical and philosophical ideas about sexual difference?

Sexing the Body in Ancient Medical and Biological Texts

In Hesiod we find the view that there are two different races – or rather one 'race' and one group of people simply equated with the human. If we call these 'genders', translating the Greek word *genos*, we won't be referring to gender in the modern sense of the term but rather to something more like our concept of 'sex'. What is the fate of the concept of two different 'sexes' if we turn to the Greek medical writers? Do they believe that the two 'sexes' correspond to two different bodies?

The question, at first glance, would appear easy enough to answer in the affirmative. Consider, for example, that in the anonymous medical texts dating from the classical era and gathered in the Hippocratic Corpus, an entire subgenre of treatises is devoted to 'women's things' (*ta gynakeia*): a proto-gynaecology that will be called upon to justify further attempts to institutionalise gynaecology in later centuries. The classification suggests that, on the whole, the early medical writers did recognise differences between male and female bodies, at least differences salient to health. Their significance is discussed by the author of the treatise *Diseases of Women* I:

At the same time, the physicians also err in not learning through accurate inquiry into the cause of the disease, but they heal as though they were treating men's diseases (*andrika nosēmata*). I've seen many women die from these kinds of troubles. But you have to interrogate the cause right away, and accurately. For the cure of women's diseases (*tōn gynaikēiōn nosēmatōn*) differs enormously from that of men's. ([Hippocrates] *Diseases of Women* I 62, Littré 8.126)

The author's remarks reveal that some physicians did fail to recognise that women have their own diseases – with deadly consequences. But his own insistence that the physician must adopt a different strategy when dealing with the diseases of women suggests that he at least understands the female body to have a nature of its own.

Before exploring the implications of this claim further, we need to pin down what we mean by 'body' and 'nature' here. Until now, I've spoken loosely of 'nature'. But the Greek term that comes to designate nature, *physis*, owes its later significance to what by the end of the fifth century BCE was being calling 'the inquiry into nature'. It's not completely clear what *physis* meant to the earliest thinkers in this tradition, such as Thales and Anaximander. But the word eventually seems capable of designating how a natural entity comes to be and develops, its stable attributes and its power to act on and be acted upon by other things, all topics that were open to investigation through the analysis of phenomenal evidence. The cosmos as a whole is approached in this way as an object of study. But things *within* the cosmos can also have natures. The first known use of the word, in Homer, refers to a plant (*Odyssey* 10.303). Even more important for our purposes, the nature of a human being is the explicit object of inquiry in some Hippocratic texts, as is the nature of women. So, too, is the nature of the body (*sōma*). In fact, as I have argued elsewhere, it's precisely by becoming an object of knowledge – and especially *medical* knowledge – that the physical body is first 'seen' conceptually in this period.[20] The medical writers serve, then, as important resources for our understanding of how the natures of men and women come to be grounded in the new concept of the *physical* body as a mostly hidden terrain of constituent stuffs.

How is the physical body used to differentiate the sexes in early Greek medicine and philosophy? Heat is critical for establishing the difference between males and females in Aristotle, but its role is more ambiguous in earlier medical and biological texts. The little evidence we have for the Presocratics indicates no consensus on whether they thought females were hotter or colder than men. Parmenides, for example, thought women were hotter; Empedocles thought they were colder.[21] The Hippocratic writers didn't agree on the answer to this question either.

These writers are all convinced, however, that women are wetter than men. The author of one Hippocratic embryological text explicitly chalks up the excess moisture of the female body to the *physis*, 'nature', of women. He asserts that, even in utero, the female is wetter than the male, with the result that the female embryo is slower to take shape: forty-two days versus thirty days for a male embryo (*On the Seed/On the Nature of the Child* 15, Littré 7.494). But most writers think that the excessive moisture of the female body decisively sets in with menstruation. The idea here is that the female body only starts to accumulate surplus blood, which is typically understood as a byproduct of food, at a later stage in its development. If all goes well, the vessels inside the girl's body widen, allowing the excess blood to move to the uterus for evacuation. But if the vessels don't expand, blood gets trapped in the body, a condition that can result in the potentially fatal 'disease of young girls', characterised by night terrors and suicidal delusions. The cure: the girl should be deflowered as soon as possible, on the principle that sexual intercourse dilates the internal passageways. Indeed, sex is necessary for keeping these paths open throughout the woman's life. Recall that Phaëthusa's problems begin when her husband goes into exile and she (presumably) enters a protracted period of celibacy. If blood fails to move through the body, all kinds of problems set in. Menstruation is so important because it's the only surefire mechanism for correcting the inherently pathological surplus in the female body.

The accumulation of blood in the maturing woman is due, in part, to the specific nature – porous and spongy – of her flesh. If excesses of this sort arise in men, they're absorbed into the glands, the only places in the male body that are comparably porous. 'The body of a mature woman', by contrast, is 'one big gland'.[22] If you want to get a sense of the sponginess of the female body, one writer describes an experiment that can be done at home:

> I declare that the woman (*gynē*) has more porous and more delicate flesh than a man . . . And indeed, if you place clean wool and a clean, closely woven cloth that is precisely equal in weight to the wool over water or in a damp place for two days and two nights, once you've taken [the fabrics] off you will find, having weighed them, that the wool is considerably heavier than the cloth. What happens is that there is always an exhalation upward from the water that is in the wide-mouthed jar, and the wool, because it is porous and soft, will take on more of the exhalation, while the cloth, because it is solid and closely woven, will be filled up, but without having received most of that drawn up. It's in just this way that a woman, being more porous, draws more moisture from the belly to her body and draws it more quickly than a man does. ([Hippocrates] *Diseases of Women* I 1, Littré 8.12)

The problems of nature are compounded by culture. Women's sedentary lifestyle and weak regimens saddle them with an even greater surplus of moisture, as Galen still believed well over half a millennium later.

The idea that the flesh is sexed shows us one way that the early medical writers understood sexual difference to be embodied. There's room in the model, it's worth noting, for variation. The flesh of some women is denser, while for others it is more porous, depending on the woman's individual constitution and sexual and reproductive experience (intercourse and pregnancy 'break down' the flesh). Moreover, some women – those who are young and pale – are wetter while others, who are older and darker, are dryer. Nevertheless, even if the female body takes on masculine traits under certain conditions, as we saw was true of Phaëthusa and Nanno, the model assumes that nature imposes a boundary that cannot be crossed. The idea of sex as a dividing line between natures is also reflected in observations like the one we saw above that women suffer from different affections from men or suffer affections in a different way. It finds confirmation in the use of treatments specific to male and female bodies and, indeed, in the very idea of a branch of medicine devoted to 'women's things'.[23]

Early Greek medical writers and philosophers establish the nature of the female body more subtly by the very hold it exercises over a woman's life, thereby inaugurating a long tradition in Western medicine and philosophy of defining women through their subordination to their bodies. The almost uncanny autonomy of the female body comes sharply into focus if we look at the phenomenon of the 'wandering womb'.

The womb looms large in Hippocratic gynaecology, despite the fact – or perhaps *because* of the fact – that the classical-era medical writers had little direct knowledge of its anatomy (the systematic dissection of the human body doesn't happen until the third century BCE, in Alexandria). The medical writers kept a close eye on its functionality, suggesting that they saw their primary responsibility as enabling women to fulfil their social role through reproduction. Unsurprisingly, the womb is, as we'll see further below, one of the most recalcitrant markers of difference between male and female bodies. Far from marking male lack, however, the womb tends to act as a liability for women. It's the usual suspect for the majority of female diseases, even in cases where the symptoms resemble those of diseases that would not seem to be sex-specific, such as epilepsy. The pathologies of the womb are often related to its movement inside the body. The problems begin when the womb isn't kept properly hydrated. Driven to seek moisture, it wanders around the body, attaching itself to the liver, the heart and even the head and producing a wide range of physical and mental symptoms that often cause the woman to lose control over herself. The natural susceptibility of women to losing control has a long and active afterlife. But it would be a mistake, as Helen King has shown, to see the origins of the modern idea of hysteria (from the Greek word for womb, *hystera*) in the Hippocratic texts.[24] The problem here is very much one of the body. It's not in the head.

Plato also thought that the womb could travel around the body. But, in his own mythmaking account of how the world and human beings came into being, the *Timaeus*, he offers a rather different explanation for its restlessness:

> In women the womb or the uterus as it's called ... an indwelling creature hungry for making children, when for a long time it's been without fruit past the proper season, bears it harshly; growing irritated, and wandering all over the body, blocking the passageways of the breath and not allowing respiration it throws the body into an extreme state of distress and causes all kinds of other diseases until the desire and *erōs* of men and women alike drive them together. (Plato, *Timaeus* 91c-d)

It's true that Plato offers as a complement to his picture of the womb a vivid portrait of a beast-like penis that, in its frenzied lusts, seeks to 'dominate everything'. Moreover, he blames these lusts on the self-willed, disobedient nature (*physis*) of the genital organ. Nevertheless, elsewhere he associates women in particular with physical necessity and subordination to the body. Earlier in the *Timaeus*, for example, we find a creation story that recalls the asymmetry of Hesiod's account. The eponymous narrator, Timaeus, claims that only men were created directly by the gods. The female race came about when some of these men failed to discipline their bodies by cultivating their souls. They were punished by being reborn first as women, then as increasingly brutish beasts. Plato suggests here that the 'race of women' represents a secondary, degraded state of being that means being enslaved to the disorderly rhythms of embodied life, with no hope of achieving true human flourishing.

The Hippocratic writers don't describe the womb as an animal. Nor do they assign it a desire for sex or sexual reproduction. Rather, as we saw above, they explain its displacement mechanically, usually as a response to a deficit of moisture. Nevertheless, the best way to keep the womb moist and healthy in the gynaecological texts is through sexual intercourse. What we find in the medical writers, then, is an account of female nature that arguably subordinates women to the physical body and, more specifically, its reproductive function, even more than Plato's account does. As Lesley Dean-Jones puts it, women's sexual appetite in the Hippocratic Corpus is a 'purely physiological phenomenon not necessarily associated with any psychological affects'.[25]

It's therefore possible to see the subordination of women to their bodies as another marker of sexual difference in ancient medical writing, one that resonates with the representation of women in other classical genres as creatures 'in bondage to their physical appetites'.[26] The contrast between the sexes along these lines deepens as writers of the late fifth and early fourth centuries BCE start to develop practices of 'care' (*epimeleia*) that allow male subjects to master the demands of their bodies and especially their desires before they are themselves mastered. These practices, which have been made famous by the work of the French historian and philosopher Michel Foucault on 'the care of the self' (*le souci de soi*), are unsurprisingly targeted at men.[27] Indeed, despite the greater independence of women in the Hellenistic and Roman worlds, women continue to be excluded from practices of self-mastery in later medical and philosophical authors such as Galen and Plutarch. The male thus continues to be defined in part against the model of a sex that cannot, by its very nature, get a handle on its physicality.

We've been focusing on some of the ways in which Hesiod's sense that women belong to a separate *genos* persists in classical Greek medical thinking. But Greco-Roman medical writers also recognise continuities between male and female bodies. Earlier, we saw how excess moisture helps to establish the specificity of female nature in the Hippocratic writings. But despite its greater dryness, even the male body in the early medical treatises is defined by fluids and fluxes. This is in part because the 'generic' body is understood primarily in terms of its constituent stuffs: bile and phlegm, fire and water, an indefinite number of juices defined by their qualities (acrid, sweet, salty and so on). The medical writers tend to blame disease on qualitative changes in these stuffs under the influence of changes in the environment, food and drink and the seasons. But while by the fourth century BCE, they're increasingly inclined to classify types of individuals by the humour believed to dominate the patient's constitution, we don't see them using the humours to divide male from female bodies. The humoural body is common territory.

Besides the humours, other stuffs move through the body according to what Laqueur calls 'the free-trade economy of fluids': food and blood, milk and semen.[28] These fluids circulate through the same set of vessels inside the body. They can share orifices as well. Blood that should be evacuated as part of the menstrual cycle, for example, might exit through the nose. Finally, these stuffs participate in ongoing processes of transformation: food becomes blood; blood becomes milk or seed. Given that these fluids are so fungible, they can easily be turned away from one purpose towards another. The wet nurse, for example, was supposed to abstain from sex to keep the blood targeted for milk from getting diverted towards pregnancy.

From another perspective, the transformation of fluids from one into another can be organised hierarchically. Aristotle's biology is dominated by stuffs distinguished by being increasingly cooked or, more technically, 'concocted' by an inborn heat. When, at the highest level of transformation in Aristotle's physiology, blood gets concocted into either the male seed or its colder, wetter, female equivalent, *catamēnia*, it's just one more step along a process of refinement shared by the male and the female. These material transformations, together with the common humoural economy, suggest that the fluid substratum of the physical body as it is imagined by the Hippocratic writers and Aristotle – and indeed, as it continues to be imagined for centuries – is unmarked by sexual difference.

From the fourth century BCE on, and especially after politically connected physicians start dissecting the corpses of criminals in third-century BCE Alexandria, the learned medical tradition increasingly emphasises the similarities between male and female bodies. It goes almost without saying that the female remains a flawed specimen. To take Aristotle's notorious formulation, 'the female is, as it were, a deformed male' (*to gar thēlu hōsper arren esti pepērōmenon, Generation of Animals* 737a26–30). Nonetheless, Aristotle thinks that the male and the female belong to the same species (he reserves the term *genos* for the genus – in this case, animals). One of most striking examples of such homological thinking is Galen's description of the female reproductive anatomy in his *On the Use of Parts* as an inverted version of male anatomy, trapped inside the body, rather than outside, due to a deficit of vital heat (Galen shares with Aristotle the view that women are colder, which is to say less perfect). The ovaries, for example, are, in some sense, inverted testes (*orcheis*) for Galen, much as they were for Herophilus, the Hellenistic anatomist credited with discovering them. Homology, it's worth emphasising, is not identity. Galen finds countless homologies between humans and animals – these homologies, after all, are crucial to justifying why his experiments with apes and pigs produce results that can be applied to people – without claiming that humans and animals are simply interchangeable. Still, the tendency of some physicians to assimilate female bodies to male bodies undoubtedly has an impact on the later Western medical tradition.

But there's a danger that the later success of Galen's homological modelling of male and female reproductive anatomy in Western medicine will lead us to see the ancient Greco-Roman sources in purely teleological terms. That's to say that when we read these sources for the ideas that are most enthusiastically elaborated in the later tradition, we risk overlooking the ideas that get lost, the points of emphasis that are gradually muted, the complications and contradictions. The caveat is all the more important in view of the fact that the impact of Galenic homology is extremely limited in the centuries prior to 1500, when *On the Use of Parts* began to circulate among influential physicians, as the medieval historians Joan Cadden and Katharine Park have pointed out.[29] Rather than the homological model dominating Western medicine for most of its history, as many historians and gender theorists have assumed, we find instead that its appearance in the early modern period 'represents a resurrection of a Greek idea that had effectively played no role in Latin (as opposed to Arabic) medical culture for well over a thousand years.'[30]

Even in Galen, the homology of male and female reproductive systems is not a procrustean model but part of a more complex picture. Like Aristotle, Galen sees sexual difference as both necessary and real. He's a devoted teleologist, committed to the belief that every part of nature has been created for a purpose and that nature always produces the best outcome possible under the conditions of the material world. So men and women are both required for sexual reproduction; the excess fluids of the female body are needed for the nourishment of the foetus. The weakness of women, moreover, is not just a quality established relative to the male. It defines the female sex as different in nature from the male. The weakness of the female sex begins in utero, where the female foetus, lodged on the less perfect left side of the womb, is nourished by watery and inadequately purified blood rather than by the pure blood that feeds her male counterpart. Once she's born, the woman is further differentiated from the man by the weakness and softness of her flesh and what Galen called the 'natural faculties', by which he means the capacity of the body and its parts to perform the functions providentially assigned to it. In fact, so attenuated are these faculties in women that Galen thought it impossible for a woman to be ambidextrous. She 'must be content to use only her right hand, and to do so in moderation' (*Commentary on Hippocrates' Aphorisms* 7.43, Kühn 18a.148). So even though he recognises similarities between the sexes,

Galen still sees the female sex as fundamentally different in nature from the male sex.

The historian of ancient medicine Rebecca Flemming has perceptively characterised Galen's corpus as overflowing with ideas and arguments that tend to resist systematisation. What sometimes looks messy to us reflects, in fact, his immersion in a culture 'in which good systems of thought were systems of plenitude and proliferation, not austerity and restriction'.[31] It's only to be expected that much of this messiness was cleaned up as Galen's works were slowly transformed into Galenism, the doctrines that dominated Western medicine for more than a millennium. But Galen's own thinking about the sexes was complicated. He combined a belief in homologies between male and female bodies with a strong sense of sexual difference at the level of the body and nature.

If we turn away from Galen, we find a whole range of opinions in post-classical Greco-Roman medicine on the question of whether male and female bodies are fundamentally different. To take one example, Celsus, the Roman encyclopaedist who, writing in the first century CE, gives us the first detailed account of the female body in Latin, largely follows the Hippocratic writers in constructing the female body as weaker, more fluid and more labile than the male body and in seeing the womb as marking the deviance of the female from a male norm. But, like his Hellenistic Greek models, Celsus also recognises significant continuities between the sexes. The female body thus appears on the stage of the learned Roman medical tradition through representations that 'veil and unveil both "hateful contraries" and "fearful symmetries"' in relationship to the male body.[32]

One of the most informative texts for what Greek and Roman physicians thought about the sexed body is the *Gynaecology* of Soranus, a Greek physician originally from Ephesus who was active, it seems, in the early second century CE. In the third book of the treatise, Soranus relates an extended debate in the medical tradition about whether there are affections (*pathē*) peculiar to women. Soranus is in the habit of approaching controversial questions by first defining the terms and reviewing the opinions of others before stating his own views, and this is exactly what he does here. He starts off by clarifying what he means by women: 'the female sex, in the sense in which woman (*gynē*) constitutes a class (*eidos*), the female (*to thēlu*) a gender (*genos*)' (Soranus, *Gynaecology* 3.1, Ilberg 1). He goes on to define what he means by 'peculiar' ('that which does not belong to another') and 'affection', which, importantly, is not simply a disease – that is, something contrary to nature – but may also be a state 'in accordance with nature', such as giving birth or lactation. And then he dives into the debate.

So what are the arguments in favour of the view that the female sex has affections that are 'peculiar' to it? The advocates of this position – an impressive roster that includes the fourth-century BCE physician Diocles of Carystus, members of the Empiricist sect and some followers of the Hellenistic physicians Erasistratus and Asclepiades – point first to the existence of midwives, who specialise in treating affections that women do not share with men. They observe, too, that the uterus and its proper functions – primarily, menstruation, conception and birth – are peculiar to women.

By contrast, their opponents, including Erasistratus himself and the other great Hellenistic anatomist, Herophilus, as well as the founders and disciples of the Methodist school of medicine, among whom Soranus counts himself, emphasise the homogeneity of the basic stuffs of the body. According to one line of argument associated with Asclepiades, the female body is made up of the same core elements (small particles and the passages they move through, according to Asclepiades' mechanistic corpuscular theory) as the male body, and women get sick for the same reasons (primarily, the obstruction of these passages) as men do. Herophilus offers another version of this argument, claiming that the uterus, despite its unique function, is made up of the same stuffs as every other part of the body. What's more, it's regulated by the same faculties, draws on the same material substances and becomes diseased from the same causes.

But Herophilus does concede that conception, parturition and the 'ripening' of the milk, as well as the 'opposites' of these things (infertility, miscarriages, problems with lactation), are indeed affections peculiar to women. Soranus's own position is similarly complex. He's willing to grant that the elementary parts might have come together in such a way that 'an original part of the whole [sc. body] was developed in women', so that a woman is affected 'in a manner unique to her' (*Gynaecology* 3.1, Ilberg 4). And, he can accept, as Herophilus does, that the female sex has affections of its own that are 'according to nature' – again, conception, parturition and lactation. But what Soranus emphatically denies is that there is an affection '*contrary* to nature' for the female as a *genos*. Soranus is following the Methodist principle here that there are only three pathological states of the body: constriction, flux or a mix. In these states, women show some peculiarities (a specific set of symptoms, for example). Yet these do not qualify as genuine marks of difference.

Soranus, it's worth remembering, is reporting a debate about differences between the sexes that are perceived as relevant to the practice of medicine, rather than a debate about sexual difference in and of itself. Still, his account is interesting because it involves two camps who disagree on whether each sex has a body peculiar to it or whether the sexes share a single basic material substratum. But notice that even the defenders of the one-body-fits-all theory have a hard time assimilating the uterus and its capacities to the unsexed norm. Soranus, like others working after dissection had better acquainted physicians with the anatomy of the reproductive system, may dismiss the idea that the uterus wanders freely in the body (it does continue to cause a disease labelled hysteria). Nevertheless, the uterus remains something that sets the female sex apart, as it continues to do in medical texts and commentaries in later antiquity and the medieval period.

The debate reported by Soranus is particularly interesting in the light of the argument made by Thomas Laqueur that the 'one-body' or 'one-sex' model is standard in antiquity and the medieval period. Laqueur's position, as we'll see further, draws heavily on the homologies alleged by ancient authors between the male body and the female body. He places particular weight on Galen's account in *On the Use of Parts*. But notice that the ancient advocates of a 'one-body' model in Soranus not only fail to introduce homology to make the uterus seem less like something peculiar to women.

They neglect homology altogether. They focus instead on the unsexed nature of the matter constituting the body.

Notice, too, that in the account given by Soranus, Aristotle's claim that the female is imperfect while the male is perfect is taken up by those who want to argue that the female sex has its own affections: 'for that which differs by the whole of its nature is also susceptible to particular affections' (*Gynaecology* 3.1, Ilberg 3). Aristotle, in other words, is the authority invoked on behalf of radical difference. By contrast, Laqueur argues that Aristotle offers the Western tradition 'a still more austere version of the one-sex model than did Galen.'[33] So who is right?

The problem lies with expecting a straightforward answer to this question. For much as we saw was true of Galen, Aristotle can be read in different ways on the question of how the body and matter in general relate to sexual difference. In fact, as it turns out, how one reads Aristotle on this point has had a good deal of impact on the stories that have been told within gender studies about ancient ideas about the nature of sexual difference. It's worth taking a closer look, then, at what he has to say.

Aristotle was the son of a physician. He also wrote extensively on biological subjects. These writings reflect different – and even, at times, competing – ways of viewing natural phenomena. True to Aristotle's interest in systematic consistency, they incorporate concepts and axioms common to his philosophy as a whole. But they also contain a wealth of detail gleaned from Aristotle's own observations – often patient, sometimes careless – of countless organisms, human and nonhuman, and these details can spill beyond the boundaries of his overarching categories. Aristotle's navigation of the relationship between theory and observation is especially tricky when it comes to his discussions of sexual reproduction, the main point of entry to his ideas about sexual difference. If we want to sort out what he thinks about male and female, we have to deal with different kinds of claims, having to do with both abstract principles and living organisms, and try to figure out how they relate to one another.

Aristotle's biology is founded on the idea that the 'first principles' (*archai*) of all generation are the male and the female. In the same breath, he defines each of these principles according to its role in generation. The male possesses the principle of movement and generation, while the female possesses that of matter. Aristotle is drawing here on more general categories and oppositions that cut across the branches of his philosophical system. Central to his ontology – his understanding, that is, of what exists – is the idea that every really existing thing is a substance (*ousia*) that has both form (*morphē*) and matter (*hylē*). Neither form nor matter exists on its own. One way of distinguishing the two principles of generation maps them onto the binary between form and matter:

> The female always provides the matter, the male provides that which fashions the matter into shape; this, in our view, is the specific characteristic of each of the sexes: that is what it means to be either male or female . . . The physical part, the body, comes from the female, and the soul from the male, since soul is the essence of a particular body. (Aristotle, *Generation of Animals* 738b20–7)

The female is thus defined as that which provides the matter and the male defined as that which forms the matter.

If we approach generation from another perspective, that of Aristotle's four causes – formal, telic (that towards which something aims, its *telos*), efficient and material – we arrive at another correlation. Aristotle believes that the first three causes, all of which are 'active', belong to that which generates, i.e., the male. The fourth cause, the material, is 'passive' and associated with that from which something is generated, i.e., the female. Aristotle thus allocates the power to create ensouled life to the male principle. The female is, in turn, categorically defined through the contribution of passive matter.

Aristotle's understanding of sexual difference, then, appears to turn on a strict dichotomy that is most crisply outlined in sexual reproduction. Male and female, from this perspective, are in fundamental opposition. The partisans of female exceptionality in Soranus seem to have read Aristotle rightly when they adopted him for their cause. In fact, Aristotle has been consistently associated with a rigid notion of sexual difference by his later readers. We find, for example, a Parisian Aristotelian arguing at the 1636 meeting of the Bureau d'Adresse in Paris that male and female principles are so incompatible that hermaphroditism is a logical impossibility:

> Because the internal and fundamental principal . . . of man is opposed to that of woman, because one consists in activity and the other in passivity, one in giving and the other in receiving, they can never coexist in the same individual.[34]

Aristotle comes out looking like the worst kind of essentialist; that is, someone committed to the view that male and female are essentially different. And, indeed, feminist scholars have often read him in these terms.

But things turn out to be a bit more complicated. The male and female principles shouldn't be confused with the male and female animals in which these principles are realised. It is true that the basically binary nature of these principles doesn't disappear at the level of the animal. After all, each sex has parts specific to it, Aristotle believes, so that the principles of male and female can be realised through sexual reproduction. And there's no getting around the fact that only the male body can heat blood up to the point where it becomes life-generating sperm. Aristotle sometimes calls the male 'the one who is able' and the female 'the one who is unable' (*Generation of Animals* 765b36). Yet it's also true that once we move from principles to individual males and females, we find Aristotle thinking not only in terms of opposition but also in terms of similarities, shared ground and continuities. The 'essentialist' label is misleadingly incomplete.

To start with, Aristotle holds that any species (*eidos*) falling under the genus (*genos*) of animals encompasses both the male and the female. Therefore, the sexes *cannot* differ in their essence without violating Aristotle's definition of a species (*eidos*), even as they embody the contraries 'male' and 'female'. Moreover, in Aristotle's embryology, the sex of an embryo isn't determined in advance by the form-giving nature of the male seed. Rather, sex emerges as the result of the interaction between the male seed and the conditions of the female material. If the matter contributed by the female ends up mastering the 'motions' of the male seed (usually because it's too cold), the seed 'changes into its opposite' (*Generation of Animals* 766b15–17), by which Aristotle means it turns female. Marguerite Deslauriers has argued that, given these commitments, Aristotle cannot see the difference between individual males and females as an *essential* difference.[35] Rather, the anatomical and physiological differences between men and women have something contingent about them. They belong to a realm more fluid and accidental than that of essence and principles – namely, the realm of matter.

It's no surprise, then, that when we move to Aristotle's discussions of sexed bodies, radical difference often gives way to a sliding scale. The model is neatly summed up in a formulation that we've already encountered: the female is, 'as it were', a mutilated or deformed male. In other words, while the female falls short of the male, she nevertheless approaches him.

If we reconsider the evidence with the idea of a continuum in mind, the binaries that structure sexual reproduction at the level of principles start to soften. Consider, for example, the capacity of the male to spark ensouled life. Aristotle is often seen as a defender of a 'one-seed' theory of sexual reproduction that assigns the soul- and life-engendering privilege to the male seed. But technically, this is incorrect. Aristotle does, at times, refer to both male and female seed. Both are 'residues' that begin as blood concocted from food. The male alone, however, has sufficient innate heat to concoct the blood further into a seed capable of transmitting the higher forms and movements that define human life. The colder female can create only the *catamēnia*, the material contribution to the foetus. From one perspective, that of capacity, her coldness stands in polar opposition to the male's hotness. But from another, that of the matter itself, we are dealing with gradations.

We might put it like this. For Aristotle, gradations of heat produce gradations in the value of the person, with the dominance of hot male seed producing males, the dominance of colder matter producing 'deformed' males – that is, females – and the dominance of excessively cold matter nullifying the conditions of generation altogether. In this context, Aristotle seems to approach sexual difference in much more fluid terms than the essentialist reading of him suggests. It is this Aristotle who underwrites the 'one-sex' model of the body advocated by Laqueur and others.

None of this means that Aristotle sees embodied sex as completely fluid. If we want to understand his views on sexual difference, we have to learn to hold together the idea of fixity *and* the idea of fluidity. Bodies aren't just bundles of matter, becoming more male or more female when the weather changes. They're also articulated – and so defined – by the principles of maleness and femaleness. A man can certainly lose what makes him male – namely, the capacity to concoct blood into the highest kind of seed, which can disappear with the loss of the penis. This is what happens to the eunuch, who ends up 'falling only a little short of the form of the female' (*Generation of Animals* 766a27–8). But at least as far as Aristotle is concerned, the female can never ratchet up her inborn heat enough to cross the boundary into maleness. There's only one way to go on the ladder and that's down.[36] And even when men do slip, their transformation is incomplete. The eunuch is still, in the end, only *like* a woman – or, as the Roman poet Catullus writes, a 'fake woman' (*notha mulier*, 63.27) – just as, for Galen, an ape or a woman is only *like* a man. The structure of homologies and analogies always involves an internal line that keeps one side from collapsing into the other. Despite the similarities between male and female bodies in Aristotle, that line doesn't get erased.

Aristotle's views on sexual difference are by any account hard to get a handle on. It's certainly helpful, when trying to make sense of them, to distinguish the polar principles 'male' and 'female' from actual sexed bodies, which are messier. But we have to face up, too, to the tangled interdependence of principles and bodies. We can see just how hard it is to pry the two domains apart if we try to follow Aristotle's claim that males have a more robust inborn heat than females do.

We've seen that the male principle is defined as the form-giving active cause. Therefore, males have to be hotter. But why does Aristotle identify the active cause with the male in the first place? One way of answering the question – or, rather, of sidestepping it – is to flip things around and make the hotness of males something that can be proven empirically (rather than something already supplied by the definition of the male role in generation, i.e., active and form-giving). Some modern scholars have done just that, arguing that Aristotle could very well have inferred the hotness of men and the coldness of women by simply observing their respective seminal residues – that is, sperm and menses. The latter just *look* more abundant and watery. It's easy to conclude, then, that they're less concocted.[37]

But in view of the metaphysical stakes, is it really 'an innocent, (objective) observation that one kind of matter' – i.e., female – 'is somehow more material than another'?[38] There's little question, after all, that, for Aristotle, matter is the denigrated partner to form. And the very premise that the observation of bodily fluids is straightforward is problematic, since phenomena can be interpreted in different ways. Remember that some Presocratics held that women are actually hotter. They, too, could offer empirical evidence in support of their claims. Parmenides, for example, argued that women *must* have a surplus of blood, or else they wouldn't be able to lose so much of it every month and remain healthy. He concluded that, because blood is hot, women must be hotter than men. Now, to be fair, Aristotle actually argues against Parmenides' inference in favour of his own on both theoretical and empirical grounds (*Generation of Animals*, 765b22–35). Nevertheless, when he observes that the female residue is less concocted and colder than the male seed, it's hard not to suspect that he has already assigned coldness – associated with a mostly passive, entirely inferior material cause – to the female. That is, given what coldness means to Aristotle, it is women who have to be cold.

But whatever you end up concluding about the role of ideology in Aristotle's biology, the topic of innate heat shows how entangled sexed bodies are with metaphysical principles in his views. More generally, we can see that Aristotle's thoughts on the matter of sexual difference are marked by what I've described as a tension between fixity and fluidity. Matter is itself unsexed, at least prior to conception, as is the seed. The seed gives rise to a male or a female body only under certain conditions in the womb. The formation of a body as sexed establishes difference at the level of the individual animal, but without the absolute polarity that characterises male and female principles. At the same time, matter is gendered as feminine, not only metaphysically but also at the level of real bodies, some of which are defined by being less formed and less capable of imposing form than others.

I return later in this chapter to the definition of the female through the materiality of sexual reproduction, as well as the gendering of matter as feminine, considering the work of feminist philosophers who have seen the double marginalisation of 'the feminine' and matter in early Greek philosophy as a devastatingly consequential move in the foundation of Western metaphysics. But first I want to return to Laqueur's arguments about the ancient 'one-sex body'. The far-reaching impact of these arguments on contemporary histories of sex and gender invites us to probe more deeply into the use of the past to define modern categories.

Sex and Gender: Ancients and Moderns

The basic thesis of Laqueur's *Making Sex*, as we saw earlier, is that until the eighteenth century, people in the West had views on sex and gender that were essentially the opposite of our own. Laqueur's arguments are based largely on the idea that the body in the premodern period is too unstable to function as the substrate of sexual difference. From antiquity to the Renaissance, the flesh offers only a continuum of qualities – wet and dry and, especially after Aristotle, hot and cold – along which individuals move all too easily, changing sex as they go. The reproductive capacities of males and females, while more perfect in the former, are homologous in significant ways. Add to all this the idea that, for the premoderns, female anatomy is basically male anatomy turned inside out and you have Laqueur's one-sex body. The unstable, reversible body makes it necessary, Laqueur argues, to locate the truth of sexual difference elsewhere, in a domain that he calls, at various points, metaphysical, sociological and political.

It's only in the eighteenth century, on Laqueur's account, that we see a shift away from the Aristotelian-Galenic model towards the idea of two absolutely different sexed bodies. The change of paradigm owes much to physicians. But we would be wrong, Laqueur insists, to attribute the change to advances in medical knowledge. Rather, the belief that men and women have different bodies was a reaction to social factors. In the face of a growing clamour for equality between the sexes, defenders of the status quo began to enlist evidence from biology and medicine about women's bodies and women's nature in support of the existing distribution of rights, privileges and responsibilities (which favoured men). Some of their arguments – for example, women were made for child-bearing and child-rearing; women are naturally unsuited for politics or maths or education – no doubt sound familiar, a testament to the persistent allure of 'naturalisation' in the age of brain science. By contrast, 'there is no effort' in classical antiquity and the medieval period 'to ground social roles in nature; social categories themselves are natural and on the same explanatory level as what we would take to be physical or biological facts'.[39]

But Laqueur's analysis didn't come out of nowhere, any more than the arguments of his eighteenth-century physicians did. To better understand what's at stake in his claims, it's worth situating them in the scholarly milieu where they developed, at the crossroads of feminism, the history of science and cultural studies.

One of the more hard-hitting critiques of the feminist development of the sex/gender binary in the 1970s has been that it has strategically 'quarantined' the concept of gender from 'the infections of biological sex'.[40] The very coherence of gender as a category, in fact, is founded on this isolation. There were some critical objections to the marginalisation of biology and the biological body as the sex/gender binary was calcifying, objections which have recently been renewed with greater force.[41] But in the 1980s, the split between sex and gender was more likely to be bridged by the critique of biology itself as another domain for the social construction of gender. No longer a mute, natural given, the sexed body was increasingly laid open to critique through inquiries into *its* historical, social and rhetorical construction. Such research went hand in hand with a push in the humanities and social sciences more generally to approach science as a cultural practice to be studied with the methodological tools of sociology, anthropology, history and literary analysis. By situating the sciences in relation to prevailing structures of power, those working in what came to be called 'science studies' challenged the claims of science to objectivity and disembodied truth.

In *Making Sex*, Laqueur, too, aims to show that however real the body may be – and he does not deny the 'real' body, although it makes only a cameo appearance in his introduction – *ideas* about the body are always constructed culturally and historically. What this means is that where sex (biological bodies) used to be, at least since the eighteenth century, we find there's only gender (cultural constructs). Renaissance drawings of the male and female reproductive systems, for example, suggest a different way of seeing 'sex' – if the word has any meaning in that period – than what we find in *Gray's Anatomy*. These differences can make us more aware of the extent to which social and cultural factors shape contemporary scientific and medical discourses about sexed bodies and sexual reproduction, discourses that tend to position themselves outside history altogether.

For Laqueur, one of the most important factors determining how we talk about the sexed body is our very commitment to the biological body as the domain of what's really real; that is, the *idea* of biological determinism at the level of sex. He's interested, in other words, in how claims on behalf of the sexed body come to acquire cultural authority in the first place. Like a number of other historians (and most notably Michel Foucault), he locates the roots of modern biology's ascendancy in the eighteenth and nineteenth centuries, a period also characterised by burgeoning demands for women's education and political equality. These social pressures seem to favour naturalised models of the 'two-sex body', with its power to legitimate institutionalised inequalities.

Laqueur isn't the only scholar who has sought to uncover the ideological and historical conditions under which sexual difference becomes embedded in the body and naturalised. The historian Ludmilla Jordanova, working a decade before Laqueur, demonstrated how, in the later part of the eighteenth century, the medical idea of 'sensibility' – that is, the nervous system's susceptibility to external influences – became a marker of female physiological specificity.[42] Londa Schiebinger, who has also argued for a strong contrast between ancient 'gender' and modern 'sex', has documented how scientists working between 1730 and 1790 went looking for evidence of motherhood as women's biological destiny in the differences between male and female skeletons.[43]

In the years since the publication of these studies, some historians have challenged the claim that the eighteenth century is the turning point for a shift to a 'two-sex' model, arguing that the shift should be pushed back to the sixteenth or seventeenth centuries.[44] Moreover, as we've already seen, there are a number of problems with assuming the dominance of a 'one-sex body' in the premodern period, problems to which I return below. But there's a widespread consensus that physicians have become increasingly preoccupied with sexual dimorphism over the course of the past five hundred years, a shift that has coincided with changes to the authority attached to claims about nature and the body. Moreover, by trying to show the implication of biology and medicine in ideological battles at the very origins of their modern institutional formation, scholars like Laqueur, Jordanova and Schiebinger have embedded this shift in the politics of sexual difference.

The politics of sexual difference have hardly gone away. We do not have to deny that the bodies of men and women diverge in some respects to see the benefits of gaining historical distance on the hunt for signs of sexual dimorphism that still dominates contemporary science, especially in its popularising guises. Too often we register reports about 'the female brain' or natural deficits in men's capacity to nurture without looking closely at which differences in the data have been made to matter; the assumptions that creep in when scientists move from observation to interpretation; the difficulties involved in pinning down 'masculine' and 'feminine' traits; and the failure of scientific studies of sexual difference, recently documented at length by Rebecca Jordan-Young, to come up with consistent results.[45] The more we can grasp that the science of sexual dimorphism has a history, the better chance that we won't simply accept new reports trumpeting its existence at face value.

The investigations of historians like Jordanova, Laqueur and Schiebinger thus complement the efforts of feminist biologists to show how contemporary scientists have consistently sought to identify sex-specific traits – and, hence, sexual difference and sex complementarity – in data that appear to tell a much more complicated story. The developmental geneticist Anne Fausto-Sterling has documented at length the ambiguities in the experimental results on which some relatively recent conclusions of strict sexual dimorphism in human nature have been based.[46] She's argued that, given these ambiguities and the complexities they suggest, we – scientists and non-scientists alike – need to recognise the radical diversity of bodies without shoehorning them into the categories of 'male' and 'female'. Writing about intersexed bodies, she turns the idea of sexual dimorphism as a biological truth on its head:

> But if the state and the legal system have an interest in maintaining a two-party sexual system, they are in defiance of nature. For biolog-ically speaking, there are many gradations running from female to male; and depending on how one calls the shots, one can argue that along the spectrum lie at least five sexes – and perhaps even more.[47]

Fausto-Sterling's appeal to nature admittedly sets her apart from cultural historians like Schiebinger and Laqueur, a difference of perspective I come back to later in this chapter. But her work confirms the need to be critically alert in the face of headlines about the natural differences between the sexes. What I want to stress is that historical literacy plays an important role, too, in helping us understand why scientists still tend to privilege differences that suggest two separate, rigidly defined sexes rather than poly-morphic diversity and common ground. It forces us to be more self-aware about our own interest in the nature of sexual difference when we look at the evidence from earlier societies.

But there are also difficulties with a 'one-sex' to 'two-sex' narrative about the history of sex and gender. The most serious of these is that it relies on a polarising opposition between the ancients and the moderns that ends up underwriting the contemporary binary between sex and gender. Laqueur, as we've seen, understands modern views as inverted versions of premodern ones. Ancient 'gender' is a metaphysical concept with the solidity of the modern notion of sex, while ancient 'sex' designates the physical realm but carries the connotations of malleability that we moderns tend to associate with gender. As we have seen, this account is too simple. But the story of an eighteenth-century rupture between premodern and modern ways of viewing the body doesn't just gloss over complexities in the ancient evidence. More troublingly, the very terms of the comparison – namely, the modern notion of gender and its antonym, sex – risk forcing ancient categories 'into modern straitjackets', as Rebecca Flemming has written.[48] The problem is this. If we want the kind of symmetry between past and present suggested by an 'inversion' model, we have to achieve it by driving a wedge between nature in the sense of masculine and feminine principles and nature as it is realised through the fleshy body. But when we do this, the binary between 'sex' and 'gender' in the ancient world becomes the product of our own model, imposed on classical antiquity from outside.

There's no need, however, to force the opposition between 'sex' and 'gender'. If we become more open to the different ways of organising the world evident in the ancient material, we find that this material doesn't confirm the oppositional logic that structures the modern sex/gender binary as much as it challenges that logic altogether.

Consider, for example, the argument about naturalisation in the ancient world. Laqueur derives the stability of ancient 'gender' in part from the fact that conventional social roles go largely unquestioned in our ancient sources. But it's worth noting that these roles could be challenged. In the *Republic*, Plato puts forth the argument that women should be excluded from politics because of their reproductive role only to have Socrates refute it. Socrates' aim in doing so is to establish women's suitability for the guardian class in the ideal city. While guardians are not rulers, they nevertheless constitute an elite political class, undergo rigorous training and form a tight community, sharing property and exchanging sexual partners through state-regulated unions. That including women in such an exclusive class is an unusual move is confirmed by Socrates' need to justify it. He does so by arguing that whether someone has a uterus or not has as little to do with their ability to be educated or perform the duties of a guardian as the presence or absence of a beard.

Now there are limits to the equality between the sexes here. It's a stretch to call Plato, who matter-of-factly holds that women remain naturally inferior in all respects to their male counterparts, a proto-feminist. But his utopian vision, for all that it continues to define women in terms of their reproductive and familial roles, doesn't allow these roles to preclude political participation. At the same time, Plato seems to be the exception rather than the rule (and the *Republic* is an exception among Platonic dialogues in this respect). The social roles of women and men, while subject to important changes in the Hellenistic and Roman periods, appear by all accounts more fixed in classical antiquity than in the eighteenth century. So Laqueur is right to observe that there would have been little need to ground those roles in nature, as we see happening in the early modern period. Even Aristotle, who's often blamed for first naturalising the political subordination of women in terms of biology, addresses female inferiority independently in his works on politics and in his biological writing. Claims made in one domain aren't required to shore up those made in another.

The idea of 'gender' in *Making Sex*, however, isn't only stabilised by the social realm. It is also – and indeed, *primarily* – held in place by the natural order (*physis*). 'What we would take to be ideologically charged social constructions of gender', Laqueur observes, ' . . . were for Aristotle indubitable facts, "natural truths"'.[49] It is precisely because these 'natural' principles are so real for Aristotle that they become the analogues of modern biological facts in Laqueur's schema (even as our rejection of these principles makes it easy to reclassify them as 'ideologically charged' constructs of gender). The twist – and here's where the inversion comes in – is that the reality of Aristotelian principles floats above the physical body, whereas the reality of modern biological facts inheres within it. But the clarity of the model rests on two problematic assumptions. The ancient 'biological' body *has* to be unstable and unreal, seeing as it has to serve as the foil to the modern body, and 'natural' principles remain, in some sense, metaphysical.

But why do we have to assume a strict opposition between the biological body and the socio-cultural domain, so crucial for our own binary view of sex and gender, in dealing with the ancient evidence? Why project our own rigid contrast between nature and culture onto the relationship in classical antiquity between the categories or principles 'male' and 'female' and sexed bodies? If, instead, we set aside the opposition between biological sex and socio-cultural gender, we're no longer obliged to define 'metaphysical' nature, here standing in for the 'cultural' domain, as the opposite of the flesh when dealing with our ancient sources. Once this contrast is set aside, it becomes easier to perceive the ways in which 'masculine' and 'feminine' principles and traits, on the one hand, and 'male' and 'female' bodies, on the other, interact in classical antiquity to create complex concepts of sexual difference. These contrasts enable a variety of ways of understanding how sexual difference is realised in and through individual human bodies. What we've seen so far of ancient medical and biological writing suggests that the category of nature, despite being set against something like 'culture' (*nomos*) in other contexts in Greek thought, doesn't support the binary that is so entrenched in our thinking about sex and gender. Moreover, at the level of individual embodied natures, we see, as I've stressed time and again, both fixity and fluidity.

If we want to understand how bodies are classed as male and female in Greco-Roman medical and biological writing, recognising that this is just one area of the culture as a whole, I suggest we try to think instead in terms of a continuum *within* material bodies along which maleness and femaleness is more or less fixed. In the texts we have, a baseline of maleness or femaleness seems to be determined at the moment the embryo is formed. Before that decisive moment, what we might call 'sex' (closely associated with reproductive capacity) is up for grabs. But after the outcome of the struggle between male and female seeds or stuffs in the uterus has been reached, the sex of the embryo is, for all intents and purposes, fixed (although in some early embryological theories, whether the foetus develops on the left or right side can have a bearing on sex or gender identity).

Nevertheless, much of the uncertainty and fluidity that characterises the meeting of male and female on the battlefield of the uterus persists within the 'gender identity' of the resulting person. The slide towards maleness in Phaëthusa and Nanno offers an excellent example of such instability. The potential for drift will become even clearer in the following chapter, where we'll see some of the ancient practices designed to stabilise masculinity from the time of infancy, when wet nurses under the Roman Empire were known to mould the foreskin to standards of propriety, through the disciplinary regimens of adolescence, to the cultivation of normative habits and desires in adulthood. The evidence for the daily vigilance required to uphold masculinity in both Greece and Rome shows that gender identity was perceived as fluid even outside medical writing. At the same time, we can see the influence of naturalising philosophy and medicine in the fact that fluidity was increasingly explained by all kinds of authors from the fifth century BCE onwards in materialist terms. The emergence of the physical body as a concept is why practices of acting on the body – and often on a mind that is itself understood to be physical – are so important to securing gender.

There are plenty of complications within this picture. Recall, for example, the debates reported by Soranus about whether the whole body is sexed or only certain parts (e.g., the uterus) or the ambiguity that surrounds the eunuch, who has lost what makes him male without having crossed over to being a female. And traits that go against one's 'proper' sex aren't always the result of how the body is managed after birth. The embryological theory found in the Hippocratic text *On Regimen* suggests that some people are fixed *as gender deviants* at the very moment sex is determined. If, for example, the male seed of the mother conquers the female seed of the father, the child is born an *androgynē*, a 'man-woman' (*On Regimen* I 28, Littré 6.502). By this the author means a male – for the androgynous type is classed among the three kinds of men – who is nevertheless congenitally effeminate, doomed to live out the confused material conditions of his conception within his gender identity. To take another example, the practice of physiognomy, which we'll see further in the next chapter, assumes that people have a particular gender identity by nature (e.g., the effeminate male), which no amount of artifice or practice can alter.

Then again, we might just take cases where gender identity is determined in utero as further evidence for a continuum along which both sex and gender are located by different authors as relatively fixed or fluid. If what we would call sex is fixed in virtually all our authors, gender, in the sense that one is 'masculine' or 'feminine', travels more freely across that continuum. At times, it, too, seems 'biologically' determined. But the more plastic gender becomes, the more susceptible it is to environmental influences, bad behaviour and practices of self-fashioning. The point I want to make is that all this happens within the scope of the physical body and its nature. Some aspects of that body are given, others are malleable. Different authors have different views on which are which. But the physical body is not quarantined from culture.

What's at stake here is not only how we read the past. It's also a question of whether the practice of history legitimates or challenges the assumptions of the present, and at what level. On the one hand, the accounts of Jordanova, Laqueur and Schiebinger have helped us see how an understanding of the biological body as the bedrock of sexual difference is contingent on historical developments. On the other hand, we cannot just assume that the ancients function as our mirror image, perfectly inverted like female to male in Laqueur's one-sex body. To do so is to cripple the power of the past to challenge the sex/gender binary itself. The story we get in *Making Sex* – first gender, then sex – implies that the whole history of thinking about sexual difference in the West has been structured by a tension between sex (nature, physical bodies) and gender (culture, malleable traits) just like our own. The very transformation of the sex/gender binary into a category that structures historical inquiry makes it into something without a history of its own, immutable and natural. Yet if we take that binary as given, we fail to see how it's precisely the polarity between biology and culture that has helped create the coherence of gender as a modern and postmodern object of study.

The ancient medical and biological writers, read differently, can help us find ways of getting past this binary by opening up different ways of conceptualising the interaction between categories and bodies. It's true that, at first glance, the material might not look very promising. What we're dealing with in antiquity are, in some sense, variations on the time-worn nature–nurture theme. More perniciously, our ancient authors tend to lean on the very assumptions that feminists and gender theorists have tried to undercut, such as the idea that women are naturally passive, emotional and ruled by their bodies. The stigmatisation in Greece and Rome of individuals who exhibit the 'wrong' gender (e.g., effeminate men) is depressingly familiar.

But nothing here justifies writing these sources off altogether. For they testify to a long and sophisticated tradition of trying to come to terms with the very plasticity of our identities as male and female, masculine and feminine, men and women in the face of a fairly stable distribution of reproductive parts among types of bodies. In recent years, we've started to think about the sexing of the body in more complex ways. But there's something to be learned from watching the Greek and Roman biological writers imagine the malleability of material selves in their own idioms, negotiating the binaries between body and mind and nature and culture in unexpected ways. To follow our Greek and Roman sources doesn't mean we have to end up in the same places they do. We may find instead the spurs of alternate paths that can help us cut through the binaries that have constrained so much modern and postmodern thinking about the relationship of materiality to subjectivity, identity and the potential for transformation.

The Gendering of Matter

For much of this chapter, we've been asking how the ancients viewed the nature of sexual difference and especially the question of whether sex is a trait fixed in the body. Here I want to step back and pose the question of the relationship of gender to materiality in classical antiquity from another angle. Did the ancients believe that nature or matter has a gender? Do they view the body as inherently 'feminine' or 'masculine'? If so, what are the consequences of their ideas? And, to put it bluntly, are they right or wrong?

The hint of an answer to at least some of these questions can be found in our earlier discussion of Aristotle's views on sexual difference. There we saw that the very principle of 'the feminine' for Aristotle is bound to the principle of matter, while at the level of sexual reproduction, matter is contributed by the female, with form being supplied by the male. It is hard to imagine better evidence that at least some ancient authors saw material bodies not only as sexed (male or female) but as gendered *in their materiality* (here, as feminine). And Aristotle offers evidence, too, for the devaluation of matter in relationship to masculine principles such as form and agency. But it's worth asking what we should *do* with this evidence. What does it tell us about ancient gender? Does it have any bearing on contemporary theories of gender?

One strategy would be to inquire into whether Aristotle's devaluing of the mother's role in reproduction can stand in for what 'the ancients' believed more generally. Here, as we might by now expect, the situation is not exactly clear-cut. It's difficult to deny that many of our ancient Greek sources, at least the textual sources that we have, seem uneasy about the female capacity to give birth. Already in Hesiod we encounter ambivalence about the role of feminine principles and especially mortal women in genesis and reproduction and a desire to locate creative force on the side of the father. The idea that men are not born from mortal mothers structured the way some ancient cities mythologised their own origins. The citizens of both Athens and Thebes claimed to have had autochthonous ancestors; ancestors, that is, who were born directly from the earth, never passing through the birth canal of a flesh-and-blood mother. Heroes on the tragic stage imagined reproduction without maternity. The young puritan Hippolytus in Euripides' play of the same name conjures up, in the midst of a tirade against women, an alternate reality where men just buy their children directly from the gods, getting what they pay for (*Hippolytus* 616–24). In Euripides' *Medea*, Jason wishes that men could reproduce on their own, a situation, he believes, that would bring about the prelapsarian paradise inhabited by the first race of men in Hesiod (*Medea* 523–5).

But even if the 'dream of a purely paternal heredity never ceased to haunt the Greek imagination', it was hard to avoid the mother altogether.[50] The next-best option seems to have been that adopted by Aristotle – namely, to downplay or downgrade the contribution made by the mother to sexual reproduction. Most notorious among such attempts, at least for contemporary readers, is the speech delivered by Apollo in his defense of matricide in the *Eumenides*, the last play in Aeschylus's *Oresteia* trilogy. Apollo argues there that Orestes should not be held responsible for the murder of his mother, Clytemnestra, on the grounds that she is virtually no relation to him.

> The one called the mother of the one born
> is not the parent, but a nurse to the newly sown sprout.
> The one who mounts engenders life while she, like a stranger for a
>   stranger,
> preserves the young shoot, unless god does it some harm.
>
> (Aeschylus, *Eumenides* 658–61)

The mother, in other words, doesn't contribute anything of her own to the life created. She's simply the foreign host of the father's seed. Apollo's argument is by no means a clear success: the trial results in a hung jury. The god's reasoning, however, appears subtly validated when Athena breaks the stalemate in favour of the matricidal son, justifying her rejection of the mother's claim by pointing out that she herself spent no time in the womb but sprung from the head of Zeus.

And yet we shouldn't pass over the doubts of the Aeschylean jury too quickly. Half a century after the *Oresteia* (458 BCE), Euripides revisited Apollo's exculpatory argument in a scene from his *Orestes* (408 BCE). Orestes is trying to assuage the anger of his maternal grandfather Tyndareus, who is understandably none too happy about the death of his daughter: 'My father begat me, your daughter bore me, she was the field that received the seed from another' (*Orestes* 552–3). This time around, the argument has a specious ring, and it only makes Tyndareus angrier.

Indeed, Apollo probably didn't have contemporary science on his side. Many of the Presocratics, including Alcmaeon, Parmenides, Empedocles and Democritus, seem to have believed – for we have to depend on later commentators for reports of their theories – that the female contributes generative matter to reproduction. The Hippocratics, as we saw above, adopt a similar approach, with our two main embryological sources (*On the Seed/On the Nature of the Child* and *On Regimen*) advancing a two-seed theory. No classical medical text, moreover, defends the one-seed position. Some centuries later, Galen is adamant that the two-seed theory is the authentic Hippocratic position and defends it vigorously against Aristotle.

Even Aristotle, however, doesn't follow Apollo in writing the mother off as a mere incubator. The female on his model contributes not only space but also matter. Moreover, as we saw earlier, the outcome of the encounter between the matter contributed by the female and the male seed determines the sex as well as some characteristics of the resulting embryo, complicating the 'passive' role of feminised matter. It's true that, despite granting the female a role in reproduction, Aristotle devalues her contribution and reserves the capacity to generate ensouled human life for the male. The compromising association of the female with the material body in Aristotle brings us back to the tendency of the medical writers and Plato to define female nature, implicitly or explicitly, as a form of subordination to the physical body. Still, Aristotle's remarks on generation are marked by a tension between the recognition that the female plays a necessary and significant role in the generation of human life, on the one hand, and the desire to privilege the contribution of the father, on the other.

These tensions can appear more muted and the relationship between women and fertility less fraught if we move beyond the confines of the canon and consider the culture of early and classical Greece more broadly. The association of women with fertility was central to the life of ancient communities. In the classical *polis*, women were the primary participants in the ritual control of agricultural production through festivals such as the Thesmophoria at Athens, festivals that undoubtedly have deep roots in even older cults. The analogies between the female body and the earth and between the womb and the ploughed field abound in our sources, as Page duBois has richly documented.[51] We can see these festivals and cultural representations as evidence that men sought to control female sexuality and fertility. But we should also be open to the cultural respect and power accorded to women – and not only because of their perceived associations with fertility – in the ancient world within the religious sphere, as well as within the household.

At the same time, there are reasons for narrowing our perspective here to take in only canonical texts and, more specifically, canonical philosophical texts such as those of Aristotle. For one thing, we would do well to make a distinction between the semantic complex represented by the earth and the more specific philosophical concept of matter (*hylē*, 'wood' or 'timber'), which Aristotle was arguably the first to introduce. That is not to say that these two concepts are not intimately related or that philosophy is somehow insulated from 'raw' materiality and its archaic representations. Rather, recognising the specificity of philosophical constructions of matter brings us back to the question I asked a few pages ago about what we 'do' with Aristotle's gendered principles.

In the last section of this chapter, I want to trace out one strategy for engaging this material – namely, the contribution made by feminist critiques of the gendering of matter in early Greek philosophy to contemporary debates about gender. How have analyses of gender at the origins of Western metaphysics informed our thinking about the very historicity of matter as a concept? What role have these analyses played in debates about the usefulness of an association between matter and women or 'the feminine' within feminist critiques of the philosophical tradition?

Let's begin by adjusting our perspective in order to ask why Aristotle and 'the Greeks' should matter to feminist critique in the first place. No one in contemporary feminist and gender theory has answered the question more forcefully and more unambiguously than the French feminist philosopher and psychoanalyst Luce Irigaray. For Irigaray, there is no moving forward without a return to the moment when, as she puts it, 'we forgot': *forgetting that we have forgotten* is sealed over at the dawning of the photological metaphor-system of the West'.[52] Or, as she puts it more bluntly in a recent paper: 'With regard to Greek culture . . . I think that we are trying to find the crossroads at which we have taken the wrong path'.[53] The ancients are foundational to Irigaray's philosophical project. Indeed, 'the history of philosophy for Irigaray', as Miriam Leonard has written, 'starts (and in some sense finishes . . .) with Plato'.[54] Irigaray's attention to Plato – Aristotle, too, figures large in her work – comes as no surprise, given her philosophical training in France in the 1960s and the 1970s. In such a context, to critique Plato and Aristotle was to mount a full-scale challenge to an intellectual tradition that drew its legitimacy from classical antiquity. The force of this challenge has sometimes been lost in the reception of Irigaray's work among Anglophone theorists of gender, many of whom lack the training in ancient philosophy that was *de rigeur* in Europe. At the same time, the increasing rarity of a 'classical education' has increased the importance of Irigaray's own readings as a point of entry to classical antiquity within gender studies. Her insistence that feminist philosophy must first *remember* the past before looking to the future can be credited with helping keep Greek texts in the foreground of feminist and gender theory.

What have we forgotten about the classical past? The answer, for Irigaray, is straightforward. The Greeks inaugurate the exclusion of 'the feminine' within Western metaphysics. I will come back in a moment to what 'the feminine' means for Irigaray. But it's worth asking first: What does it mean to uncover an absence? Trained in both philosophy and psychoanalysis, Irigaray appropriates the tools of both disciplines to reread texts from the philosophical canon by inhabiting, as it were, the logic that governs them. Her patient, probing and disruptive rereadings pioneer a technique of bringing to light what is not simply missing from these texts but what eludes all modes of direct representation. One way of describing this technique is as excessive or strategic mimicry. Irigaray's texts are woven from quotations, paraphrases, rhetorical questions, sentence fragments and subversive inferences in a style that resolutely resists summary. To see what Irigaray is up to, let's look at an extract – translated into English by Gillian C. Gill – from her long essay 'Plato's *Hystera*', originally published in French in 1974 in *Speculum of the Other Woman*.

The passage in question 'mimics' the famous Allegory of the Cave in Plato's *Republic*. The philosopher has just exited the cave, leaving its puppet-representations – shadows of the truth – for the genuine reality above ground. Bracing himself, he turns to face the light of the sun.

> And since the power of fantasy is now circumvented in/by the star, 'last of all' man 'will be able to look at the sun itself'. One might add: this is what he will wish to do. This will be his only desire, even. The sun has a monopoly on attraction. And if the sight of its 'reflections in water or any other medium' could hold the attention of one unaware of the waste involved in such reduplication and procreation; if it was necessary to retrace the links in the chain of 'copies' in order to sustain proof of the model they are based on; if the struggle with childhood, with the blindness correlated with birth (in another body) was unavoidable and demanded to be methodically pursued in order to purge the sight of its fascination with the charms of the senses – perhaps with all this behind it, the preliminary education, the formation, has arrived at its goal now. At its first goal. The Sun. Quit of the 'mediums' that permitted his reproduction in images of more or less good, truth, and beauty, freed from the matrical and material support [*ce support encore matriciel, maternel*] he had needed in order to spawn so many more or less bastard offspring whom the apprentice philosophy had put up with in the childhood of philosophy, now the Sun at last will be envisioned in his omnipotence. His sovereignty. His autonomy. Himself, 'in his own proper place, and contemplating him as he is'.[55]

If you go back and read Plato's original, the scene may seem like an unusual choice. For you'll find that it doesn't have much to do with 'the feminine' or 'the masculine' at all. Nor does Irigaray's restaging, at least at first glance, seem to uncover these terms. Yet on closer examination, the world disavowed by the philosopher's attraction towards the sun begins to emerge in subtly feminine terms: the blindness 'correlated with birth (in another body)'; the 'charms of the senses'; 'the support', *matriciel* and *maternel* in Irigaray's punning French, that has enabled the engendering of 'bastard offspring'. The gender of the philosopher – and of the sun itself – starts to sound, in turn, insistently masculine. The passage is animated by the inexorable movement towards a goal, accompanied by ever more intense purging until the philosopher arrives at 'himself, "in his own proper place"'. What Irigaray is after is the simulation of a phantasmatic 'feminine' at the very moment that it's quietly abandoned on the path to (paternal) truth, suppressed within the terms of philosophical representation. Irigaray faithfully – which is to say subversively – reproduces those terms to show what they ignore and, in so doing, what they betray.

Notice that the dynamics of the passage follow the movement from support and dependence to autonomy and sovereignty. Behind these stages we can glimpse the outlines of 'another body' that is ultimately left behind on this quest: the body of the mother. Each of these terms, 'body' and 'mother', has a powerful resonance for Irigaray. For the ground disavowed by metaphysics is matter. We can see this particularly clearly in the short essay 'How to Conceive (of) a Girl' (also in *Speculum*), whose epigraphs are drawn from Aristotle's writings on sexual reproduction and sexual difference. Irigaray focuses on the last of these citations, where the material residue of women is associated with 'prime matter' (*prōtē hylē*), a difficult concept in Aristotle that often eludes definition. For Irigaray, the very impossibility of knowing that's built into the concept is the symptom of an exclusion. Might prime matter be, she asks, 'the body of the mother, and the process of becoming flesh within the mother'?[56] The maternal body functions here as the very soil 'in which the logos can grow'.[57] Irigaray's point is not that Aristotle excludes matter altogether. Rather, she finds the points when he takes matter into consideration suspicious, for the reason that such philosophical discussions – and here Irigaray shows her psycho-analytic inclinations – point to a repression taking place far below the exclusions of matter being enacted in the text. What is hidden is the dependence of *all* logos on what she calls *la mère-matière*, 'mother–matter': 'Every utterance, every statement, will thus be developed and affirmed by covering over the fact that being's unseverable relation to mother–matter has been buried'.[58]

Irigaray interrogates the exclusion of 'mother–matter' most exhaustively in 'Plato's *Hystera*', her reading of the *Republic*. For classicists, a second Platonic text has offered a crucial figuration of the double movement by which the maternal body is both appropriated and disavowed at the origins of philosophy: the *Symposium*. In a dialogue that unfolds in the all-male space of the symposium, we find, in the influential reading of David Halperin, 'the paedagogic processes by which men reproduce themselves culturally' – most notably elite pederasty – invested most enthusiastically 'with the prestige of female procreativity'.[59] I want to focus, however, on another Platonic text: the *Timaeus*. If Irigaray's engagement with the *Timaeus* is less developed than her treatment of the *Republic*, it's nevertheless the *Timaeus* and, to some extent, Irigaray's reading of the *Timaeus*, that has become a privileged site for engaging the gendered dynamics of matter at the origins of Western philosophy. Indeed, Irigaray's reading, together with the readings of Julia Kristeva and Judith Butler, offers a microcosm of debates about the meaning and the priority of sexual difference at this ostensibly foundational moment.

The *Timaeus* represents one of the first attempts in ancient Greek philosophy to think through the nature of something like matter (it's Aristotle who first uses the term *hylē* of matter). The narrator, Timaeus, openly acknowledges that what he has to say is speculative. His topic, after all, is the physical world, with its drift and turmoil. Still, the dialogue's account of cosmic genesis became a classic in later ancient and medieval philosophy, wielding considerable authority.

Timaeus first posits two kinds of being: unchanging Forms, on the one hand, and imitations, created and embodied, on the other. Eventually he introduces a third kind, which he labels at one point the 'receptacle' (*hypodochē*) and, at another, *chōra* ('land' or, more abstractly, 'place' or 'space'), glossed as the 'nurse of all generation'. The *chōra* contributes nothing to generation. It is, rather, entirely sterile and passive. And yet, it's the necessary space of mediation between the two other kinds of being, a point of passage for the Forms before they are realised through bodies in another world. The *chōra* is, as such, the condition of all embodied existence. In a crucial passage, Timaeus likens it to a mother, part of a triangle that also includes the paternal Forms and the created offspring.

> At the present time, then, we must conceptualise three kinds: that which is being generated, that in which generation takes place and that which the thing being generated is naturally made to resemble. And in fact it is fitting to liken the receiving thing to a mother, the source to the father and the nature in between these things to the offspring and to recognise that if the imprinted copy is to take on every variety of form, the thing itself in which the model is fashioned would only be sufficiently prepared if it lacks the shape of all the forms it is about to receive. (Plato, *Timaeus* 50c-e)

Timaeus's ontology is thus firmly implicated in the dynamics of sexual reproduction. The *chōra* that functions as the site of inscription is compared to the mother, while the source of the offspring's form acquires the name of the father.

But how should we understand Timaeus's apparent conflation of the material and the maternal? Note, first, his shift into the mode of likeness. He doesn't say that the receptacle (*hypodochē*) or the *chōra* actually is a mother. He says it is *like* a mother. It's useful to recall here Irigaray's distinction between 'the feminine' that is represented within philosophical discourse (here in the form of likeness) and 'the feminine' that can register only as a spectral presence within the discourse that it makes possible. Irigaray, in her own reading of the scene, emphasises that the *chōra* has no proper form or being of its (her?) own: 'needed to define essences, her function requires that she herself have no definition'.[60] Instead, 'she' stands outside the system of representation altogether as its ground, the blank surface that mirrors the image of the Forms without remembering their imprints or contributing to the 'children' created. But, of course, what we have here is still a representation, albeit one that represents the *resistance* to representation. For Irigaray, the very figuration of the *chōra* in terms of a mother who receives without giving symbolises the suppression of both matter and 'the feminine' on the stage of philosophy.

Irigaray isn't the only feminist philosopher to have turned to Plato's *chōra*. Julia Kristeva, in a text published the same year as Irigaray's *Speculum* and translated into English as *Revolution in Poetic Language*, approaches the *Timaeus* from a rather different angle.[61] Kristeva takes onboard Plato's likening of the *chōra* to the mother but recasts the *chōra* as what she calls the 'semiotic' or pre-symbolic realm. The semiotic, according to Kristeva, describes a space where the infant's body remains entangled with the mother's, a space organised by drives not yet expressible in language (and accessed in adult life only under the privileged conditions of poetic language). Kristeva believes, as Irigaray does, that Western metaphysics emerges through the exclusion of the *chōra*, understood in terms of the maternal body, and that this exclusion continues to define philosophy. But whereas Irigaray seeks to revisit canonical moments in the tradition in order to simulate the displacement of 'mother–matter', Kristeva works to reclaim the maternal *chōra* for her own theoretical project, investing it with novel signification.

What Irigaray and Kristeva seem to agree on is the sense of a fundamental bond between the maternal and the material, a bond that is devalued by the metaphysical tradition founded in Greece. The equation of maternity and materiality, however, is not without its problems. Indeed, both Irigaray and Kristeva have been criticised for their alleged belief that 'the maternal' is an essence that persists unchanged throughout history. But rather than going into those debates, I want to approach the role of the matter–maternity coupling at the origins of Western metaphysics through Judith Butler's reading of the *Timaeus*, which is also a reading of Irigaray's reading of the dialogue.

Butler rejects outright the strategic appropriation of the *chōra* as the locus of a rival feminist ontology or ethics, a position that she associates primarily with Kristeva. She instead focuses her critical energy on Irigaray's identification of 'the feminine' and, more specifically, 'the maternal', with the 'constitutive outside' of the *Timaeus*; that is, that which the dialogue excludes from representation – namely, matter in Irigaray's sense of the unspeakable materiality that grounds all representation. The problem here, Butler argues, is the uncritical identification of 'the outside' and 'non-thematisable materiality' with 'the feminine'.[62] By contrast, the gendering of matter is, for her, a *product* of metaphysics itself, and one that is pernicious and tenacious. The idea that matter has a (feminine) gender becomes, in Butler's hands, a myth to be exploded.

For Butler, then, what we're witnessing in the *Timaeus* is one moment in the creation of the formless, material feminine *as* a philosophical figure. For by adopting the terms of sexual reproduction (with the active lined up with the male, the passive with the female) to structure the relationship between the Forms, matter and the world of things, Plato inscribes sexual difference into the conceptualisation of materiality. But it's a mistake, Butler insists, to accept these terms, to 'secure and perpetuate a constitutive violation of the feminine'.[63]

In her epoch-making *Gender Trouble*, published three years before the reading of the *Timaeus* in *Bodies that Matter*, Butler had proposed resistance along similar lines to the strategy of taking the mother's body as the disavowed site of representation. According to the critique outlined there,

> the maternal body would no longer be understood as the hidden ground of all signification, the tacit cause of all culture. It would be understood, rather, as an effect or consequence of a system of sexuality in which the female body is required to assume maternity as the essence of its self and the law of its desire.[64]

In *Bodies that Matter*, the construct of the female body (and bodies or matter as feminine) acquires a history. In her first chapter, Butler announces that she'll pursue 'a consideration of the scenography and topography of construction'. Her project turns out to include the return to the ancients.[65]

But if something has been forgotten at the beginning of the Western tradition in Butler's view, it's not mother–matter, as it is for Irigaray. Rather, it's the knowledge that the association between 'mother' and 'matter' is created by philosophy. The critical imperative isn't to remember the excluded maternal body or the lost intimacy of mother and infant but to expose the way in which matter comes to be represented at the origin of metaphysics.

What's at stake for Butler in the return to the *Timaeus*, then, is a challenge to the relationship between matter and 'the feminine' not just in Western philosophy but in feminism itself. As the passage from *Gender Trouble* suggests, that challenge is part of a larger critique that Butler was pursuing in the early 1990s, one that had an enormous impact on the future course of gender studies. At the heart of this critique was Butler's repudiation of the category of Woman around which traditional feminism had been organised. That category had come under attack before, most seriously for its blindness to racial, cultural and class differences (a problem that Butler also draws attention to). But she takes a different tack, mounting an aggressive offensive against the essentialist underpinnings of the category of Woman and, more specifically, the idea that sexual difference is rooted in the body.

Butler developed this line of argument by pointing to the heterosexual bias of much feminist theory from the 1970s and 1980s. Butler's position builds on the work of the French philosopher Monique Wittig. Wittig has argued that the very idea of sexed bodies (male and female) is a cultural fiction designed to naturalise heterosexual norms ('heteronormativity') in the interest of promoting reproductive sexuality. In the confines of such a system, 'woman' is a term that makes sense *only* within a heterosexual relationship with a man: the lesbian, strictly speaking, is not a woman.[66] Butler doesn't see heteronormativity as the only system of power that constrains the expression of gendered identities. Still, she sees it as exercising considerable power over the formation of gender norms, with the result that some gender identities, such as the butch lesbian, become literally unintelligible within the dominant logic of sexuality.

If we go back to the *Timaeus*, we can see these arguments being developed in the crucible of the Platonic dialogue. By challenging the alignment of 'the feminine' with matter in Irigaray's reading, Butler dislodges the proprietary claim of 'the feminine' on the position of the 'excluded Other' in Western metaphysics. Indeed, on her analysis, Plato's cosmogony produces a whole range of excluded Others that come to be identified in ancient Greek philosophy with materiality, including slaves, children and animals.

At the same time, Butler continues to see Plato's representation of his ontological triad in reproductive terms as significant. One reason the scene remains important is because it's where Plato most starkly equates the *chōra* with formless femininity. But Butler shifts our attention slightly to Plato's insistence on the receptivity of the *chōra*, which stands in contrast with the phallic agency of the father. From this perspective, the binary excludes the possibility of a female who acts (through penetration) or a male who's acted upon (is penetrated). These taboos make heterosexuality, with its strict regulation of penetration, a necessary precondition of the stability of Plato's ontology, as necessary, in fact, as the identification of formless 'matter' with the mother. For Butler, then, the *Timaeus*'s heterosexual dyad is a point of resistance in its own right. She aims to crack open the dyad's oppositional logic to reveal the wider range of gendered positions that it hides.

On the one hand, then, Butler embraces Irigaray's use of mimicry to upset the Western philosophical tradition from within. The *Timaeus*, by virtue of its position at the head of that tradition, remains a strategic text for such a project. On the other hand, her own reading multiplies the places where subversive mimicry is practiced: 'if there is an occupation and reversal of the master's discourse, it will come from many quarters.'[67] Every attempt to delimit the 'elsewhere' of discourse will produce another 'constitutive outside'. At the same time, this 'elsewhere' remains implicated in the gendered history of materiality, a history that takes the ancients as a point of origin.

The positing of the ancients as foundational is especially interesting in light of the interpretations of ancient medicine and biology that we saw earlier, where the premodern functioned as the inversion of the modern. Butler uses Plato's text to take up a different angle on matter in Greek philosophy. She's interested in going back to the *Timaeus* in part in order to undermine the idea that matter preexists language and culture by demonstrating its history. Her project participates in the post-structuralist impulse to show the difficulties inherent in the concept of a 'real' that exists outside all representation. More often than not, theorists working in this tradition have represented the 'reality' of the body and matter as something that comes after language, not before, which is to say as something always already implicated in discourse, ideology and culture. Butler, working along similar lines, argues that the claim of matter and bodies on the real, much like the alliance between matter and 'the feminine', is produced by a history of representations that are ingrained in our cultural consciousness. Her main aim in doing so is to undercut the legitimacy of the material body as the bedrock of gender identity. Describing her work in *Gender Trouble* a decade after its initial publication, she writes:

> My effort was to combat forms of essentialism which claimed that gender is a truth that is somehow there, interior to the body, as a core or as an internal essence, something that we cannot deny, something which, natural or not, is treated as given.[68]

In this struggle it becomes imperative to expose the sexed body as an *effect* of the cultural and political dynamics of gender. The reconstruction of the history of the body through a return to 'the Greeks', while less pronounced than in Irigaray, is one part of this strategy.

Butler thus reaches a conclusion similar to the position of historians of science like Laqueur and Schiebinger: the sexed body is not a natural given. Rather, the use of matter and materiality to secure sexual difference is entangled in a long tradition of representing bodies. And like Laqueur, in particular, she uses the ancients to build her case. Where Butler diverges from these scholars is in her understanding of matter or, rather, the material body as the stable, unquestioned ground of sexual difference. For Laqueur and others, working primarily in ancient medicine and biology and privileging the body, the ancients see the body as too fluid to stabilise sexed identities. It gains the necessary stability only in the eighteenth century. Butler doesn't dispute that the ancients characterised matter as fluid and formless – after all, this is what makes it so feminine in the philosophical tradition. But working from a more theoretical perspective and thinking primarily about matter, she finds in the ancient sources – and, more specifically, in Plato – the looser idea that matter exists prior to cultural markings and significations. Such sources represent, for her, the distant origins of modern commitments to the materiality of sex.

Laqueur and Butler represent two ways of incorporating the ancients into a history of the nature of sexual difference: one that turns on a point of rupture between the ancients and the moderns; one that travels back to the fourth century BCE as a foundational moment for the West. Yet in both cases, history becomes part of a project that uses the concept of gender to set us free in the twenty-first century from the limits – ultimately deemed imaginary – of sex. Laqueur sets as his goal a demonstration of how both the one-sex and the two-sex models of the body 'have constrained the interpretation of bodies and the strategies of sexual politics for some two thousand years' in the interest of shedding these constraints.[69] Butler, looking more squarely at the future, writes:

> If sex does not limit gender, then perhaps there are genders, ways of culturally interpreting the sexed body, that are in no way restricted by the apparent duality of sex . . . If gender is not tied to sex, either causally or expressively, then gender is a kind of action that can potentially proliferate beyond the binary limits imposed by an apparent binary of sex.[70]

For Butler, too, the more we recognise the messy entanglement of sex in gender, the better positioned we'll be to break out of the straightjacket of binary thinking.

I suggested earlier in this chapter that we need to be on guard against another binary within gender studies, namely, that between nature and culture. Of course, the argument that claims about sex are really just claims about gender is itself a challenge to the barrier between nature and culture. But if we look more closely, we see that the way the challenge works is by letting culture take over nature: there's no nature that's not subordinated to culture (or, rather, there's no nature that we can access without our cultural blinders). The problem is that such a strategy risks reinstating the nature/culture binary by fencing off nature completely. I raise the problem here because the charge that gender studies is founded on a pernicious 'anti-biologism' has been rapidly gaining ground in recent years. It has been targeted, in particular, at work like Butler's reading of the *Timaeus*. I want to close by taking a very brief look at this charge and reflecting on the *absence* of the ancients from this critique's claims to legitimacy.

The charges of anti-biologism have been made most forcefully by theorists associated with a loose movement that's come to be called New Materialism. The allegation, more specifically, is that the types of analysis – cultural, discursive, literary, social – that dominated sex and gender studies in the last decade of the twentieth century are characterised by an implicit resistance to the domain of the biological. What we have seen in this chapter suggests there is some truth to the charge that gender has entirely edged out sex (or rather, what 'sex' represents).

It would be misleading to say that, until now, there have been no feminist engagements with the biological beyond the rejection of science as ideologically biased or simply reductive. Indeed, some of the most critically sophisticated work of the past three decades has been done by feminists with training or interests in the sciences, such as Anne Fausto-Sterling, whom I mentioned earlier, Donna Haraway and Lynda Birke. These theorists have not been able to avoid the tension between the 'modern' commitment to material evidence and the belief in realism it implies, on the one hand, and the 'postmodern' distrust of truth claims, on the other.[71] Rather, they approach the physical sciences both as ways of knowing the natural world and as products of the cultural, intellectual and historical context at any given time. By keeping channels of communication open with the sciences, these theorists do not rule out that science might have something useful and surprising to tell us, even – or maybe especially – about the sexes.

The belief that science may push the critical edge of gender studies is a driving force of the New Materialism. Indeed, feminist engagements with the sciences – cognitive neuroscience, quantum physics and evolutionary biology, to name a few – are entering a new phase of intensity, excitement and growth. The most important insight of such work is undoubtedly that nature and material bodies are much messier, much more fluid and much more *interesting* than the old stereotypes about biological determinism imply. If the biological study of both humans and animals has led to the reaffirmation of 'natural' sexual difference in some quarters, it's also gone in the opposite direction towards an embrace of the unruly diversity of material bodies, as we saw earlier in Fausto-Sterling's defense of a spectrum of sexed bodies. The question of what it means for a body to be sexed is thus finding a whole range of new answers. Theorists of sex and gender are grappling, too, with the implications of a material world that seems to be far more plastic and unpredictable than the ordered Newtonian cosmos, far more layered and diverse in its intelligences than the stereotypes of 'brute' matter imply. The primacy of plasticity has led to a renewed interest in the ways in which materiality 'plays an *active* role in the workings of power' and in 'how biological complexity impels the complications and variability of culture itself'.[72]

From the perspective of the New Materialism, then, we shouldn't just dismantle the truth claims that have been made on behalf of the nature of sex by extending the domain of culture. We need a different understanding of nature itself. The sciences are part of this reconceptualisation. For by bringing us face to face with material bodies that are malleable, creative and unpredictable, the sciences have the potential to open up new paths for feminism, gender studies and indeed any theoretical enterprise with investments in political and social transformation.

There are plenty of risks involved in embracing science naively. It would be foolish to turn our backs on what we know now about the permeable boundaries between the lab and the culture outside its doors, about the complex processes by which a set of numbers is turned into a headline in the *New York Times*, the ways in which research agendas are formed in the first place. But there is also an opportunity at the present for theorists of gender to take up the biology of the body and the materiality of the world as opportunities for critical and creative engagement. The physical world is far too fascinating to bracket it off as an inaccessible 'real', the sciences far too important cultural players to keep at arm's length.

Does that mean that we have to leave the 'ancients' behind? The rhetoric of the New Materialism, unfolding as it has in the tenses of the present and the future, seems to suggest that the answer is yes. I believe, however, that the past does still matter, for at least two reasons.

First, there's certainly still a case to be made for tracing the long and tangled history of materialism and the material body in the West. Despite the work that's been done, we still need a better understanding of where our concepts of matter and the body come from if we want to maximise the radical potential of the natural sciences, which are hardly immune to inherited assumptions and conceptual habits. The ancients aren't the be-all and end-all in this story. But they stand at the head of a long tradition of trying to come to grips not just with the physical world but with our own physicality. The research being carried out in, say, cognitive science and evolutionary biology can challenge our thinking about our material selves. But it doesn't solve the problems posed by our status as both creatures of nature and naturally cultural agents. To grapple with these problems productively, we still need the critical distance afforded by the practice of history.

Second, the newfound critical energy of matter conceptualised as flux invests the dynamics of fixity and fluidity that we traced earlier in our ancient sources with renewed potential. The very qualities that make matter and material bodies problematic for ancient philosophers can be seen to open up fields of possible recuperation and regeneration. We might appropriate the malleability of the ancient self, once seen as the condition of decline or perversion, as the condition under which blurred and multi-faceted gender identities are cultivated. Moreover, the ancient philosophical tradition is not simply the scene of a crime against matter and women. There's more to it than Plato and Aristotle. When the twentieth-century French philosopher Gilles Deleuze set out to trace the origins of a tradition of 'reversing Platonism', he began in antiquity with the major Hellenistic philosophies of Stoicism and Epicureanism.[73] The history of Epicureanism, in particular, is inextricable from the history of materialism in Western philosophy. It thus forms a necessary part of any engagement with Spinoza or Bergson, Nietzsche or Marx. Figures like Lucretius can facilitate interventions in the present that emphasise the latent potential of the past to generate new avenues of thought across chasms of history, as Michel Serres has argued in juxtaposing the Roman poet with twentieth-century physics.[74] The ancients can become agents of what Nietzsche called the 'untimely', 'acting counter to our time and thereby acting on our time and, let us hope, for the benefit of a time to come'.[75] In short, we need the past, not only to know where we've come from but to get outside our present selves and imagine the future afresh.

In this chapter, we've explored some of the ways in which mostly ancient Greek writers (and a few Romans) imagined the nature of male and female and how they conceptualised the gender of nature and matter. Despite ostensibly talking about the history of 'sex', our real subject has been 'gender': how canonical ancient authors have constructed sexual difference as naturalised and embodied and how matter itself has been theorised in gendered terms from Plato to contemporary theorists like Irigaray and Butler.

In the next chapter, we'll shift gears to explore the views of Greek and Roman writers on the relationship of male and female natures to gendered identities; that is, identities constructed around ideals of femininity and especially masculinity. I pay particular attention to perceived perversions of gender, such as the effeminate man, whose 'gender' is misaligned with his 'sex'. That figure, it turns out, was not only a source of considerable anxiety in ancient Greece and Rome. The attempt to define him from the perspective of the present has proved to be one of the most contentious issues in the ancient history of sex and sexuality and a lightning rod for contemporary debates about homosexuality.

CHAPTER II

THE PRACTICE OF GENDER, THE GENDER OF PRACTICE

Gender's Zero-Sum Game

At the beginning of the last chapter, we met two female Hippocratic patients, Phaëthusa and Nanno, whose incomplete masculinisation has fatal results. In the fourth book of Ovid's *Metamorphoses*, we find a story about a slide in the other direction. Deep in the region of Lycia in Asia Minor there is a spring that makes any man who bathes in it soft (*mollis*) and weak. Ovid, or rather his surrogate narrator – in this case, a Theban princess named Alcithoë – goes on to explain the origins of its power.

The son of Hermes and Aphrodite, at the age of fifteen, has set off to see the world. Arriving in Lycia, he comes across a marvelously clear pool. This turns out to be the home of a naiad named Salmacis, who shuns the hunt in favour of gentler pursuits: grooming herself, bathing, gathering flowers. She is, in fact, out picking flowers when she sees the intruder.

Now, in classical myths, the scene of a young girl in a blossoming meadow usually cues an imminent rape. Here, though, it triggers a long series of gender inversions. The naiad is the one who, seeing the stranger, is gripped by desire and takes the lead. She approaches and offers herself to the boy as a potential wife. He recoils, however, and she retreats. That would seem to be the end of the story. But as soon as the boy, thinking he's alone, slips into the water, Salmacis sees her opportunity. She leaps in and clings to him 'as the ivy is accustomed to enfold great tree-trunks, or as the octopus holds its ensnared enemy below the surface of the sea, its tentacles encircling him on every side' (*Metamorphoses* 4.365–7). He fights Salmacis off, but the gods are on her side. She appeals to them for eternal union, and they consent, joining the bodies into one, 'no longer two, but with twofold form, neither to be called woman or boy: they seemed both neither and both' (4.378–9). The son of Hermes and Aphrodite, registering with horror his transformation into a 'half-man' (*semivir*), turns to his parents for help:

'Grant this favour, father and mother, to your son, who has the name of both: whoever comes into these waters as a man, let him leave a half-man [*semivir*] and be made soft [*mollescat*] at the touch of the waters'. Moved by the words of their two-formed son, his parents fulfilled his request and tainted the waters with that defiling power.
(Ovid, *Metamorphoses* 4.383–8)

It's for this reason that men who bathe in these waters today leave a good part of their masculinity behind when they emerge.

Ovid's telling of the myth of Hermaphroditus, written in the Augustan period (late first century BCE to early first century CE), is not the first or only variant. The evidence for the story goes back at least to the fourth century BCE, and a Hellenistic (first- or second-century BCE) inscription containing another, more positive version of the myth has been discovered near Bodrum, an ancient Lycian city.

Ovid's version focuses attention, however, on the anxieties of a society where masculinity is a fragile trait. The belief in gender's plasticity is also betrayed in some of the other contemporary accounts of the spring's power. In *On Architecture* (2.8.11–12), Vitruvius explains the spring's reputation by reporting that Greek colonists established an inn near the fountain of Salmacis where the once tough locals, the Carians and the Leleges, were eventually 'softened' by the Hellenic comforts on hand (the Greeks are often cast by Roman authors as contagious hedonists, although here 'softening' is more akin to civilising the barbarian natives). The waters, Vitruvius concludes, thus acquired the reputation of feminising those who came in contact with them. The Greek geographer Strabo, a contemporary of Ovid's, dismisses claims about the Lycian spring's emasculating powers by arguing that effeminacy is a condition caused by a life of wealth and wanton pleasure (*Geography* 14.2.16). The alleged dangers of the pool are thus the dangers faced by every Roman male at a time when Rome, having succeeded in building a vast empire, is awash in foreign luxuries. What's unnerving is that it's impossible to contain these threats to a spring in Asia Minor.

Still, it is Ovid's story about the mythical emergence of the 'half-man' that best captures the threat such a figure embodied for men, and especially, it seems, for elite men, in Rome. Hermaphroditus's gender identity, for one thing, is dangerously malleable. He's at an age, it is true, when boys were believed to be especially vulnerable to competing influences. But effeminacy was something even adults had to worry about. The persistence of the threat created a need, as we'll see, for practices designed to uphold masculinity in the face of its natural plasticity.

Notice, too, that the catalyst for Hermaphroditus's metamorphosis is a sexually rapacious female. In a sequence that begins with her audacious proposition and ends with her literally enveloping the boy in her desire, Salmacis ends up forcing her prey into a passive role. Ovid's description of the nymph's behaviour points to the ancient idea of sex as a zero-sum game: you're either active or passive, dominant or submissive, a winner or a loser. Any man who fails to exercise mastery finds himself enslaved to another. In the story of Hermaphroditus, the void of power is filled by female lust. But a man could just as easily be represented as capitulating to his own appetite for sexual pleasure. By failing to master himself, he was thought to become like a woman, conquered by desire and available to others to be used sexually.

The fusion of the two bodies leaves the son of Hermes and Aphrodite neither a woman nor a man. Like Phaëthusa and Nanno, he's caught in a no man's land of sex and gender. Yet at the same time, like them he seems to stand closer to one sex than the other, more a compromised man than a masculinised female. The clue to such an interpretation lies in Hermaphroditus's prayer that other men suffer the same fate as he has by being 'made soft' by the pool. The language of 'softening' (*mollescere*) permeates Roman discussions of men whose masculinity falls short. In Ovid, it signals to the reader that the pool's future victims will be effeminised. Forced to forfeit the role of a proper male, these 'hermaphrodites' will join the ranks of the gender deviants whose perversity is best expressed, in both Greece and Rome, by the figure of the *kinaidos* (Latin: *cinaedus*), a male who seems to have been defined by his desire to be penetrated. The story of Hermaphroditus is thus a story of lost masculinity rather than complete metamorphosis. Still, the loss is catastrophic. If the blurring of male and female in the cases of Phaëthusa and Nanno poses a threat to life itself, the confused state of the 'half-man' is arguably no less anxiety-inducing. What it leads to is a kind of social death.

My major concern in this chapter is how our ancient evidence deals with the relationship of masculine and feminine traits to male and female bodies. I pay particular attention to what I call 'practices' of gender in the ancient world, by which I mean the different ways that individuals upheld or violated gender norms. These practices are associated in our sources primarily with the cultural ideal of masculinity. The concept of femininity still matters in this context, but only as it serves as the opposite of masculinity, designating those traits thought to compromise masculine integrity. Who, after all, would try to be feminine? Being a woman was viewed, as we saw in the previous chapter, as a condition dictated by nature. Masculinity, by contrast, is something you have to work at. The techniques designed to keep nature in line are, accordingly, directed at men.

The very concept of practice, in fact, is conventionally gendered in both Greece and Rome as masculine. The male is defined again and again in our sources as the one who acts, not only on himself but also on others. Clement of Alexandria gives a neat summary of an axiom that had operated for centuries before him: 'to do is the mark of the man; to suffer is the mark of the woman' (3.19.2). Masculinity is defined in antiquity through relationships of domination organised around active and passive roles, gendered as masculine and feminine, respectively. Nowhere are these roles and the asymmetries of power they imply more starkly realised than in the act of sexual penetration. It comes as no surprise, then, that the language of sex is inseparable from the language of power in both our Greek and Roman sources, while relationships of inequality (master/slave, conqueror/conquered) are often figured in both gendered and sexualised terms. The impossibility of disentangling sexual acts from categories of gender, together with the gendering of power, obliges any analysis of ancient gender to take into account the history of sexuality, loosely defined as the history of how sexual meanings, attitudes and practices were constituted in Greece and Rome.

The study of gender in antiquity has also intersected with the history of sexuality understood in a narrower, more contested sense. According to one influential line of argument, the very category of sexuality is a product of modernity, one that shapes our experience in historically contingent ways. Defined in modern terms, sexuality is something each of us has. It makes us who we are – most obviously, at least from the later part of the nineteenth century onwards, into homosexuals or heterosexuals. But it wasn't always like this. Before the emergence of sexuality, there weren't any homosexuals or heterosexuals, for the simple reason that in the premodern period, identity wasn't determined by whether you had sex with men or women.

If we look at the Greeks and Romans more specifically, we find that what matters to your identity is not whether you're having sex with men or women but whether you're on top. That's to say, the rules are organised primarily by the binaries that we've just seen – active and passive, male and female – and the hierarchies they create. Sex is primarily about power. That, anyways, is the central argument of the study that first put Greek sexuality on the map, K. J. Dover's *Greek Homosexuality*, published in 1978.[1] For Dover, power in ancient Greece is wielded most visibly through penetration and the idea of penetration; to be penetrated, conversely, is to submit to the power of someone else. What's come to be called the 'penetration model' of sex hasn't gone unchallenged, as we'll see below. Yet, together with the claim that sexuality has only been around about a hundred years, it's forever changed the way we think about ancient sexual practices and attitudes and fundamentally destabilised the modern categories of homosexuality and heterosexuality.

For our purposes, the significance of these arguments is twofold. First, by privileging the fundamentally gendered active/passive binary over the modern terms homosexuality/heterosexuality, scholars have incorporated the study of sexual relations and sexuality in classical antiquity into the larger field of gender studies. The ancient historian David Halperin has gone so far as to argue that, in systems of sex and gender like those found in ancient Greece and Rome, 'the notion of "sexuality" is dispensable because the regulation of conduct and social status is accomplished by the gender system alone'.[2] In such a system, men can have sex with other men without compromising their masculinity, as long as they occupy the active role (pederastic relationships, where freeborn boys take a passive role, are usually seen as straining these rules). But occupying that role isn't enough to prove you're a real man. The codes of gender turn out to be implicated in a range of practices and behaviours in premodern societies, as scholars have begun to see more clearly now that masculinity has been uncoupled from heterosexuality. The dynamics of gender have thus come to define much of the space once covered by the categories of homosexuality and heterosexuality in the study of classical antiquity.

Second, the arguments in favour of trading sexuality for gender in our analysis of the ancient evidence have had an enormous impact on the present, and in very real ways. As the history of sexuality (or its premodern antecedents) took off in the late 1980s and 1990s, Greece and, more slowly, Rome began to function as privileged sites for exploring the rules of a conceptual and social system seemingly indifferent to the categories so entrenched in our own understanding of sex, desire and sexuality. As James Davidson has remarked:

> . . . the radical difference of ancient Greek sexuality has been presented as one of the most vivid demonstrations of the efficacy of cultural constructions in the field of experience, desire and subjectivity, and one of the most widely credited; claims for the radical otherness of the early modern self . . . become much more cogent in the light of the demonstrable otherness of the ancient Greek experience of sexual desire.[3]

By 2000, the historian Ruth Mazo Karras could observe in a review essay for the *American Historical Review* that while it was once ancient models of democracy and empire that attracted the attention of modern historians, 'today, if modern historians think about ancient Greece and Rome, they are quite likely to do so in the context of the history of sexuality'.[4] The impact of the field went well beyond the academy. By shaking up ideas about homosexuality as a transhistorical category of identity, scholars working on sex in antiquity have raised difficult questions about what it means to do the history of homosexuality and the very importance of history to modern categories of identity and struggles for political recognition. Indeed, these debates have found their way into some of the most important court cases on gay rights over the past two decades, as we'll see later in this chapter.

But it would be a mistake to see the study of Greco-Roman sexuality as a unified field. Ancient historians have vigorously disagreed among themselves about how the history of sexuality should be done and the significance of gender within it. At stake in what Marilyn Skinner has trenchantly called the 'sexuality wars' of the 1990s were not just different definitions of sexuality in ancient Greece and Rome.[5] These debates also turned on competing accounts of historical rupture and continuity, each with its own view of how classical antiquity should be brought to bear on contemporary political struggles organised around sexed, gendered and sexual identities. Besides debating the sameness or the difference of the past, historians wrangled, too, over the fact that the subject in most histories of sexuality was, by default, male.

One name, in particular, came to stand as the fulcrum of these debates: Michel Foucault. Foucault did not define all the terms of the debates around the history of sexuality. Most classicists, moreover, have felt at best ambivalent about his readings of ancient authors. Nevertheless, the name of Foucault became synonymous with classical scholarship that denied there were sexual identities akin to homosexuality and heterosexuality in antiquity. As a result, the sexuality wars were often fought around Foucault's work, particularly the three volumes of the *History of Sexuality*.

It's worth starting, then, with a brief introduction to Foucault's work and his engagement with classical antiquity. Even though I can offer only a schematic overview here, it's still valuable to get some sense of his larger project before looking at the debates he has catalysed among classicists. I then focus on the two areas where Foucault's impact has been most pronounced: first, the pursuit of the history of sexuality and the introduction of other categories – including gender – to analyse ancient sexual activity and identity formation; and, second, the use of the ancients in ongoing political struggles around sex and gender. The debates about Foucault's work have taken place within dense networks of theoretical and political affinities. Here, too, my survey will be relatively brief, with the aim of clarifying the main issues at stake.

Given these practical decisions, I should emphasise that the analytic category of sexuality cannot simply be reduced to that of gender, however much, in the words of Eve Kosofsky Sedgwick, 'particular manifestations or features of particular sexualities are among the things that plunge women and men most ineluctably into the discursive, institutional, and bodily enmeshments of gender definition, gender relation, and gender equality'.[6] It's true that the masculine/feminine binary appears endemic to Greek and Roman reflections on sexuality. But we also have to remain aware of the limitations of our sources, which tend to reflect dominant ideologies and social hierarchies. These limitations skew our perceptions in other ways. A more thorough survey of Greek sexuality would work harder to recover the unruly, polymorphous desires that flourish beyond the moralising and prescriptive texts that constitute most of Foucault's corpus. It would bring in the evidence for female same-sex desire. But that is not the survey I offer here. Instead, I accept the terms of the sexuality wars as they've been fought most publicly, exploring them from within and showing how they've shaped debates about the contemporary relevance of ancient sexuality.

In the last section, I take a closer look at the complex dynamics of masculinity in ancient Greece and Rome. My aim here is to move the idea of masculinity out of the structural and theoretical binaries where it resides for most of this chapter and give it some of its texture as a lived experience in antiquity, at least for elite men. By examining texts that speak of the practices involved in achieving and upholding masculinity, we can also begin to get a richer sense of how acts of mastery over others extended to the mastery of the self and especially the mastery of the body and its behaviours. Many of these texts dovetail with Judith Butler's concept of performativity, inviting us to reflect on the subversion of masculinity and, in turn, the subversion of gendered structures of power more generally – the subject of the following and final chapter.

Foucault's Ancients

The idea that sexuality, which seems like our most basic and irrepressible instinct, is actually a product of the eighteenth and nineteenth centuries may seem counterintuitive. From Foucault's perspective, it's supposed to be. In the first volume of the *History of Sexuality*, he makes our resistance to seeing sexuality as historically determined an important part of his argument.

To understand why this is, we have to recognise first that, as is true of many of Foucault's major works from the 1960s and 1970s, the project of the *History* is a 'history of the present'.[7] We have to understand, too, that Foucault takes it as axiomatic that when we stand inside systems of knowledge and power (what he called *epistemes*), the objects of knowledge around which these systems coalesce appear to us as natural, given and timeless. One example of such an object would be the modern concept of mental illness, which Foucault examined in his *Madness and Civilisation* (1961). Another is what he calls the 'medical gaze', analysed in the *Birth of the Clinic* (1963). These objects generate subjects with identities that seem essential and immutable. The modern heterosexual and his counterpart, the homosexual, are produced in just this way, their identities borrowing a veneer of naturalness from something that goes by the name 'sexuality'. Foucault wants to show in this case that sexuality isn't a stubborn natural drive but rather, 'an especially dense transfer point for relations of power', embedded in the rise of the modern state, capitalism, industrial production and bourgeois society.[8] It only *looks* natural because of the way power works to legitimate itself. The 'natural' identities to which sexuality gives rise are themselves products of the dynamics of power within a given society.

Foucault's strategy for practising history thus begins with uncovering the constraints and procedures that govern what can be said or thought in any society, what he called 'discourse'. Fundamental to his approach is the belief that something like sexuality doesn't stand behind discourse as a real object that we talk about. It is, rather, an 'apparatus' (*dispositif*), which he has defined as

> a thoroughly heterogeneous ensemble consisting of discourses, institutions, architectural forms, regulatory decisions, laws, administrative measures, scientific statements, philosophical, moral and philanthropic propositions – in short, the said as much as the unsaid. Such are the elements of the apparatus. The apparatus itself is the system of relations that can be established between these elements.[9]

The concept of the apparatus is crucial to understanding Foucault's position on sexuality. Foucault is sometimes criticised for talking about sexuality as a nineteenth-century invention when he should be talking about discourses of sexuality. But from his perspective, there is no sexuality before the discursive formation that *produces* it in a specific historical period. The task of the historian, therefore, can't be to track the manifestations of some timeless entity over the course of history. It is, rather, to identify discontinuities in the field of discursive possibilities where new apparatuses, and eventually new forms of subjectivity, emerge. Over the course of his career, Foucault increasingly sought to uncover the forces and events responsible for these tectonic shifts of power. These two methods of historical analysis – 'archaeology' and 'genealogy', respectively – were Foucault's tools for exposing the radical contingency of all discursive formations, including those that govern the present. It's precisely because he wanted to excavate the foundations of modern configurations of power and knowledge that

Foucault focused for much of his career on the seventeenth, eighteenth and nineteenth centuries.

In 1976, Foucault published the first volume of the *History of Sexuality*, in which he introduced his plan to submit sexuality to a genealogical analysis over the course of a multi-volume work. He begins the book by attacking what he calls the 'repressive hypothesis', according to which the rise of the bourgeoisie and the modern state in eighteenth-century Europe entailed a widespread attempt to banish sex and sexuality from the public domain. The alleged repression was believed to include a moratorium on talking about sex, a moratorium whose force persists today, despite our supposed sexual liberation. Foucault polemically takes the opposite view. What he sees when he looks to the eighteenth and nineteenth centuries is not silence but 'the grandiloquence of a discourse purporting to reveal the truth about sex, modify its economy within reality, subvert the law that governs it and change its future'.[10] The very subjugation of sex, he argues, incites people to talk about it. It makes them see sex everywhere they look.

Foucault starts his story with early Christianity. It is here that he locates the rise of deep-seated anxieties about sex and, in the Catholic institution of confession, the origin of a demand to talk about sex. But his narrative really takes off in the eighteenth and nineteenth centuries, when sex explodes into visibility as never before. Foucault draws attention to the imperative to discuss sex as a matter of state-managed population control and the proliferating medical and psychiatric investigations into nervous disorders, sexual perversions and 'frauds against procreation', such as masturbation. These emergent discourses, he argues, succeed in inventing sexuality as an object of regulatory control. Indeed, he eventually defends the stronger claim that *sex itself* comes into being under these conditions as something that makes it possible

> to group together, in an artificial unity, anatomical elements, biolog-
> ical functions, conducts, sensations and pleasures, and . . . enable[s]
> one to make use of this fictitious unity as a causal principle, an
> omnipresent meaning, a secret to be discovered everywhere.[11]

For Foucault, then, the idea that sex is an irrepressible force erupting from the inner core of the self, a force that must be *constrained* by power, has nothing to do with the nature of sex. Rather, sex is a concept generated, paradoxically, out of the historical formation of sexuality. It is nothing other than the very deployment of sexuality that 'has lifted up from deep within us a sort of mirage in which we think we see ourselves reflected – the dark shimmer of sex'.[12]

Foucault's language of the self's hidden depths points to one reason why sex came to attract his attention. He had always been interested in the modes of becoming a subject (*assujettissement*, 'subjectivisation') that are possible at different historical moments. But in the *History*, the constitution of subjects and, eventually, selves comes to occupy an exceptionally important role. At the heart of the first volume lies a shift from the 'juridical' modes of prohibition that Foucault sees as characteristic of the institutions that dominate the period from early Christianity to the eighteenth century – especially canon law and civic law – to eighteenth- and nineteenth-century technologies of disciplinary control. The juridical mode operates by prohibiting certain sexual acts, such as sodomy. By contrast, modern technologies of power forego interdiction in favour of *regulating* what are now seen as perverse or peripheral sexualities. In so doing, these technologies create new modes of subjectivity.

The proliferation of newly minted subjects in the domain of sexuality comes about in part because of the nature of regulatory power, which increases itself by multiplying the sites where sexuality is discovered and policed. The process is aided and abetted, especially in the nineteenth century, by the medicalisation of sexuality and the corresponding rise of techniques to identify types of individuals who should be subject to medical control: the masturbating child, the Malthusian couple, the adult pervert, the homosexual. Here, for example, is Foucault's explanation of how these developments forge the modern category of the homosexual:

The nineteenth-century homosexual became a personage, a past, a case history and a childhood, in addition to being a type of life, a life form and a morphology, with an indiscreet anatomy and possibly a mysterious physiology. Nothing that went into his total composition was unaffected by his sexuality. It was everywhere present in him: at the root of all his actions because it was their insidious and indefinitely active principle; written immodestly on his face and body because it was a secret that always gave itself away. It was consubstantial with him, less as a habitual sin than as a singular nature. We must not forget that the psychological, psychiatric, medical category of homosexuality was constituted from the moment it was characterised . . . less by a type of sexual relations than by a certain quality of sexual sensibility, a certain way of inverting the masculine and the feminine in oneself. Homosexuality appeared as one of the forms of sexuality when it was transposed from the practice of sodomy onto a kind of interior androgyny, a hermaphrodism of the soul. The sodomite had been a temporary aberration; the homosexual was now a species.[13]

The emergence of the homosexual thus illustrates perfectly the shift from juridical to regulatory power and the emergence of new, more effective modes of subjectivisation. Before this shift, the homosexual literally doesn't exist as far as Foucault is concerned.

I'll confess that I have not chosen this passage as simply one example among many. As it happens, Foucault's vivid portrait of the nineteenth-century homosexual has proved to be one of the major battlegrounds in the history of sexuality, especially as that history has been defined in terms of a rupture between the ancients and the moderns.

But before taking a closer look at the battles fought on this terrain, I want to follow Foucault's *History* a bit further in order to give some sense of his own, increasingly complex encounter with antiquity. Foucault had pitted the premoderns against the moderns in the first volume of the *History*. But in that text, it is the early Christians who are his starting point. In the second and third volumes, the position of origin is handed over to the Greeks and Romans. The shift of focus leads Foucault to stake out an uncharted phase in the history of sexuality, one that conforms neither to the juridical regime nor to the modern regime of disciplinary power. The ancients, on Foucault's account, approach sexual conduct as an object of ethical concern to be managed through 'the care of the self'.

Eight years elapsed between the initial publication in French of the first volume of the *History of Sexuality* in 1976 and the publication of the second and third volumes in the year of Foucault's death. In those years, Foucault shifted the scope and the aims of his project considerably. In the introduction to the second volume, he identifies three axes constituting sexuality: the sciences (*savoirs*) that take sexuality as their object; the systems of power that regulate the practice of sexuality; and the forms through which individuals can and must recognise themselves as subjects of this sexuality. For the first two axes, Foucault says, his earlier work provided him with the necessary tools of analysis. But in the course of his research, he realised that his methodological resources were inadequate to an understanding of the third axis; that is, how people constitute themselves as subjects of sexuality. He reports that he thus decided to devote the second and third volumes of the *History of Sexuality* to the history of the 'desiring subject' in the West and the different ways in which individuals, embedded within specific cultures, have granted meaning to the experiences that eventually come to be classed under the rubric of sexuality. The revised project, he determined, would require a further shift, namely, a long detour into the cultures of ancient Greece and Rome aimed at mapping out the early development in the West of a 'hermeneutics of the self'. The resulting two volumes of the *History* are focused, accordingly, on classical antiquity: Greek medical and philosophical texts (primarily from fourth-century BCE Athens) in the second volume and largely prescriptive texts, both Greek and Roman, from the first two centuries CE in the third.

Foucault remained committed to a genealogy of sexuality in these later works. But, in part under the influence of the work of Pierre Hadot, the French historian of ancient philosophy, on 'spiritual exercises' in Greek and Roman philosophy, he became increasingly interested in the care of the self understood more broadly.[14] The ancient desiring subject who takes shape in the second and third volumes of the *History* regulates his sexual behaviour – and, as we'll see, the subject is unquestionably male – as part of a regimen of self-reflexive practices that Foucault terms 'arts of existence'; that is:

> ... intentional and voluntary actions by which men not only set themselves rules of conduct, but also seek to transform themselves, to change themselves in their singular being, and to make their life into an *œuvre* that carries certain aesthetic values and meets certain stylistic criteria.[15]

Foucault's interest in ancient self-fashioning suggests a shift of outlook in his later work. Rather than emphasising the subject's formation under coercive regimes of power, he came to focus on how people fashioned themselves as subjects through practices that he at times characterised collectively as the practice of freedom.

Foucault was admittedly cautious about painting antiquity as a lost Golden Age. In response to an interviewer who asked whether the classical Greco-Roman concept of the care of the self might be updated for use in the present he replied:

> Absolutely, but I would certainly not do so just to say, 'We have unfortunately forgotten about the care of the self; so here, here it is, the key to everything'. Nothing is more foreign to me than the idea that, at a certain moment, philosophy went astray and forgot something, that somewhere in its history there is a principle, a foundation that must be rediscovered.[16]

For Foucault, the return to the past is not about remembering what has been forgotten, as it is for Irigaray. Nevertheless, he casts the ancients as a deeply useful resource for thinking through the nature of ethics in the present. The last two volumes of the *History* have, in turn, revitalised the role of Greco-Roman texts in contemporary debates about ethics.

If we step back, we can see that Foucault made antiquity relevant to contemporary questions concerning sex, sexuality and gender in at least two ways. On the one hand, he radically historicised sexuality – and, indeed, sex – by turning it into a product of the eighteenth and nineteenth centuries. Once the concept of sexuality had been restricted to the recent past, scholars started to look at the premodern period – including classical antiquity, although Foucault himself doesn't go this far back in the first volume of the *History* – in terms of sexual acts rather than identities. On the other hand, when Foucault himself turned to the Greeks and Romans, he didn't just see acts. He saw an originary moment in the history of the (masculine) Western subject, organised around self-reflexive practices of care that ultimately went beyond sexuality. These dual lines of influence make the Foucault invoked by critics and defenders alike something of a hybrid figure, defined both by his denial of sexuality to the premoderns and by his affirmation of a version of Greco-Roman ethics.

I want to turn now to the debates that Foucault's work on antiquity has provoked over the past few decades. These debates have often been fractious and sometimes turn on seemingly arcane points. So what's the point of rehearsing them here?

Foucault's claims about sexuality provoked a searching examination of what really was different in ancient Greek and Roman ideas about sexuality, gender and power compared to our views today. The task of identifying those differences has been very much an exercise in defining the present, with tangible results for how sexuality has been understood as a category of identity in recent years, both inside and outside the academy. Moreover, the very urgency of these debates led to the development of a playbook of strategies for implicating the ancients in contemporary struggles. By following the unfolding of these strategies, we can gain a better sense of how they can and should be deployed in the future. Finally, these debates are valuable to the extent they produced one of richest fields of research on ancient life and values in recent years. Later in this chapter we'll take a closer look at some of this research and what it suggests about the inextricability of gender from games of power.

Before Sexuality? The Past and Its Uses

The debates that have swirled around Foucault's *History* converge on several related questions. First, are sexuality and the corresponding notions of homosexuality and heterosexuality really modern constructs? Second, if there is no sexuality in the premodern period and, more specifically, in classical antiquity, what do we find instead? And, finally, are there any relevant lines of continuity between ancient beliefs and practices and modern sexuality? Or are we better off focusing on the differences?

To start with the first question, Foucault's claim that sexuality, together with homosexuality and heterosexuality, is a recent invention has proved endlessly provocative (to say nothing of his stronger claim that sex itself is a relatively contemporary concept dependent on the deployment of sexuality). It's also been highly influential in defining the terms of subsequent debate. Foucault quickly came to be seen as the major theoretical resource for the 'constructionist' position; the idea, that is, that sexual experience acquires its form and meaning through language and culture. His name was also invoked on behalf of the more specific argument that the forms taken by same-sex desire and sexual activity are so radically unlike one another in different historical periods and societies that a continuous history of homosexuality is impossible.

The approach to the history of sexuality identified with Foucault has not gone unchallenged. Eve Kosofsky Sedgwick has argued that the project of identifying successive historical models of same-sex relations has ended up producing a notion of 'modern' homosexuality that is falsely coherent and, therefore, politically counterproductive. If we're really interested in a critique that can 'denaturalise the present', she argues, we should tackle the modern definition of homosexuality and heterosexuality not as a clean break with the past but as a complex, internally contradictory field.[17] Others, such as the classicist Bruce Thornton, have taken issue with constructionism itself, caricaturing it as the claim that everything is discourse.[18]

And yet some version of the constructionist argument eventually came to pervade almost every corner of the debates around Foucault. Even a scholar regularly identified as 'essentialist', John Boswell, is more than willing to admit that, at least in some respects, 'pre-modern patterns of sexuality were fundamentally different from modern ones'.[19] Most scholars, in fact, seem to accept Foucault's arguments that a specific historical formation called 'sexuality' is generated out of modern power structures; that this formation creates historically specific identity categories ('homosexual' and 'heterosexual'); and that this formation and these categories lack clear premodern parallels.

Now the strict Foucauldian would say that even if you accept these arguments, you haven't accepted Foucault's position at all. You can't have 'pre-modern patterns of sexuality' if you accept with Foucault that there *is* no sexuality prior to the eighteenth century. To see sexuality as something timeless that is expressed differently at different times and places, the Foucauldian would argue, is just to advocate for a banal version of historical relativism. But the purist critique risks underestimating the remarkable effect that the weaker 'Foucauldian' argument has had on the study of sexuality, especially ancient sexuality. After all, something like this argument underwrites the very practice of a *history* of sexuality. The more relevant debate, then, at least for my aims here, has to do with what we have 'before sexuality', to borrow the title of a pioneering collection of essays that became emblematic of Foucault's approach.[20] So what do we have if we don't have sexuality?

One of the interpretations of Foucault's arguments in the first volume of the *History* is that, before the modern era, sexual acts didn't index a sexual identity, let alone a type of subjectivity more broadly understood. In premodern Western societies, sodomy, for example, was primarily understood to be 'a category of forbidden acts' proscribed by civic and canonical codes. The sodomite was someone accused before the law of committing these acts. The paraphrase of Foucault's argument at its most abbreviated is collapsed into a simple opposition: 'premodern sexual acts' versus 'modern sexual identity'.

The stark opposition of past and present in these terms recalls the schematic contrast between premodern and modern views on the binary between sex and gender in the previous chapter. Like that contrast, it turns out to be misleading. The two classical scholars who have been associated the most (and have most identified themselves) with Foucault, the late John J. Winkler and David M. Halperin, have both emphasised that the 'acts versus identities' position often ascribed to Foucault is too simplistic to capture the meaning of homoerotic relations and sexual behaviour more generally in classical antiquity (and Halperin has argued that it doesn't accurately reflect Foucault's own views on the matter).

The most serious challenge to the claim that the ancients lack a concept of sexual identity is the figure of the *kinaidos*, a man apparently defined by his desire to be penetrated, as we saw above. Winkler has used the *kinaidos* to offer an influential rebuttal to the acts-versus-identities position:

> The *kinaidos*, to be sure, is not a 'homosexual' but neither is he just an ordinary guy who now and then decided to commit a kinaidic act. The conception of a *kinaidos* was of a man socially deviant in his entire being, principally observable in behaviour that flagrantly violated or contravened the dominant social definition of masculinity. To this extent, *kinaidos* was a category of person, not just of acts.[21]

Halperin, citing Winkler's formulation, repeated and defended this position more forcefully eight years later, concluding:

> The *kinaidos*, in short, is considerably more than the juridical subject of deviant sexual acts. To recur to Foucault's terminology, the *kinaidos* represents at the very least a full-blown morphology.[22]

Such a figure, in the words of the ancient historian Maud Gleason, was a '"life-form" all to himself', whose condition was 'written all over him'.[23] Roman social historians, too, have argued that the *cinaedus* was a recognised social identity in the Roman period. The gap between the ancients and the moderns begins to look less yawning than the abbreviated 'Foucauldian' story implies.

Yet difference doesn't only reside in straightforward oppositions. Part of the challenge is that when we evaluate the ancient material, we need to deal with acts *and* identities, categories whose precise intersections are often difficult to recover from our ancient texts and continue to thwart easy classification in the present. Acts definitely do matter in antiquity. In both Greece and Rome, as we've seen, sexual taxonomies are organised by who does what, and the Romans, in particular, cared a great deal about the body parts involved (touching the genitals with the mouth, for example, was considered especially degrading). That much seems clear. It's also clear that the desire of men to penetrate *other men* was not problematised in and of itself in classical antiquity – a crucial point of difference between their sexual mores and our own. On the other hand, taking the passive position, however it was defined, seemed to pose a risk to masculinity. The tough question, then, is to what extent doing certain things (or having things done to you) in Greece and Rome determines who you are.

It's worth returning at this point to Halperin and Winkler. Both scholars, as we have just seen, have contested the 'acts versus identities' position by emphasising the morphology of the *kinaidos*. But is a morphology an identity? Halperin has emphatically denied the slide from one to the other. He's done so in part by defending the view, associated with Foucault, that sexual preferences of any kind – either for a given sexual role or for a given sexual object – just didn't constitute sexual *identities* in antiquity:

> Before the scientific construction of 'sexuality' as a supposedly positive, distinct and constitutive feature of individual human beings . . . certain kinds of sexual *acts* could be individually evaluated and categorised, and so could certain sexual tastes or inclinations, but there was no conceptual apparatus available for identifying a person's fixed and determinate sexual *orientation*, much less for assessing and classifying it.[24]

Halperin's claim goes beyond removing *kinaidoi* from the category of the homosexual. It also undercuts the idea that references in ancient texts – the fourth-century CE *Erotes* attributed to Lucian is usually cited in this

context – to people who have a preference for sexual partners of a particular sex (boys or women) indicate a modern concept of sexual orientation.
You can have a sexual preference, Halperin argues, without it determining
the very sense of who you are. The preference for sex with boys is, he
suggests, rather like being a vegetarian.[25] In an age of increasingly rigid
dietary restrictions, a better analogy might be the one Holt Parker draws
between having a thing for women (as opposed to boys) and being a 'breast-
man' as opposed to a 'leg-man'.[26] The point, at any rate, is that preferences
don't qualify as full-fledged orientations. More specifically, the desire to
play the receptive role in sexual encounters doesn't constitute, at least for
Halperin, an identity in the ancient world.

The relationship between the desire for the receptive role and the
morphology of the *kinaidos* is complicated in other ways. How much does
it matter that he gets pleasure from being penetrated? If we go back to the
citation from Winkler above, we'll notice that he defines the *kinaidos* as
'socially deviant in his entire being'. The *kinaidos* violates the protocols of
masculinity. The real issue, in other words, isn't sexuality or sex but gender
and, more specifically, gender norms. The condition that's 'written all over'
the *kinaidos*, to borrow Gleason's language, is effeminacy, diagnosed through
a host of signs that I come back to later in this chapter. The desire to be
penetrated, from this perspective, is the most spectacular symptom of radical
gender deviance rather than a defining feature of identity (and, in fact,
there's plenty of evidence that the *kinaidos* could play the active role with
both men and women). Craig Williams has argued that gender trumps
sexuality among the Romans as well.

> The deviance of *cinaedi* is ultimately a matter of gender identity rather
> than sexual identity; their predilection for playing the receptive role
> in penetrative acts is not their single defining feature, but rather a
> sign of a more fundamental transgression of gender boundaries.[27]

Indeed, the *cinaedus*, on Williams' analysis, is the crowning example of
'gender trouble' in ancient Rome.[28] His Greek counterpart, on this analysis,

is also a unique cultural form. The morphologies in question, then, must be seen as systematic inversions of historically specific ideals of masculinity. What they express are cultural anxieties, not about men having sex with other men but about gender, as we saw with Hermaphroditus in the passage from Ovid. They're the projections, in short, of men whose greatest phobia seems to have been becoming women. Winkler, in fact, has suggested that the *kinaidos* was nothing *but* a cultural fiction designed to keep elite men in line.

Now one objection to this position, at least as far as the Greeks are concerned, is that even with the subordination of sexuality to gender, it still puts too much emphasis on penetration as the axis for gender inversion. The charge has been made most vigorously by the social historian James Davidson, who blames the distortion on the outsized importance that the 'penetration model' has come to assume in discussions of ancient sex more generally. Indeed, Davidson has heavily criticised both Dover and Foucault for promoting that model and, in a recent and controversial book, he has tried to move the conversation about ancient sex away from penetration altogether.[29] In his view, the problem with males who are labeled *kinaidoi* in Greece or excoriated as *euruproktoi* (roughly 'having a wide asshole'), isn't that they like getting screwed. The slurs point to an insatiable appetite for pleasure.[30] The real problem, then, has everything to do with self-mastery (*enkrateia*) and its failure. The better-attested models for sexual morality and practice in Greece, he concludes, 'require neither winners nor losers and . . . relate much more directly and explicitly to central concerns about appetite, gender and status'.[31] Davidson thinks that the Greek evidence has been misread in part because scholars have extrapolated too much from Roman models of sex based on dominance and submission. But Rebecca Langlands has recently questioned whether the 'penetration model' even had much currency at Rome, and Williams himself, cautioning against an 'overzealous' application of the model, has resisted a simple equation between sex and penetration.[32]

Davidson is right to push for a more expansive and more nuanced view of ancient sexual practices and attitudes, especially one that can accommodate relationships of greater complexity and reciprocity than the mechanical 'penetration model' implies. What's more, there *are* important differences between sexual practices and mores in Greece and Rome that have been brought to light in recent years.

But there's no need to deny the significance of penetration altogether, especially at Rome, where the legitimacy of the model has been demonstrated by a number of scholars.[33] For one thing, the idea of penetration makes the concepts of phallic agency and domination starkly visible. The language of penetration is thus a useful and vivid shorthand for talking about relationships of power in general. What's more, the sharply binary nature of these relationships is reinforced by the language of gender. These three axes – the roles in the 'penetration model', the active/passive binary and the opposition of masculine and feminine – neatly come together in the Younger Seneca's pronouncement: 'women were born to be penetrated' (*Letters* 95.21).[34] The triple weave of sex, gender and power brings us back to Aristotle's *Generation of Animals*, where sexual reproduction enacts a whole range of ontological hierarchies (form/matter, active/passive) in the register of gender. These texts remind us of one of the great insights of early feminist scholarship on gender and sexuality. Sex is never just about sex in classical antiquity.

Despite numerous cultural differences between Greece and Rome and different historical periods, then, sex throughout classical antiquity functions as a space, both conceptual *and* literal, where free men establish agency and the right to dominate inside and outside the bedroom in relationship to a passive and feminised partner. The concept of penetration remains indispensable to making sense of the ancient language and imagery of sex and its implications for identity and legitimacy in the ancient world because of the work it does to represent the dynamics of zero-sum competition: I win when you lose.

Moreover, we don't have to trade the language of penetration for that of self-mastery, as Davidson would have it. Rather, the two discourses work in tandem. For the practice of mastering the self is just another way of casting the active role. The passive role is played here not by the object of someone else's action but by the subject who fails to master himself, thereby falling victim to his desires and his own physicality. Significantly, as Davidson stresses, such a subject is stigmatised in terms of gender. As we saw in the previous chapter, women are often portrayed as enslaved to their appetites or subjected to the tyranny of their bodies. The natural passivity of women works as a foil to define the agency that men exercise over their own bodies and desires. Practice itself, as I pointed out earlier, is gendered.

But practice, of course, isn't just about representations, however much representations shape experiences. All the while that talk about sex is being used to express cultural anxieties about masculinity and power, the Greeks and Romans are still having sex. And if there's no sense in the ancient world of a homosexual 'orientation' that divides men who sleep with boys from men who sleep with women, it remains true that sex shaped the way people thought about themselves, not just as ethical subjects but as mortal creatures, as Giulia Sissa has shown in depth.[35] The control of *erōs*, erotic desire, was a major part of the practice of mastering the self in Greece, as we've seen, and it remains so at Rome. Yet *erōs* constituted a far richer vehicle for imagining the self and the tyranny of the passions than the prescriptive texts suggest, not just bitter but sweet, as an unforgettable fragment of Sappho reminds us. In the beginning, after all, *Erōs* was a god, whose domain encompassed the entire cosmos – land, sea and air – and straddled the divide between mortals and immortals. 'Dynamic, mobile, elusive, ever renewed, erotic energy circulates in all zones of existence.'[36]

There is, in fact, a wealth of data that attest to the broad cultural preoc-cupation with desire and sexuality as crucibles of subjectivity in ancient Greece and Rome. At the same time, when we try to probe the experience of sexuality and the realities of sexual practice, we hit up against problems in our evidence. The ancient historian isn't like the anthropologist or soci-ologist conducting fieldwork. He or she can't just go and interview the Greeks and Romans about their sexual attitudes and behaviours. There are no Kinsey Reports for the ancient world. Moreover, the evidence we do have is heavily tilted towards the reproduction of dominant cultural atti-tudes, expressed by elite males interested in shoring up their own positions of power. So, for example, despite the extent to which 'the feminine' informs the fields where sexuality and power are defined, we don't meet many female subjects of desire in our corpus of evidence from Greece and Rome. Those we do meet, such as Salmacis, tend to be creations of male authors. The same could be said for those males who were stigmatised as effeminate. How should these gaps in our evidence affect the histories that we write of sexuality in the ancient world?

The question has been posed with particular urgency in the past twenty years in response to Foucault's history of the desiring subject in the ancient world. For Foucault has virtually nothing to say about women as desiring subjects, especially in the second volume of his *History*. It's true that his sources, predominantly philosophical, medical and prescriptive texts, are especially concerned with and targeted at free men. Still, Foucault's feminist critics have argued that his omissions are not innocent. By reproducing the exclusion of women from these texts without comment, Foucault fails to acknowledge – let alone analyse – the gendering of the ethical subject of care. He is thus complicit in his sources' equation of the subject with the male subject and their implicit denial of female subjectivity, 'underwrit[ing] and absorb[ing] the masculine ideologies of the past as part of the process of living out those of the present', as one of his critics, Lin Foxhall, has written.[37] By taking the ancient ideologies at face value, Foucault misses the opportunity to explore the ways in which they might be ironised and challenged.

Amy Richlin, Foucault's fiercest feminist critic, has argued further that his narrow choice of texts produces a skewed picture of sexuality in the ancient world, one that covers up the brutality of ancient discourses about sex on display in genres like Roman satire. Roman sexuality on Richlin's analysis becomes the obscene underside of Foucault's care of the self, best expressed by 'genital and copulative practice and language perceived by their subjects as shaming'.[38] In a realm where objectified women and other Others consistently operate as crude foils to the male self, it's impossible to ignore gender. Foucault's portraits of 'contemplative, self-disciplined and married pederasts', Richlin argues, unconscionably ignore the abuse of those needed to shore up the coherence of the elite male self.[39]

Part of the problem here is that Foucault's very choice of sources facilitates his gender bias. Many feminist scholars have argued that the history of the desiring subject and Greek and Roman sexuality could and should be told differently. Foxhall, for example, argues that Foucault fails to take gender into consideration in part because he neglects the broader social and cultural context of sexuality in the ancient world. If we move outside the prescriptive texts, we find various forms of agency exercised by women within the household, in ritual and festival contexts and over their own sexuality.[40] Ellen Greene has argued that Foucault's model of sexual relations, with its 'masculine' emphasis on hierarchy and domination, is guilty of neglecting the more reciprocal 'feminine' model that she and others have found in the fragments of Sappho.[41] Richlin imagines an alternative *History* that includes, among other texts, the verses of the Roman poet Sulpicia, who gives voice to her erotic anguish; epigraphic inscriptions produced or paid for by women; and Imperial-era philosophical texts with female addressees.[42]

There is a good deal of truth in the charge that Foucault's limited perspective cannot just be chalked up to the gaps and biases of the sources but is, rather, complicit in making the history of the desiring subject in the West into a history of the *masculine* subject. The portrait he paints is plagued by other omissions and distortions as well, as a number of prominent scholars have observed. Halperin and Winkler, too, despite their widely acknowledged gifts for close reading and cultural analysis and their interest in moving beyond the sources utilised by Foucault, have often been faulted for using a limited group of chronologically and geographically disparate texts, almost all of them Greek, to construct a sweepingly misleading narrative about the ancient world as a whole.

Nevertheless, we should hesitate before writing off the Foucauldian line on ancient sexuality as irremediably flawed. For Foucault's attention to practices of self-fashioning, together with Judith Butler's work on performativity, which I discuss further below, has helped open up an enormously fertile area of study at the intersection of gender and sexuality in ancient Greece and Rome. By focusing on the ways in which desire itself was problematised and managed, we not only find the tools to move past taxonomies like 'homosexuality' and 'heterosexuality'. We can also start to work towards a more complex idea of what it might have meant – and still means – to be a subject of desire. That's to say, rather than starting with sexual identities, we enter a strange terrain that challenges us to think about the relationship between acts, including acts performed on ourselves to discipline desire, and the constitution of identities and subjectivities. Later in this chapter, we'll examine some of these practices in more detail.

There is also a question of the extent to which we can recuperate alternative perspectives from the historical record. The research of feminist and gender-sensitive scholars has proved that we don't have to be constrained by the dominant voices in the canon. The evidence for a richer picture of sex, desire and sexual attitudes in the ancient world is there. But challenges remain as to how to characterise such evidence. Can we recover, for example, a 'female' or 'feminine' perspective on sex and sexuality, especially from fragments and male sources? Should we even assume that there is a uniform perspective determined by sex, either in the ancient world or across time?

Here we need to be careful. The risk is that in the face of fragmentary evidence, coupled with what's often a strong desire to recover lost voices, we are too quick to discover traces of a 'female' perspective with which women today can identify. At the same time, we neglect the potential of cross-gendered identifications. The French feminist theorist Hélène Cixous, for example, has written that when she first read Homer, she identified with Achilles.[43] And even a brief scan of recent scientific research on 'female' or 'feminine' sexuality reveals the pitfalls involved in defining what exactly this is, even for our own culture.[44] Moreover, when it comes to lived experience in the highly stratified societies of the ancient Mediterranean, it's questionable how uniform the category of women is, as we saw in the first chapter. I discuss the challenges of identifying 'feminine' perspectives and positions at greater length in the next chapter. Here I want to pursue the problem of recovering the viewpoints of marginalised subjects as it's been debated with respect to the *kinaidos/cinaedus*.

The difficulty with the *kinaidos/cinaedus* is that, as with women, the portraits we have are overwhelmingly – if not exclusively – the products of hostile sources. Can we say, then, just who this elusive figure was? Remember that Winkler believed he was mostly just a scarecrow designed to force men to adhere to gender norms and a blunt weapon deployed in high-stakes political arenas. Halperin, basically accepting this position, has elaborated the social utility of such a figure in Greece. On the one hand, in his 'universalising' capacity, the *kinaidos* embodies the perversion of masculinity that threatens every man who doesn't sufficiently police himself. On the other hand, he functioned in a 'minoritising' way, representing a special class of deviant individuals marked by a constitutional defect of masculinity. Halperin's second classification suggests that, *pace* Winkler, there really were people consistently picked out by the labels *kinaidos* and *cinaedus*, an interpretation supported by our evidence from Rome. In fact, by late antiquity, medical writers could diagnose effeminate men (*molles*) as suffering from a verifiable clinical condition, characterised by the desire to dress and act like a woman and outsized lust (Caelius Aurelianus, *On Chronic Diseases* 4.9.131–2). But would anyone have seen themselves in those labels? If so, how would *they* have defined the terms of their identity?

The idea that men would have willingly laid claim to being a *kinaidos* or a *cinaedus* seems, to some scholars, absurd. From their perspective, these are labels of abuse, designed to keep men from stepping out of line, to attack enemies and to stigmatise anyone deviant with respect to their gender. But others have argued that there were men who defined themselves either through their gender deviance or through the expression of sexual desires and behaviours demonised by society as a whole. Richlin has adopted the view that there was a class of men at Rome who desired to be penetrated sexually by other men and has tried to uncover the evidence of their lives.[45] Richlin acknowledges the differences between the *cinaedus* and the modern homosexual. But she also argues that *cinaedi* at Rome were defined – and that they defined themselves – primarily by their deviant sexual role (passive in male-on-male sex). Given the social stigmatisation that accrued to this identity, she argues, we can see the *cinaedus* as the historical counterpart of the modern-day homosexual. 'It might be possible', Richlin concludes, 'to historicise homosexuality without losing it as a concept'.[46]

Rabun Taylor has further developed the case for a quasi-homosexual subculture or, rather, two such subcultures in the Roman period, one in religious cults built around self-castration (the *Galli*), the other something of an urban underground in the imperial capital.[47] For Taylor, quasi-homosexuality is defined not so much by desiring to be penetrated but by sexual reciprocity and the preference for male partners beyond the age when they were considered legitimate targets of desire. Like Richlin, however, he is resisting the collapse of sexuality into gender in the work of Halperin and Winkler. Surveying the available evidence to find out what it was like 'on the inside of same-sex adult male relationships in Rome', Taylor provocatively positions his research as 'a case study for the development of homosexual subcultures in the face of adversity'.[48]

Richlin and Taylor are both well aware of the difficulties involved in extending the term 'homosexuality' to antiquity. But they insist on reclaiming it in order to establish a continuous history of homosexuality. Part of the motivation is simply the desire to do our sources justice, to get the past 'right' as much as possible. At the same time, Richlin is upfront about how she sees the political implications of practising what she calls an 'essentialist' history of sexuality; that is, a history committed to the persistence across time of categories not just of sexual identity but of sex (i.e., 'women' and 'men'). If we see categories of sex and sexual identity as historical constructs, she argues, we forfeit the very tools we need to do the history of women or the history of homosexuality, the tools that allow us to unmask the *continuities* between practices of oppression in Greece and Rome and the oppression of women and homosexuals today. The risk is that we leave undocumented the history of present systems of domination.

Yet how we tell the history of sexuality also has serious political stakes for those who have identified a sharp rupture between the ancients and the moderns in the domain of sex and sexuality. Foucault is sometimes accused of having his own agenda in looking to the ancient Greeks and Romans.

His accusers are right. He did have an agenda. He described his turn to the ancients as 'a philosophical exercise', the object of which was 'to learn to what extent the effort to think one's own history can free thought from what it silently thinks, and so enable it to think differently'.[49] In this spirit, Winkler and Halperin have argued that narratives about 'the Greeks' are necessarily implicated in contemporary systems of dominance and resistance. By telling the story of the past differently, the ancient historian sets out to disrupt these systems in order to allow power to circulate more freely, to open up new identities to contemporary gay men and women, for example, or to expose structures of domination over women. As Halperin describes it, the ultimate aim of an 'enlightened historicism' is

. . . to accede, through a calculated encounter with the otherness of the past, to an altered understanding of the present – a sense of our own non-identity to ourselves – and thus to a new experience of ourselves as sites of potential transformation.[50]

What makes the ancients so powerful for Halperin is precisely their otherness. Winkler, too, aimed to challenge the long-standing philological maxim that the past is transparent by learning to 'read against the grain'. The 'ambiguities and contradictions' of the ancient evidence become, accordingly, 'an occasion to struggle against the tacit, conventional and violent embrace in which we are held by the past'.[51]

Despite their differences, then, all these scholars have passionately argued that what we say about sex and gender in the ancient world matters, not only to how we define ourselves today but to the struggle to build a just society. Indeed, the sense of urgency explains, at least in part, why tempers flared so high in these debates. A lot was at stake in getting it right. Davidson, too, in contesting the 'penetration model', wasn't just worried about historical inaccuracies. What he was railing against was its toxic perpetuation of 'an obnoxious myth-making of sexual intercourse as essentially dominating, and of gay sex as gestural and instrumentalising, motivated by a quite self-conscious and opportunistic desire to undermine the already strongly contested identity of a sexual minority'.[52] Once again, we find the history of sexuality invested with considerable power to shape the present.

The questions that historians of Greco-Roman sexuality have struggled with cut to the heart of the debate about essentialism and constructionism and the nature of homosexuality as an identity category. Do we need to affirm the presence of gays in the past to legitimate homosexuality as something more than a 'lifestyle choice' today? Or is the recognition of radical historical difference the best way forward? How important are sexual acts to gay identities today? What about the subversion of gender norms? And, finally, what role should the past play in legitimating or challenging the present?

That the struggle to answer these questions can have tangible effects on the present has been made particularly clear by several recent court cases about gay rights in the United States. The case that illustrates most obviously the concrete implications of the debate over constructionism is *Lawrence v. Texas*, decided by the Supreme Court in 2003.

The background to the case is complex, and I do not have space here to discuss the legal intricacies involved. But one of the most important pieces of the puzzle is a 1986 Supreme Court decision on an earlier case, *Bowers v. Hardwick*, that had challenged a Georgia statute criminalising sodomy. The Court had concluded on that occasion that it was not willing to confer what it called a 'fundamental right to engage in homosexual sodomy'.[53] One of the interesting twists of that decision is a statement by Justice Warren Burger, appended to the majority opinion, elaborating the 'ancient roots' of the prohibition against sodomy and, more specifically, homosexual sodomy.[54] He frames any attempt to overturn the Georgia law as the rejection of 'millennia of moral teaching' based not just on Judeo–Christian standards but also on Roman law.[55] The dissenting opinion, authored by Justice Harry Blackmun, excoriates the argument from ancient precedent. The validity of ancient precedent will resurface seven years later in Colorado as a contentious issue in another crucial case for gay rights, *Romer v. Evans*, to which I'll return. First, however, let's look at the sequel, as it were, to *Bowers v. Hardwick*: *Lawrence v. Texas*.

Lawrence v. Texas took aim at a Texas law against homosexual sodomy and, unlike *Bowers v. Hardwick*, it succeeded, taking down the Georgia anti-sodomy law as well. Looking back with some regret on the *Bowers* decision, the majority opinion in the case aims to rectify the earlier 'failure to appreciate the extent of the liberty at stake' by affirming that adults may choose to pursue sodomy in the privacy of their homes without forfeiting their dignity as free persons.[56] What is important for our purposes is the strategy adopted by Justice Kennedy, writing on behalf of the majority, to neutralise the earlier arguments about the 'ancient roots' of the proscription against homosexual sodomy.

The crux of Kennedy's argument is the scholarly 'Foucauldian' position that homosexuality has emerged only recently as a category of identity. With this in mind, Kennedy revisits early American sodomy laws and concludes that they aren't directed against homosexuals but against non-procreative sex more generally. After all, he argues, there simply weren't any homosexuals who could be targeted by the earlier laws. But, he cautions, that doesn't mean present-day non-discrimination statutes shielding gays are baseless. It is precisely because they are discriminated against as a class now that homosexuals require legal protection. In one of the most important court decisions for gay rights in the US, then, 'constructionism saved the day'.[57]

The ancient world plays a more direct role in the case I mentioned above, *Romer v. Evans*. The case began life as a challenge to a ballot initiative narrowly passed by the voters of Colorado in 1992. Amendment 2, as it was called, prohibited the state from taking any action to prevent discrimination on the grounds of 'homosexual, lesbian or bisexual orientation, conduct, practices or relationships'. Its constitutionality was subsequently challenged in court. One of the arguments advanced against the amendment was that it had its basis in religious sentiments – more specifically, its antipathy to gays was derived from Christianity – and so violated the First Amendment's clause on the establishment of religion. In response, the defendants decided to bring in the Oxford moral philosopher John Finnis to show that the intolerance of homosexuality could be traced back to classical Greek theories of natural law. Finnis offered in support of this claim a passage from Plato's *Laws* suggesting that homosexual copulation is 'against nature' (*para physin*) and a shameful abomination. The plaintiffs invited the classicist and philosopher Martha Nussbaum to the stand to refute Finnis's argument.

Nussbaum adopted a multi-pronged strategy in her testimony. She brought in evidence, including evidence from Plato and Aristotle, of the general acceptance of sex between males (within the parameters of the penetrative paradigm) in classical Greece. She also tried to shift attention away from homosexuality to sex itself by recasting the lines from the *Laws* in terms of the anxiety expressed by many Greek authors and by Plato in particular about *all* bodily pleasures. In order to emphasise the differences between ancient and modern approaches to sexual behaviours and desires, she went so far as to cite Foucault's claim, which we have just seen, that history can allow us 'to free our thought from what it silently thinks, and so enable it to think differently'. Finally, at one point in her testimony, she introduced passages demonstrating Plato's enthusiastic endorsement of homoerotic desire under certain conditions.

Despite the wealth of ancient evidence supporting Nussbaum's position, the court battle came down to her attempt to explain away a single troubling word that Plato uses to characterise homosexual sex in the *Laws* passage (636c): *tolmēma*. Finnis, following standard translations, had argued the word has connotations of shamefulness or audacity. (The Loeb translation, referring to those who have sex with members of their own sex, reads 'those guilty of such enormities were impelled by their slavery to pleasure'.) Nussbaum, stressing Finnis's lack of credentials as a scholar of Greek, claimed that existing translations laboured under old prejudices about homosexuality. She advocated instead a more neutral translation – 'those who first ventured to do this', i.e., engage in sex with members of their own sex – backing her position up with reference to the standard Greek lexicon.

The problem was that the lexicon in question was not, in fact, the standard revised edition used by virtually all philologists (Liddell, Scott and Jones) but a late nineteenth-century version (Liddell and Scott) that conveniently lacked any entry for the word *tolmēma* involving connotations of shamefulness. Nussbaum's opponents, not just Finnis (who published a response to Nussbaum's testimony)[58] but also his former student Robert George, a professor of constitutional law at Princeton who was brought to the stand to refute Nussbaum, seized on what they presented as a deliberate sleight of hand. They succeeded in turning the case into one of academic integrity. In the end, it's not clear whether any of this had an impact on the court's decision to rule the Amendment unconstitutional in Denver or the later Supreme Court decision backing up the Colorado court. But neither the ancients nor the academics came out looking particularly good.

Much ink has been spilled about what went wrong in *Romer v. Evans*. But one of the most suggestive – and troubling – speculations about its unfortunate dénouement was raised by the critic and classicist Daniel Mendelsohn. Mendelsohn mused that there might be a fundamental incompatibility between 'the narrow requirements of legal discourse as it actually proceeds' and 'the expansive nature of serious humanistic inquiry'.[59] His conclusion may be too pessimistic. Consider, after all, the salutary impact of the Foucauldian line of argument that homosexuality is a category of recent vintage in *Lawrence v. Texas*. Yet it is undeniable that the complexities of what Plato thought about same-sex desire and behaviours, to say nothing of his views on sex, desire and the body more generally, got lost in the pressure to commit to the record what the ancients thought once and for all about homosexual sex.

It's hard not to feel something similar happened in the 'sexuality wars'. By this I don't mean to say that those involved were blinkered in their consideration of the evidence – far from it. The scholarship in the field of ancient sexuality represents some of the most rigorous, sophisticated and probing research on classical antiquity of the past two decades. But the terms in which the debates unfolded can feel like forced disjunctions: acts *or* identities; sexuality *or* gender; penetration *or* self-mastery; the past as continuous with the present *or* the past as completely alien. Now that the smoke has settled, it's easier to see that these binaries, like others that we've considered, offer false choices. What the sexuality wars make clear, too, is the lesson to be drawn from such distortions. The more urgently the past presses on the present, the greater the risk that the ancients are relegated to what Marilyn Skinner has aptly called 'the function of trope'.[60] The challenge for those who study the past is to resist this kind of narrowing as much as possible without forfeiting the hope of making resonant, effective connections between the past and the present.

I'd like to turn now to a brief survey of recent research as it has come to inform our understanding of masculinity in the ancient world. The techniques developed to achieve masculinity, together with the dangers represented by marginalised figures, represent a fascinating body of evidence for concepts of gender identity and gender deviance in antiquity. The growth of the field can be seen in part as one of the happy outcomes of the shift that we've been following towards thinking about ancient Greek and Roman sexual practices, especially same-sex practices, through the lens of gender norms. It has been encouraged, too, by Foucault's work on the care of the self, which has shown how important practice is to upholding norms of masculinity in the face of the body's unstable materiality, as well as by Judith Butler's theory of performativity and Pierre Bourdieu's concept of the *habitus* (roughly an embodied and enacted social identity). As classical scholars have documented the labour involved in shoring up masculinity and the anxieties that surround this labour, they've helped us see masculinity in ancient Greece and Rome not just as a sterile ideal but as a space of contestation in the lives of real men. They've helped us see, too, that masculinity in antiquity is not just a privilege. By exploring the strictures it imposed, we can perhaps better understand the costs exacted by rigid gender norms in ancient Greece and Rome.

Practices of Masculinity

How do you identify a man in ancient Greece or Rome? You might, if you're dealing, say, with an infant, look for a penis. If that's not possible, you can focus on the signs that signal an underlying male physiology: a beard, for example, or a deep voice. But how can you be certain that you're dealing with a *real* man, a man in the proper sense of the word (in Greek, *anēr*, versus the unmarked *anthrōpos*; or, in Latin, *vir*, versus *homo*)? A lot depends here on how we understand what counts as real in ancient Greece and Rome. Are we asking how we can identify a 'biologically' real man as opposed to, say, a woman dressed as one or, more troublingly, women who have acquired masculine features, such as Phaëthusa and Nanno? Or are we asking, rather, how we can tell the difference between men by birth and men who've proved their masculinity through their behaviours, character traits and actions?

As we saw in the previous chapter, it has become common to see the ancients as collapsing sex into gender and locating gender identity along a single continuum, where identities travel from one pole to the other, unconstrained by a sexed body. But such a picture is too simple. The sexed body remains a useful and necessary concept for making sense of the ancient evidence. At the same time, masculinity and femininity are promiscuous terms in antiquity, attaching themselves to both men and women. The misalignment of gender with the sexed body poses real problems, especially for freeborn men, who have the most to lose if they don't uphold the cultural norms of manhood: legal status, political power and social privilege, to name a few possible casualties of shoddy performances. Failure is understood in such cases as the capitulation of masculinity to what Winkler memorably called the '"internal émigré" of masculine identity': the feminine within.[61] Such capitulations are ever-present possibilities. Speaking of the Roman culture of masculinity, Williams observes that 'vigilance was crucial . . . In the balancing act of masculinity, one stumble can ruin the entire performance.'[62]

The slide towards femininity could be triggered, first, by what a man did or was accused of doing. From the *Iliad* onwards, men became real men on the battlefield. Paris, whose masculinity is always somewhat suspect, admits himself that he is not much of a fighter. In Virgil's *Aeneid*, Turnus taunts his rival Drances by asking whether his fighting spirit is found only in his quick tongue and flying feet (11.389–91), while the Italian leader Numanus mocks the Trojans' 'feminine' outfits on the battlefield, telling them to 'leave arms to men and keep from the sword' (*sinite arma viris et cedite ferro*, 9.620). It's no coincidence that the Greek word for courage is *andreia*, from the marked word for 'man' (*anēr*). In Athens, those who failed to perform their military service or fled the battlefield forfeited the right to advise their fellow citizens in political deliberations. The Latin word *virtus* (from *vir*) initially has the connotation of military valour, although it could also be used of the honour won on the battlefield of Roman politics. Indeed, as the Roman Empire expanded, we see a split opening up between the common soldier, whose social status and subordination to his superiors precluded him from being a true *vir* in the eyes of the elite, and elites who were largely spared military service.[63] As a result, in the late Republican and early Imperial periods, masculinity is defined primarily in the spheres of politics and oratory, as we'll see further below.

But already in Athens the right of a citizen to address the city was contingent on the extent to which he had managed his appetites and used his body in ways consistent with the protocols of masculinity. These protocols are in abundant evidence in a mid-fourth-century BCE speech by the Athenian orator Aeschines, who had been charged with treason by his political opponents. He responded by subjecting one of his accusers, a man called Timarchus, to a process known as the 'testing of speakers' in an attempt to strip him of his right to address the city (and, by implication, his right to pursue the case against Aeschines).

Aeschines ingeniously uses hearsay and innuendo to reconstruct a damning account of Timarchus's early manhood, alleging that he prostituted himself in exchange for financial support from a series of older lovers. He comes back again and again to his opponent's boundless, enslaving appetite for pleasure and his willingness to be used by others sexually. The speech builds to the thundering accusation that Timarchus, despite being a man 'with a male body', has nevertheless committed the offences of a woman (*Against Timarchus* 185). No one in his right mind, says Aeschines, would punish a woman for acting according to her nature: obviously, she can't help herself. But if the citizens start taking advice from a man who has 'abused himself against nature', the city is in serious jeopardy. Aeschines, in singling out sexual passivity and excessive appetites as Timarchus's vices, is taking a page from what was already by the fourth century a well-worn playbook at Athens, one that goes back at least to Old Comedy, as Nancy Worman has shown.[64] But his speech is especially useful in showing us the stakes involved in challenges to a citizen's masculinity in the city's public arenas.

Roman orators interested in smearing political opponents frequently made similar allegations of sexual and gender deviance. In his *Second Philippic*, Cicero accuses his enemy Marc Antony of having betrayed his masculinity the moment he passed the threshold of adulthood by becoming the 'wife' of another man:

> You assumed the toga of men, which you made into that of a woman in short order: in the beginning, [you were] a common whore; the price for your shameful acts was set, and not low at that. But Curio quickly stepped in. He led you away from the prostitute's trade and, just as if he'd given you the matron's robe, he settled you in a sure and stable marriage. (Cicero, *Second Philippic* 2.44)

Cicero, like Aeschines, mixes allegations of gender inversion with charges of prostitution and wifely subordination to imply that Antony's 'feminine' lack of control over his own body renders him unfit to participate in the political process. The accusation isn't that Antony has, in fact, become a woman. 'Public charges of effeminacy [at Rome]', as Anthony Corbeill has observed, '. . . never entirely negate the masculine vices of the accused'. The problem with the effeminate male is that he 'cannot recognise that the biological and social construction of maleness must coincide'.[65] He is living a life – or so his enemies claim – defined by the perversion of gender, not by the exchange of one gender for another.

The perversion of gender is all it takes, though, to endanger the benefits and privileges associated with elite male status. In the examples from Aeschines and Cicero, calling one's target a woman is shorthand for a bid to bar him from the arenas of political power. Winkler has argued that we shouldn't mistake the scrutiny to which public figures at Athens were subjected – scrutiny equally evident in Rome – for what went on in everyday life. It was only men in the public eye who had to uphold such rigid standards of masculinity. David Cohen, by contrast, is less sanguine about the constraints under which the general male population laboured, arguing that these norms exercised real power across the class spectrum at Athens.[66] In the end, it's hard to know, given the limits of our evidence, to what extent masculinity was policed beyond the stomping grounds of the rich and famous. But while it's true that the allegations of Aeschines and Cicero arise in a hothouse world where social norms and expectations were intensified, it seems likely that these norms were, if anything, reinforced by their regulation in the public sphere. What is clear is that such allegations feed on entrenched cultural attitudes about masculinity and power.

Beyond what you do, how you look determines how you're judged as a man in both Greece and Rome. Indeed, it's often through visible signs that inferences about what happens behind closed doors are made. Aeschines recalls an occasion when Timarchus threw off his cloak in the Assembly to reveal a body ravaged by years of debauchery, taking the flesh as a clear indictment of Timarchus's private life (*Against Timarchus* 26). The orator Scipio Aemilianus, in a speech from 142 BCE, assumes that because his target, Publius Sulpicius Galbus, wears perfume, plucks his eyebrows and wears a long tunic, he has done everything that *cinaedi* habitually do (Aulus Gellius, *Attic Nights* 6.12.5). Such signs can also index hidden 'softness' more directly. If a Roman man wore an elaborate hairstyle or exotic clothing, if he depilated his chest or legs, he could be suspected of compromised masculinity, regardless of whether he was also accused of sexual passivity (though the accusations often went together). Roman authors also take it for granted that an effeminate man is revealed by his gait and posture. At the same time, rusticity carried a social taint all its own, reminding us that the quest for masculinity was not just about abandoning refinement and care. The challenge for the elite Roman man, rather, was to cultivate a look of urbane authority without crossing the line into the kinds of adornment and artificiality associated with women.

The very fuzziness of that line helps explain why charges of effeminacy were such an effective weapon.

The surfaces of the body and its behaviours are so rich in information about character in antiquity that a whole technique of deciphering corporeal signs develops in the fourth century BCE and spreads through the Hellenistic and Roman worlds: physiognomy. The central axis of the physiognomic system, as Maud Gleason has deftly shown, is gender.[67] For if gender isn't constrained by sex – that is, if male bodies don't necessarily express masculine qualities, nor female bodies feminine ones – the sexed body isn't a secure predictor of gender. Sometimes, perversions of gender are obvious. But in other cases, transgression can be detected only via professional semiotic analysis. Here is the second-century CE physiognomic writer Polemo describing the practice of his art:

> You may obtain physiognomic indications of masculinity and femininity from your subject's glance, movement and voice, and then, from among these signs, compare one with another until you determine to your satisfaction which of the two sexes prevails. For in the masculine there is something feminine to be found, and in the feminine something masculine, but the name 'masculine' or 'feminine' is assigned according to which of the two prevails. (Polemo 2, trans. Gleason)

The practice of physiognomy thus invests certain corporeal zones with the power to yield clues about the gender identity of the specimen under consideration. The femininity latent in a man might be betrayed by the fold of his eyelids, a gesture of his hands or the twitching of his lips.

My language of 'clues' is not accidental. The physiognomist is always on the lookout not only for conflicts between the sex of the person and his gender identity. He's also alert to contradictions between the gender identity the person presents publicly and his 'real' nature. Deception is, unsurprisingly, rampant, given how much is at stake in the social validation of masculinity. The would-be physiognomist is thus advised to look for signs that are spontaneous and natural. Anything too affected or extreme – examples include working too hard at firming up a flaccid neck and overzealously cultivating a 'rustic' look – betrays the efforts of a man trying to mask his true (feminine) gender.

The physiognomist's emphasis on deception undoubtedly reflects his professional position in a highly competitive social milieu where prestige was won by catching out the effeminacy of men who had been passing for legitimate males. Yet the physiognomic interest in 'true' nature also points to a pervasive tension within Greco-Roman disciplines of self-fashioning: between a commitment, on the one hand, to an ideal of natural masculinity untainted by the careful grooming that characterises the 'soft' man and an equally strong commitment, on the other hand, to practices of shaping the body and one's behaviour to cultural expectations.

Such tension seems to have been especially acute in late Republican and early Imperial Rome, where we notice a heightened sensitivity to the risks to 'natural' Roman manhood posed by imported (especially Greek) artifice and newfound luxuries. If we watch Cicero negotiate the relationship between art and nature in *On the Orator*, for example, we find him subtly but systematically folding the former into the latter. All taint of Greek artfulness and training disappears behind the image of an orator whose eloquence effortlessly expresses the nature of the Roman character and, through this, the order of nature itself. Cicero thus 'preserves the Roman republican orator as a natural entity', as Joy Connolly has observed, 'free from the need of training and thus *free* in the fullest sense, free for the active pursuit of civic participation', *libertas* being the defining attribute of the citizen male under the Republic.[68] The orator understood in these terms literally embodies the perfect citizen, whom Connolly equates with the perfect (masculine) self. He stands before the public 'as the site of political unification and emotional identification'.[69]

Yet Cicero's ideal of natural eloquence, no less than the ideal of natural Roman masculinity, stands in marked contrast to the energy devoted to rhetorical training and education in the Republic and especially in the Imperial period. Schools and performance arenas were crucial sites for the institutionalised production of masculinity as an attribute of both body and mind.[70] The perfect orator, the elder Cato said, must be first and foremost a *vir bonus*, 'good man', a definition the authors of later rhetorical handbooks take very much to heart (Quintilian, *Institutio oratoria*, 1, *praef.* 9; 12.1.1). Indeed, manliness appears to be the true aim of the remarkable disciplining of the body required of the orator and would-be orator in these treatises.

The attention to discipline is due, in part, to the plasticity of the young male pupil. If all goes well, the student is moulded properly. Describing himself after he emerged from his training under the rhetorician Molon of Rhodes, Cicero writes: 'the straining of my voice was relaxed, along with my style of speaking, which had been, as it were, feverish; my lungs and fairly weak body gained strength' (*Brutus* 316). He exits his training having shed the unstable gender identity of the pubescent boy for stable masculinity. But the formation of the young orator may also go awry. The voice on the threshold of manhood is easily corrupted by bad practices. The young man is susceptible to being seduced by showy, effeminate styles of speaking. For this reason, the student must be carefully shepherded to the cultivated manhood best exemplified by the Roman orator.

The energy devoted to disciplining the rhetorical self can also be explained by the orator's acute awareness that the signs produced by his body will be scrutinised alongside his words as indices of his legitimacy to speak as a *vir bonus*. The word gains its authority through the body that delivers it. The required vigilance is especially clear in Quintilian's first-century CE rhetorical handbook, the *Institutio oratoria*. It doesn't just matter, Quintilian writes, how the orator speaks, although speech, too, must be regulated lest it become lowly, mean or effeminate or lest it 'emasculate' the subject matter with an overly lucid and variegated style (8, *praef.* 20). It also matters how the orator wears his toga: just to the knees in front and to the middle of the knee in the back, Quintilian advises. Anything else veers towards the length proper to a woman at one extreme or a centurion at the other (11.3.137). It matters what the orator does with his eyes: nothing sexy or soft, no sidelong glances, nothing, in short, to suggest the look of a sexually passive partner (11.3.76). And, finally, it matters how he moves: he should stand straight and tall, limit the scope of his movement, restrain gesticulation; he should be careful not to tilt his neck in a feminine way or move too languidly; he should avoid flicking his fingers. In short, the ideal orator should 'govern himself in his entire frame' (Cicero, *Orator* 59).

But the need to exhibit self-governance is always up against the demands of an audience. The pressures of performance push the orator to borrow the tricks of the actor and the singer, as Quintilian observes:

> But contemporary taste has adopted and requires a rather more excited delivery, and in some cases this is appropriate. Still, it must be kept in check lest while we seek the elegance of the actor, we lose the authority of the good and serious man. (Quintilian, *Institutio oratoria* 11.3.184)

In fact, the rhetorical treatises betray considerable anxiety about the proximity of oratory to other forms of performance, particularly acting. The actor, together with the singer and the dancer, is a degraded figure at Rome, regularly reviled in our sources and assigned a low-level civil status akin to that of men pegged as 'soft' (although it's the case, too, that actors could achieve considerable popular celebrity, and Cicero thought the actor Roscius to be a fine model for the aspiring orator). Actors are condemned in part because their desire to please an audience is, in itself, the mark of a woman. Then there's the problem that they readily adopt female as well as male roles, 'imitat[ing] the sex denied men by nature' (Columella, *On Agriculture* 1, *praef.* 15).

But perhaps what makes actors most troubling is the very fact that they imitate. For Roman authors, like Plato in the *Republic*, are suspicious of mimesis: the fluidity of identity it implies; its adaptability to the tastes and pleasures of the crowd; and its associations with pretence and theatricality. Still, there is no oratory – and, indeed, no education in Roman manhood – without mimesis. From the earliest stages of his training, the student looks to the tradition of heroic epic for models of masculinity and actions and attitudes to emulate. The practice of rhetorical declamation, increasingly important as the student grows older, requires him to expertly manipulate character types and channel the language of others (a Caesar, for example, or a Demosthenes). The orator-in-training acquires his habits by imitating the older man who serves as his model. Mimesis itself, then, is an object of discipline in oratory, carefully circumscribed and managed in the service of higher ends. The difference between actors and orators rests tenuously, in the end, on the claim that the former are *imitatores veritatis*, 'mimes of truth', while the latter are *actores veritatis*, 'agents of truth' (Cicero, *On the Orator* 3.102, 214). The art of performance, in short, is both assiduously cultivated and strategically effaced.

The highly public nature of oratorical performance draws attention to what Gleason calls the 'forest of eyes' within which elite masculinity was more generally practised in Rome and under the Roman Empire, as it was in Greece. But the very unease surrounding the pretences of performance led Roman authors to cast rhetorical training as a disciplining of the self *for* the self. Erik Gunderson neatly sums up the message of the rhetorical handbooks: 'we are being taught how to become ourselves, not how to pretend to be good men'.[71] The naturalisation of artifice, in other words, is meant to convince those practising it as much as those judging the performance from the outside.

The strategies of controlling the body that we see in the rhetorical treatises thus form a continuum with practices of caring for the self, which, encouraged by the Hellenistic philosophical schools and Greco-Roman medicine, flourished under the Roman Empire. Like rhetorical training, these practices require vigilant self-scrutiny, perhaps best exemplified by the journals of Marcus Aurelius, as well as an intimate audience of friends capable of providing helpful feedback. But whereas the rhetorical authors worry about the slackened gesture or the swaying hip, the ethical philosophers, while no strangers to concerns about self-presentation, are alert to the eruption of 'the feminine within' by other means, usually through appetitive desires or weakness in the face of pain or death. Nevertheless, the outcome is the same. The man who fails to master the unruly body, either through neglect or through the pursuit of a decadent and 'feminine' way of life, sinks to the level of a woman.

Foucault, as we have seen, did much to turn our attention to these reflexive practices of care. Yet he doesn't sufficiently address the anxiety about the failure to uphold masculinity that we see in so many ancient, especially Roman, authors. For these practices are as much about destabilising the masculine self as they are about constituting it. As Gunderson has observed of Quintilian, 'the irony of Quintilian's process . . . is that the endless process of training and threats of failure make the category *vir bonus* fundamentally unstable'. The fragility of elite masculinity at the intersection of acts and identities is a concept that resonates especially powerfully with Judith Butler's theory of gender identity as a naturalised product of repeated performances. Indeed, it is with Butler that Gunderson reads Quintilian.

In the previous chapter, I introduced Butler's arguments for understanding 'sex' and, more specifically, the materiality of the sexed body as an effect of dominant cultural and philosophical discourses and practices. The concept of practice turns out to play an important role in these arguments. For, on Butler's account, it is through repeated practice that the illusion of a sexed body as the *cause* of gender identity is formed:

> . . . Acts, gestures and desire produce the effect of an internal core or substance, but produce this *on the surface* of the body, through the play of signifying absences that suggest, but never reveal, the organising principle of identity as a cause. Such acts, gestures, enactments, generally construed, are *performative* in the sense that the essence or identity that they otherwise purport to express are *fabrications* manufactured and sustained through corporeal signs and other discursive means. That the gendered body is performative suggests that it has no ontological status apart from the various acts which constitute its reality.[72]

The sense we have of ourselves as sexed and gendered is thus created through the enactment of gender in a thousand small gestures, some conscious but many unconscious (Butler repeatedly stressed after the publication of *Gender Trouble* that gender is not like a set of clothes you decide to put on in the morning). It is just these gestures – and here we might think of the micro-adjustments a young elite Roman man makes to his stance, the changes of pitch he manages in his voice, the way he behaves with a lover – that produce the phantasm of a stable essence lying behind them. That phantasm can be described as a sexed body that somehow stands before and outside culture and political power and discourse. But it can be seen, too, as the natural *vir bonus* of Roman rhetoric. In both cases, the distance between acts and identities that we saw earlier in this chapter collapses. Identities are created out of acts, some – but not all – of them sexual.

But if the illusion of an inner 'core' of gender identity is to persist, the real – that is, the artificial – origins of gender have to be effectively concealed, as they are, in fact, in Cicero's language of naturalisation. Butler's project in *Gender Trouble* is to counteract the invisible labour performed by gender norms by exposing the ontological fragility of 'male' and 'female', using the concept of performativity to lay bare the mechanisms that keep the fiction of the sexed body alive. Her aim is to create space for identities that, while not necessarily *unconstrained* by gender norms, are, at least, capable of subverting and reinventing those norms. For example, the drag queen and the butch lesbian, whose gender identities most obviously violate assigned sex, hold a unique potential to expose the non-necessary, historically contingent, *artificial* relationship that always binds a body to a gender. But disruption is also possible and, indeed, inevitable, within the repetition of gender norms as they're enacted every day. This is because if repetition naturalises the idea of gender, repetition is also gender's Achilles' heel. The moment you slip up in performing masculinity or femininity, the contingency of that identity becomes nakedly clear. The 'regulatory ideal is . . . exposed as a norm and a fiction that disguises itself as a developmental law regulating the sexual field that it purports to describe'.[73]

Quintilian, of course, doesn't read the instability of gender as an occasion for subversive gender performances. Nor is he interested in pursuing alternative masculinities. Nevertheless, as Gunderson observes:

Quintilian's instruction ... explicitly opens up a space of contestation. He offers to train the bodies of men that they might be more themselves. In so doing Quintilian also exposes a latent crisis in the authoritative man: the *vir bonus* cannot automatically assume that he will successfully be himself without Quintilian's aid. In this sense Quintilian would agree with Butler: drag queens really do matter since the political stakes of bodily performances are always high, and so too are they also a question of the manliness of men.[74]

Quintilian, in the end, isn't so unlike Butler after all.

What Gunderson calls the 'latent crisis' of the *vir bonus* is spectacularly realised in those figures classed as effeminate or full-fledged *cinaedi*. It's an open question, as we saw above, whether *cinaedi* deliberately, or at least self-consciously, subverted gender norms. Remember that scholars don't even agree that the word designates a class of flesh-and-blood individuals. But if we look past these debates, we can ask whether the idea of subversion that such figures embodied exercised a pull of its own on those who officially recoiled from any hint of effeminacy.

In fact, in fifth- and fourth-century Athens, it seems that those political figures imagined to have boundless appetites – the tyrant is emblematic here – did function as more than phobic symbols of disgraced masculinity. Through what she calls 'symptomatic' readings of canonical Athenian texts from the later fifth century, Victoria Wohl has argued that citizens at Athens may have secretly desired and identified with such transgressive figures precisely because they violated ideals of self-mastery and democratic moderation.[75] One reason for this, we might imagine, is that those ideals exacted real psychic costs, not just for those who served as anti-ideals – women, slaves, foreigners – but also for those who upheld them (and the costs of upholding gender norms defined through dominance undoubtedly fed the abuse of those on the other side). The fantasy of transgression makes good sense in such a context. Moreover, it is supported by other sources. For example, the performance of tragedy, as Froma Zeitlin has influentially argued, can be understood as a civic space where citizens were able to explore the limits and the inversions of the masculine self by inhabiting 'the feminine'.[76] For the tragic stage doesn't just permit but actively encourages embodied and feminised expressions of suffering and vulnerability (on a stage full of men dressed up as women) that were elsewhere tightly circumscribed for men. This is precisely why Plato believed, as he writes in the *Republic*, that in a better world men, and especially young men, wouldn't be allowed to act in tragedies.

The situation appears similar in Rome. Kathleen McCarthy has suggested that the popular success of the so-called 'clever slave' in Roman comedy derives in part from the opportunity afforded by the character for masters to entertain the fantasy of occupying the slave role. The pleasure of stepping outside the anxieties of exercising authority is coupled with the security of knowing that order will be restored in the end.[77] If we turn to Roman love elegy, we find the first-person narrator regularly embracing a position of sexual submissiveness and even enslavement to his female lover, who, in turn, is figured as his master. The inversion of sexual roles works in tandem with the elegiac poet's rejection of military service for the fatherland – and the normative masculinity associated in this period with the duty of a citizen soldier – in favour of combat on erotic battlefields. These role reversals, Marilyn Skinner has speculated, seem to reflect the desire of elite males to occupy 'alternative subject positions permitting scope for voluptuous emotive fantasy' without having to sacrifice male prerogative.[78] The strategic embrace of *nequitia*, 'vice' or 'depravity', as in Ovid's *Amores* (2.1.2), or vulnerability, as when Catullus appropriates an image of lost virginity from Sappho to describe his own sense of erotic violation (11.21–4), carves out space for a new breed of masculinity, one with its own claims on social status. By giving voice to a sense of helplessness, these poets, writing in the first century BCE and the early first century CE, may also be registering a growing sense of impotence among social and political elites as the Republic was changing into an empire where power was concentrated in one man.

In conclusion, the imposition of gender norms doesn't simply regulate and constrain behaviour. It also generates violations of masculinity that have psychic, political and pragmatic functions of their own. If these usually seem to serve the dominant gender regime, that may be a result of our sources. But it is likely that subversions of this regime, deliberate or not, could destabilise social norms. It's probably no coincidence that the combative history of early Christianity, for example, is riddled with strategic gender-bending. The politics of subversion will concern us at more length in the next chapter, where I focus not on men courting femininity but on women who challenge men in power and the ways in which these proto-feminist icons have been appropriated for contemporary political struggles.

The idea of acting as opposed to being acted on is, as we've seen in this chapter, fundamental to social status and values in both Greece and Rome. It is also gendered to the core. The binaries of active and passive, male and female are realised most concretely in sex. The language of sex, in turn, travels far beyond the bedroom as part of the endless jockeying for position in ancient arenas of power. At the same time, practice – that is, acting on oneself – is central to the constitution of masculinity, understood as an achieved state identified by culturally specific signs.

The strangeness of a landscape defined by these terms, rather than our own categories of homosexuality and heterosexuality, has made classical antiquity a privileged domain for debates about sexual identities in the present. But the ancient terrain is also easily recognisable, insofar as it's defined by gendered hierarchies that were often brutally upheld and restrictive gender norms that invested the practice of masculinity with considerable anxiety. The task of negotiating between the unfamiliarity of ancient sexuality, on the one hand, and the familiarity of a pervasive and oppressive gender system, on the other, has been one of the biggest but also one of the most exciting challenges for historians of Greece and Rome in recent years.

In the next chapter, I shift genres to focus on the role played by Greek and Roman myths and literary texts in the contemporary theorisation of sexed and gendered identities and a more adventurously gendered politics. I also shift genders, turning from elite masculinity to powerful but fiction-alised representations of women who mount deep challenges to the social and political hierarchies that relegate them to positions of submission. The fact that these figures are products of canonical male-authored texts raises tough questions about whether they had anything to do with the lives of real women or offered genuine opportunities for subversive identifications. I largely set these questions aside, however, to concentrate instead on how iconic figures like Demeter, Clytemnestra and Antigone have been used by contemporary thinkers to probe questions of female subjectivity and to reimagine – and indeed to *reshape* – a political landscape that, for most of Western history, has largely failed to accommodate women as legitimate civic agents.

CHAPTER III

THE POLITICS OF GENDER, THE GENDER OF POLITICS

Variations on a Murder

What would it be like to live in a land where women were in charge? The Greeks could imagine the possibility. In fact, the only surviving tragic trilogy from classical Athens, Aeschylus's *Oresteia*, begins with just such a scenario. The first play, *Agamemnon*, opens with a watchman, propped up on his arm on the palace roof as he has been every night for a year. He's waiting, he tells us, for a light, for the last flame in a string of beacons stretching from Asia Minor to Mycenae that will announce the sack of Troy and the imminent return of the king, Agamemnon. He waits and watches under the orders of the queen, Clytemnestra, a woman he describes as having a heart hardened by male resolve (*androboulos*). His waiting stands as an image of her own taut endurance, sustained over the ten years since Agamemnon killed their daughter Iphigenia to launch the expedition to Troy. Less than twenty-five lines later, the flare has appeared, setting in motion a cycle of vengeance broken only once the scene has shifted to the nascent court of law in Athens two plays later.

The watchman gives us a snapshot of the state of affairs at Mycenae. Clytemnestra's iron-fisted control of the situation is expressed as a gender inversion that suggests a deeper confusion of power relations in the city. For while her husband's absence gives her the right to rule Mycenae, she has laid claim to the masculine position as her own with her 'man's mind', a position that seems cemented when, at the end of the play, she emerges from the palace with the bloody corpse of her husband. But Clytemnestra is not simply a power-hungry woman. She is also a mourning mother. Her tenacious resolve is driven by her desire to avenge her daughter's murder, and it is in these terms that she justifies her murder of Agamemnon. The equation of the mother with a raw thirst for vengeance will be redrawn once Clytemnestra herself has been murdered and her Furies, the Erinyes, are pursuing the matricide Orestes seeking retribution for the crime. But whether as man-minded queen or avenging mother, Clytemnestra's rule is untenable. The rest of the trilogy aims to correct the perverted hierarchies of the *Agamemnon* by ultimately establishing a new kind of political order.

The remaining plays thus build up to the triumph of Athens and its patron goddess Athena over a nihilistic family curse and the resolution of conflict between Olympian and chthonic powers. As the gendered politics of the first play had led us to expect, the hard-won outcome of the final play, the *Eumenides*, systematically privileges the male over the female and the father over the mother. The play opens with the Pythia, Apollo's priestess, recounting how ownership of the oracular seat at Delphi passed from a line of goddesses (Earth, Themis and Phoebe) to Phoebus Apollo. Clytemnestra appears briefly as nothing more than a fading ghost. And her Furies, whose power was ascendant at the close of the second play, are first shown asleep, lulled to powerlessness by Apollo.

The trial at Athens strikes a further blow to the mother. Apollo, as we saw in the first chapter, defends Orestes' matricide by naming the father the parent of the child, relegating the mother to the role of temporary host. If his argument does not sway a majority of jurors, it is nevertheless ratified by Athena. The tragedy concludes with Athena appeasing the Erinyes by promising them a place of honour in the *polis*, upon which they return to the earth, their powers decisively contained and circumscribed. The trilogy thus offers a glorified genealogy of classical Athens' institutions of justice while celebrating the benign incorporation of the archaic forces of vengeance, dark and female, into the city's ritual landscape. The struggle to establish the proper boundaries of the city, together with the proper hierarchies of power, is structured throughout by the opposition of male to female and father to mother. It is resolved by subordinating the mother's Furies to a political order that is underwritten by allegiance to the father. Myth is poised here on the cusp of history to legitimate the classical city and the order it imposes on the world.

The *Oresteia* shows the extent to which gender functions in Greek mythology as a way of organising relationships of power in the cosmos, the city and the family. The recognition of gender as one of the cardinal axes of Greek mythology has made the mythological tradition a privileged area for studying the construction and functions of 'masculine' and 'feminine' in antiquity. Moreover, in contrast to the relative scarcity of sources about historical women, classical mythology is full of richly drawn female figures, figures who exercise a degree of power that appears outsized in light of the limited roles of women in ancient communities. Their appeal is no doubt one of the reasons why mythology has been the preferred point of entry to classical antiquity for feminist philosophers, poets and visual artists, who've appropriated characters from the mythological tradition in endlessly inventive ways. The robust popularity of Greco-Roman mythology has meant that the tradition, in addition to being plumbed for ancient constructions of gender, has also served as one of the most active and pluralistic areas for contemporary negotiations of sexed and gendered identities in relationship to the past.

Take the *Oresteia*. In the final play, the powers of the mother decisively give way to those of the father. One way of reading the father's victory is to see it as the trace of a vanished historical moment, namely, the transition to the rule of fathers from what J. J. Bachofen, the most famous nineteenth-century exponent of this view, called 'mother-right' (*Mutterrecht*).[1] Bachofen's views have never been all that popular among classical scholars, and the initial interest of archaeologists has given way to a hard-hitting feminist critique of the archaeological foundations for the theory of a lost 'matriculture', as we'll see further below. But the idea of a prehistoric matriarchy has proved resilient over the past century-and-a-half, from Friedrich Engels' elaboration of Bachofen's theory to Jane Ellen Harrison's writings about goddess worship in prehistoric Europe to the popularising archaeology of Marija Gimbutas and the contemporary Goddess movement.

The idea that the *Oresteia* is a valuable witness to the defeat of the mother at the origins of Western culture has also been developed by feminist philosophers. Luce Irigaray has written that Freud, when hypothesising a primal murder of the father in *Totem and Taboo*, 'is forgetting an even more ancient murder, that of the woman–mother, which was necessary to the foundation of a specific order in the city'.[2] She goes on to read the matricide in the *Oresteia* as a murder decreed by the new regime of the father in the interest of appropriating the powers of a mother allied with the earth. Building on Irigaray's work, the Italian feminist philosopher Adriana Cavarero has worked to 'steal' the figure of the mother back from the matricidal tradition of early Greek myth and philosophy. Her readings of archaic and classical Greek texts seek to coax out 'the continuing presence of a transition that carries within it the fresh traces of this shift and the memory of what has been lost to patriarchal domination'.[3] For Irigaray and Cavarero, Greek myth is a valuable discourse because it conserves the memory of a world before patriarchy.

Perhaps, though, we should read the spectre of matriarchy in the *Oresteia* not as evidence for a lost world but simply as a haunting but effective myth. The anthropologist Joan Bamberger has spoken of the 'myth of matriarchy' in a contemporary South American tribal context as a story that, by recounting how women once had power but abused it, functions as a 'social charter' purporting to offer a historical explanation for why women are denied power in the present.[4] In her classic reading of the *Oresteia*, Froma Zeitlin adopts Bamberger's idea for a reading of the trilogy in terms of an entrenched concern in early Greek thought about the division of power between the sexes. 'The vigorous denial of power to woman', she writes, 'overtly asserts her inferiority while at the same time expressing anxiety about her persistent but normally dormant power that may always erupt into open violence'.[5] The trilogy succeeds in finding an appropriate place for the power embodied first by Clytemnestra and then by her Furies by shifting it from the political to the ritual realm.

From this perspective, the *Oresteia*, like Hesiod's variants on the Pandora myth, affords us the opportunity to investigate the semantic range of 'the female' and 'the feminine' in archaic and classical Greek culture and the work these terms perform in an Athenian myth of political origins. Drawing on structuralist interpretations of mythology, according to which binary oppositions, especially the polarity of male and female, are implicated in one another, Zeitlin argues that the male–female relationship in the *Oresteia* 'provid[es] the central metaphor that "sexualises" the other issues and attracts them into its magnetic field'.[6] After the metaphor does its work, the myth of matriarchy goes back underground.

The *Oresteia* is not only a text to be interpreted as a historical document. It also offers a jumping off point for rewriting and creative elaboration, as is the case, for example, in Christa Wolf's brilliant novel *Cassandra* and, less directly, in Elizabeth Cook's short story 'Iphigeneia's Wedding'.[7] In fact, one of the most significant areas within contemporary feminist approaches to classical mythology has been the return to canonical myths as material for new narratives. There's something strange about this, as Vanda Zajko and Miriam Leonard have pointed out, given that so many of these myths underwrite the most basic negative assumptions about women in the androcentric societies that produced them.[8] But myth is slippery, always created anew in variants and retellings. It turns out to be tailor-made for appropriations designed to shift angles of viewing, explore gaps and divert outcomes.

The ancient Greek and Roman poets were well aware of the slipperiness of myth. Euripides retells the myth of the *Oresteia* more than once, each time introducing new elements – unappeased Furies (in the *Iphigenia at Tauris*), a second, failed 'matricide' (the attempted murder of Helen in the *Orestes*) – that magnify the horror of the mother's murder and subvert the Aeschylean drive towards resolution. The Romans adapted Greek myths to their own ends, as when the proselytising Epicurean Lucretius vividly depicts the sacrifice of Iphigenia to illustrate the savagery of traditional religion in *On the Nature of Things* (1.84–101). Nor was mythmaking confined to canonical ancient authors. Lillian Doherty has argued that the supple nature of myth, together with its adaptability to various social contexts, must have already in antiquity encouraged variants to develop in ways that incorporated the perspectives of socially marginalised figures such as women.[9]

As myths move through the centuries and across cultures, the possibilities for investing them with new meanings proliferate. The rise of modern and postmodern feminisms, in particular, has fostered conditions that allow these myths to be inhabited from unexpected angles. Hélène Cixous' recuperation of one of the most hideous exemplars of the mythological feminine, the snake-headed Medusa whose gaze turns men to stone, enacts a classic shift in perspective: 'You only have to look at the Medusa straight on to see her. And she's not deadly. She's beautiful and she's laughing.'[10] If, as a number of scholars of myth have stressed, 'mythology' should be understood as a body of stories that are always in flux – that is, stories that must be understood in relation to other stories and other variants of the 'same' story – the reinvention of classical myths is always transforming our relationship to earlier variants, including those handed down from antiquity.

One of the advantages of taking not just mythology but the *reception* of mythology into account is that it helps us counter the tendency to see myths, and especially canonical textual variants, as originary moments that, imbued with the weight of a distant, even prehistoric past, resist critical analysis. On the other hand, we have to recognise that it's often precisely the antiquity of classical mythology and the resulting cultural legitimacy – remember the use of ancient precedents in the court cases described in the previous chapter – that makes it so appealing in contemporary feminism and gender studies. Consider, for example, feminist appeals for a return to the representations of women in early texts as the necessary precondition for liberation in the present. The poet Adrienne Rich has famously described 're-vision – the act of looking back, of seeing with fresh eyes, of entering an old text from a new critical direction' as 'more than a chapter in cultural history' for women: 'it is an act of survival.'[11] The uncovering of a peaceful prehistoric matriarchy often works in the service of the idea that feminists can recover this lost utopia. The almost talismanic power of the ancients is at work more subtly in contemporary appropriations of Antigone, where we witness again and again a strategic return to Sophocles' play as the repository of hidden truths.

So as we examine how ancient myths have been used to conceptualise gender and gendered identities, we have to get used to myth's two sides. On the one hand, myth can be deployed in the service of a monolithic reading of the past or an appeal to ancient, immutable truths. On the other hand, its mutability makes it useful to those who want to reimagine the relationship of gender to power, political subjectivity and resistance. These two aspects sometimes work together, as when creative rereading masquerades as the excavation of buried wisdom. The point is that myth is always old *and* new.

The double-sided nature of myth forces us once again to confront history itself as a loaded term. Many of the feminist artists, writers and philosophers who have turned to classical myth have been driven by the desire to embrace the past not as foreign or distant but as the source of rich material for exploring and challenging sexed and gendered identities in the present. The license for free-form inventiveness that myth provides creates an opportunity to make the past one's own. But what does it mean to take ownership of the past? What kinds of limits, if any, should be imposed on those who make claims on history? And where does the history of readings of the past fit into all this? Can claims on the past ever be disentangled from the contexts in which they are made? Is there something to be gained by taking these claims on their own terms?

These questions can help us see the clash of competing expectations for the role of history. In fact, the study of feminist and gender-sensitive engagements with the classical canon has gone a long ways towards making us aware of the various meanings of 'history' that crowd the burgeoning field of reception studies more generally: first, history as the object of academic disciplines with claims to method and accuracy; second, history as a trope used to legitimate or challenge the present; and finally, history as the history of engagements with classical antiquity. Each of these aspects of history is in play in this chapter.

One last term, or, rather, pair of terms, is destabilised in this chapter: Woman and 'the feminine'. If in the first chapter we touched briefly on the internal complexity of these terms in the ancient world, here we see how they've been appropriated in different ways for contemporary readings of ancient figures. For while myth can be a powerful tool to interrogate concepts of masculinity in Greco-Roman mythology, most interventions in classical myth from a gendered perspective have been undertaken in the name of women and 'the feminine'.

But these names designate contested ground. Indeed, the wild inter-pretive potential coiled in myth is nowhere clearer than in the polyphony of feminist readings and appropriations. Consider, for example, two different creative representations of the parting of Clytemnestra and Iphigenia before Iphigenia's sacrifice. Irigaray sees this as a paradigmatic moment that testifies to the severing of female lines of descent in Greek prehistory and the epoch-making loss of mother–daughter intimacy.[12] In Elizabeth Cook's short story 'Iphigeneia's Wedding', which draws loosely on Euripides' *Iphigenia at Aulis*, the separation is, rather, a moment that reveals the different and irreconcilable subjectivities of mother and daughter.[13] For all that myth has been put in the service of affirming the solidarity of women in the past (and of women in the present with women in the past), it's been used, too, to experiment with a range of subject positions that end up exceeding definition through gender alone. And there aren't simply competing views on whether Woman represents a single identity or many. There's a question, too, of whether 'the feminine' is a necessarily sexed position or whether it might name a position with no relationship to a person inhabiting a sexed body at all but, rather, a structural relationship to power and, more specifically, to political power.

It is, in fact, in the domain of the political that the question of defining what it means to act as a woman or in a feminine mode has proved partic-ularly thorny. To a remarkable degree, figures from Greek mythology have been central players in this debate, perhaps reflecting political theory's strong sense of its roots in classical Greece. These roots are, at first glance, unpromising for feminism. The representation of Clytemnestra in the

Oresteia sums up the view of many ancient authors that women act as a menace to political and social order. In the modern period, the German philosopher G. W. F. Hegel influentially cast Antigone as the embodiment of Woman, who destabilises the state in defending the interests of the family. In recent years, feminist readers have vigorously contested Hegel's essentialising reading, as well as its ancient antecedents. But they have also valourised the outsider status of women in classical myth as the toehold on a rival world with its own superior system of values, complicating the place of ancient Greece in feminist political theory.

In what follows, I focus on two mythological figures who have captured the imagination of modern readers interested in the relationship of women and 'the feminine' to civilisation, social cohesion, hegemonic discourses and oppositional politics: Demeter and Antigone. Each figure defies a male ruler. Demeter, the Greek goddess of agriculture, mounts one of the most effective challenges to Zeus in Greek literature in response to the rape of her daughter (and his) Persephone. Antigone's refusal to obey Creon's orders in Sophocles' *Antigone* has become one of the most recognisable symbols of political resistance in the modern period, from Argentina to Nazi-ruled Paris to Nigeria, as well as a catalyst for debates about the gendering of non-political space and challenges to the dominant order.

Each of these figures has also been used to explore alternative political, social and ethical worlds. Taken as the archetypal mother, Demeter has been held up by some readers as representing an older civilisation where motherhood was valued and women, especially in their capacities as mothers, determined the values of their societies. For others, Demeter represents a classic position of resistance within a patriarchal culture that persists today. The extraordinary fascination with Antigone, especially over the course of the past decade, poses the question of the relationship of women or 'the feminine' to the political realm from a different angle. For Antigone challenges us to reflect on the representation of the space of the anti-political or the apolitical as feminine and, indeed, what we mean when we speak of the 'outside' to a political community (or the rule of law or morality or the symbolic order). She has thus become the major vehicle for a debate not just about the age-old struggle for power between male and female but about the gendering of power and resistance in political theory.

I begin with the *Homeric Hymn to Demeter*, the best-known and oldest narration of the myth of Demeter and Persephone, dating from the seventh or sixth century BCE. I focus first on close readings that cast the two figures in an archetypal 'mother–daughter romance', before considering how the figure of a mother Goddess has informed feminist appropriations of a pre-historic or mytho-historical past. In the second part of the chapter, I shift our attention to Antigone, considering how the rapid rise of interest in Sophocles' heroine dovetails with the ascent of gender studies itself. I suggest that Antigone's popularity reflects, at least in part, the desire for a less maternal figure to appropriate for feminist or feminine challenges to the political order.

Demeter, Persephone and the Great Goddess

The Legacy of Demeter

The *Agamemnon* opens, as we've seen, with a scene of waiting. A crime has been committed – the sacrifice of Iphigenia – and, after ten long years, the father will be made to pay with his own blood. The *Hymn to Demeter* also begins with a *fait accompli*:

> Demeter, fair-haired, awesome goddess, I begin to sing
> of her and of her slim-ankled daughter Persephone, whom Hades
> seized; Zeus, deep-thundering and all-seeing, gave her away
> without the consent of Demeter of the golden sword and glorious fruit,
> as she was playing with the deep-breasted daughters of Ocean,
> gathering flowers in a lush meadow; roses, crocuses and beautiful violets,
> and irises, and hyacinth, and the narcissus
> which the Earth brought forth to be a snare for the blooming girl
> as a favour to the Host-to-Many (Hades) in accordance with Zeus's plans
> a wondrous and radiant flower, a marvel for all to see,
> both for deathless gods and for mortal men.
>
> (*Homeric Hymn to Demeter* 1–11)

Like Iphigenia, Persephone has already been seized when the poem begins. In the middle of this long opening sentence, however, we cross seamlessly from the retrospective gaze of the poet into the narrative frame itself and the threshold of the traumatic event.

The temporal dynamics of the *Hymn*'s opening scene thus make it clear that we're dealing with a text in which the separation of the mother and the daughter has already happened. At the same time, the *Hymn* projects us into events as they unfold in the moments after the abduction. As long as Persephone is still above ground, she hopes to see her mother again. That doesn't happen before she disappears into the underworld, but Demeter *does* hear her cry. The daughter's hope becomes the mother's response: her search and eventually her defiant mourning, which threatens to destroy humanity. In the *Oresteia*, the sole option available to Clytemnestra is vengeance: the payback of a deed that cannot be undone, within a cycle of bloodlust that only the city can stop. By contrast, the *Hymn* dwells for the most part in a space that is animated by resistance to the plan of the father and the possibility of reversing it. That possibility is, in the end, both realised and thwarted. Demeter succeeds in having her daughter returned to her, but Persephone's taste of a pomegranate seed in Hades consigns her to spending part of the year there. The nature of the mother's success is thus ambiguous.

Given this ambiguity, it's no surprise that Demeter's resistance has been read and appropriated in very different ways by contemporary readers. For some feminist classical scholars, what makes the text so intriguing is its sympathetic identification with Demeter. Marilyn Arthur, in an article first published in 1977, has described the poem as one of the few texts from classical antiquity to offer a 'peculiarly feminine sensibility', despite its likely male authorship.[14] For Arthur, the 'feminine' consciousness encoded in the poem through Demeter's experience is corroborated by psychoanalytic models of female experience and, more specifically, by different stages in Freud's account of female psychosexual development. In other words, Demeter's story enacts the development of the girl in terms of a 'quasi-historical' narrative that refers not to the real fall of a prehistoric matriarchy but to early Greek ideas about women and power, what we saw referred to earlier as 'myths of matriarchy'. For the poem seems to begin with a matriarchy of sorts, or at least within the cocoon of mother–daughter intimacy. But its narrative unfolds in an order where the ascendancy of fathers is guaranteed (a possible subtitle for the poem, Arthur suggests, would be 'How to be a Mother Goddess in a Patriarchal Society').[15] It's because the poem takes place under *already fixed* conditions that despite our sense that Demeter's resistance could upset the entire cosmic order, her story reproduces the experience of every little girl or, as Arthur puts it, of 'all women, who must struggle to achieve self-definition in a social and psychic world which values male attributes more highly and depreciates females'.[16]

Arthur shows no nostalgia for the closed mother–daughter relationship glimpsed in the poem's first lines. Rather, tracing a narrative arc that begins with the 'naïve' symbiosis of Demeter and Persephone described early in the poem, 'produced by their mutual antipathy toward the male and encasement in an enchanted world of virginity', and closes with reconciliation and the emergence of a form of female solidarity that recognises the necessary bonds each woman has with the male, she characterises the poem's closure in positive terms as the discovery of a female community within a patriarchal 'new world order'.[17] Arthur stresses that, despite the fact that the poem's ending confirms Zeus's power, Demeter's honour and special privileges are also affirmed. The poem validates, too, a uniquely female form of agency associated with renewal and rebirth as these processes are enacted in the agricultural cycle and through the rites of the Eleusinian Mysteries, which Demeter instates in the course of the poem. In the end, the 'feminine' perspective of the poem represents its successful expression of bonds, powers and values designated, either implicitly or within a psychoanalytic paradigm, as 'female' or 'feminine' within a patriarchal world. Arthur seems to suggest the poem's resolution as a template for the individual negotiation of femininity under patriarchal conditions in the twentieth century.

Helene Foley has also emphasised the *Hymn*'s unique perspective on the experience of women in ancient Greece. She, too, draws attention to the text's sympathetic portrayal of Demeter's grief, intimacy between mother and daughter and the cross-generational affective bonds between women. By validating the mother's mourning and Demeter's defense of the maternal bond in the face of patriarchal control, the poem, she argues, stands in striking contrast to the *Oresteia*. Like Arthur, Foley describes the closure achieved by the poem in positive terms. Again like Arthur, she draws on psychoanalysis to explain its success, assimilating the narrative structure to the model of the 'mother–daughter romance'.[18] More specifically, she sees the ending of the poem as resonating with the clinical experiences described by feminist psychoanalysts like Nancy Chodorow insofar as both the mother and the daughter are granted greater capacities for nurture after their bond has been renegotiated in the wake of the daughter's separation and sexual maturation. At the same time, she suggests that the Eleusinian Mysteries offer the initiate a kind of 'maternal plenitude' that obscures any rift between mother and daughter and Demeter's compelled integration into a patriarchal order.[19] The poem's resolution is thus a complex but ultimately successful negotiation between Demeter's demand to be reunited with her daughter and the compromise she must make.

The literary critic Marianne Hirsch has offered a similar reading of the end of the *Hymn*. Even if Demeter fails to 'repair the breach' in the mother–daughter relationship, Hirsch argues, the text manages to break free of the linear plots and 'deathly closures' characteristic of other myths of young girls alienated from their mothers (Electra, Antigone) and enact an alternative narrative structure organised by cyclicity.[20]

Arthur and Foley are deeply sensitive to the historical and cultural context of the *Hymn*. Both of them offer readings that track the original text closely. Nevertheless, the effect of turning Demeter and Persephone into actors in a timeless psychosocial drama is the collapse of distance between past and present, between myth and individual experience. These interpretations thus form a continuum with readings of the Demeter–Persephone myth in terms of universal symbols. For example, Carl Jung, the early twentieth-century thinker best known for his concept of the collective unconscious, saw the two goddesses as expressions of the psychic archetypes Mother and Maiden. The idea that these mythic figures are universal archetypes has also resonated with the many poets and novelists who have reworked the Demeter–Persephone myth, especially in the years since what Andrew Radford has called a 'virtual cult' of the two figures sprung up in European artistic and intellectual circles in the second half of the nineteenth century.[21] Arthur closes her essay with a poem by the modernist poet H.D., which lays claim to the figure of Demeter through the use of the first-person voice:

> The mysteries remain
> I keep the same
> cycle of seed-time
> and of sun and rain;
> Demeter in the grass
> I multiply,
> renew and bless
> Iacchus in the vine;
> I hold the law,
> I keep the mysteries true,
> the first of these
> to name the living, dead;
> I am red wine and bread.
>
> > I keep the law,
> > I hold the mysteries true,
> > I am the vine,
> > the branches, you
> > and you.
> > > 'The Mysteries' VI[22]

The use of the first-person goes hand in hand with a powerful present tense. Together, these rhetorical strategies enact the concepts of continuity, persistence and fidelity: the endlessly renewed presence of an ancient past in the here-and-now.

The unifying ground for the meeting of past and present – for Arthur and Foley, as for many of the writers and artists who have taken up the myth of Demeter and Persephone – is a universal female subject who tends to be allied with fertility, nurture and other women against an aggressive, sexually invasive and destructive male force. The very presupposition of such a subject has been sharply challenged within feminism and gender studies. But before considering these criticisms in more detail, I want to look first at some more radical appropriations of the gynocentric, that is female-centred, mythology hinted at by the *Hymn*. These versions move the narrative out of the world of myth into history, or, rather, prehistory. Moreover, they designate Demeter's resistance to Zeus and Hades as the model not for triumphing under the terms of patriarchy but for triumphing over patriarchy altogether by righting ancient wrongs.

Earlier in this chapter, we touched briefly on Luce Irigaray's view that Aeschylus's *Oresteia* bears witness to a primal matricide resulting in the ascent of a patriarchal order. The return to Greek mythology is, for Irigaray, a critical element in a larger project of recovering what she calls 'female genealogies'. Such acts of remembrance, which Luisa Muraro has aptly described as elements in a politics of 'witnessing',[23] are urgently needed, Irigaray argues, to reverse the damage of that consequential act of violence. 'If we are not to be accomplices in the murder of the mother we also need to assert that there is a genealogy of women'.[24] But what needs to be remembered is not only the murder of the mother. The lines of female ancestry have been broken, too, by the father's theft of the daughter's virginity when he exchanged her in marriage. Like the matricide, this 'original sin' leaves traces in Greek myth and tragedy, above all, Irigaray claims, in the story of Demeter and Persephone.

The larger framework of female genealogies explains why Irigaray focuses above all on the mother–daughter bond in her most extensive reading of the myth of Demeter and Persephone in the essay 'The Forgotten Mystery of Female Ancestry'. It's interesting to compare this reading to Irigaray's treatment of the myth in the *Marine Lover of Friedrich Nietzsche*. In *Marine Lover*, Irigaray resists characterising Persephone (or rather Kore,

'Girl', as she calls her, following one ancient tradition) as either a piece of property circulated among men or the daughter torn from the mother's arms: 'her depth, in all its dimensions, never offers itself up to the gaze, whatever the point of view may be'.[25] By contrast, in 'The Forgotten Mystery', Kore is primarily a pawn. Her identity remains inseparable from that of her mother, and she is innocent to the end (Irigaray dismisses later variants that hint more directly at Persephone's complicity in her seduction as attempts on behalf of the patriarchal order to make the woman bear responsibility for its crimes). The mother and the daughter are a fused unit symbolising the chain of female genealogy.

Irigaray recognises that the *Hymn* takes place – as do all the texts we have from classical antiquity – within a world already organised by patriarchy. She takes Demeter's failure to turn to her own mother Rhea in her grief, for example, as symptomatic of bonds already broken. Moreover, the crime against Kore cannot be undone, despite the eventual reunion of mother and daughter. The world remains haunted by the theft of the daughter's virginity, the trace of which survives in the pressure on young girls to fashion themselves as objects of male desire. 'None of this could happen', Irigaray writes, 'if she [sc. Kore] had not been separated from her mother, from the earth, from her gods and her order'.[26]

Yet Irigaray also recognises the possibility of reversing course. On other occasions she describes the present state as a world 'which is *not yet* an order of respect for and fertility of sexual difference'.[27] In the 'not yet' lies the possibility of generating that respect by reestablishing a bond between mothers and daughters. Here is where myth as history, what I referred to earlier as the *trope* of history, comes into play. For such a bond, Irigaray insists, must be generated and sustained not only in specific familial relationships but also through a collective return to the past:

> If the rationale of History is ultimately to remind us of everything that has happened and to take it into account, we must make the interpretation of the forgetting of female ancestries part of History and reestablish its economy.[28]

Myth itself has a special status in this enterprise to the extent that it commu-
nicates history in a way that, on Irigaray's argument, recalls female, matrilineal traditions. If in her earlier work Irigaray seems to suggest that to
remember is simply to mark the point of erasure, here she stresses the
importance of rescuing what has been forgotten from invisibility. To recuperate the image of the relationship between Demeter and Kore as one of
loving reciprocity is an act of political resistance to the tyranny of 'male'
values organised around violence, power and money. By restoring 'female'
respect for sexual difference, she argues, we can once again divert the path
of civilisation, putting it back in harmony with the natural world.

The reading of the Demeter myth offered by Adriana Cavarero honours
the spirit of the project outlined by Irigaray while plotting the route from
the mythological past into the future along slightly different lines. For
Cavarero, the core principle of the myth is the generative power of the
mother. Such power depends, she argues (as does Irigaray), on the reciprocal visibility of mother and daughter. What this means is that as long as
Persephone stays close to Demeter, each seen by the other, the natural world
continues to flourish. But when this bond is broken, the other side of
Demeter's power comes into play, namely, the power to *refuse* to generate.
Cavarero makes this refusal into the sign of what she calls the 'universal
sovereign subjectivity' of the mother, which stands in opposition to the
patriarchal model of maternity as 'mere reproductive function'.[29]

For Cavarero, as for Irigaray, the logic of the Demeter myth has real
implications for the contemporary political landscape. Despite the triumph
of Zeus and the ensuing patriarchal order, the mother's sovereignty persists.
In the contemporary world, it is symbolised above all by elective abortion.
Cavarero's aim here isn't to advocate abortion. What she's interested in,
rather, is the durability of the practice. The fact that women continue to
make choices about whether to give birth or not proves, she believes, that
the sovereign subjectivity embodied by Demeter is still operating in the
present. It can serve, then, as a strategic point from which to develop a
mother-centred philosophy of birth. Such a philosophy wouldn't deny
sexual difference in the name of a universal neuter subject, who is always,

as feminism has long argued, masculine by default. Rather, it would acknowledge 'the dignity of being alive (as either woman or man), thanks to our common maternal origin, before our social integration into the fathers' political order'.[30]

It's worth pausing for a moment on Cavarero's appeal to a space prior to politics. For it raises a question that runs through appropriations of Greek mythology for the project of feminist political resistance. Must 'feminine' or 'female' space exist outside the boundaries of the state? On the one hand, Cavarero defends the separation of the home from the state as necessary for securing an autonomous maternal domain. On the other hand, she concludes by imagining the state gradually taken over by a rival female symbolic order. Demeter would thus seem to stand for both the need to stake out a strictly maternal space *and* the possibility of a new politics. The tension between these two alternatives – *either* the anti- or pre-political *or* a new political order – becomes even more acute in discussions of Antigone. Before turning to Antigone, however, let's take a closer look at the idea of a mother-centred domain that Cavarero and others believe predates the political and represents its most viable future.

Matriarchal Prehistory

Irigaray and Cavarero suggest that screened behind texts like the *Hymn* or the *Oresteia* is a phase in history before the rise of patriarchy and its violent appropriation of the female body. Such a phase is characterised by the absence of domination, the sovereign power of the mother and a harmonious relationship with the earth. The belief in a prehistoric matriarchy or matriculture, usually seen as devoted to the worship of a single Mother Goddess, has, in fact, found a wide range of adherents over the past century-and-a half. Its roots have been traced to the rise of European Romanticism, a movement defined by its veneration of wild, uncultivated nature, on the one hand, and cultural primitivism, on the other. The idea of a Great Goddess, first suggested by the German scholar Eduard Gerhard in 1849, quickly took hold of both the scholarly and the popular imagination. It gained further support from excavations of Neolithic sites in southeastern Europe later in the century, which began to turn up figurines appearing to be representations of women with exaggerated hips, bellies and breasts (the Venus of Willendorf, discovered in what is now southern Austria in 1908, is perhaps the most famous example). These figurines were widely identified with the worship of the Great Goddess. The latter half of the nineteenth century also saw the dissemination of J. J. Bachofen's arguments, mentioned at the beginning of this chapter, for a primitive matriarchy. Bachofen characterised this matriarchal phase as an early stage in civilisation marked by close ties to nature and the dominance of corporeal life. By the early twentieth century, a fairly robust picture of prehistoric societies ruled by women and organised around the veneration of a single goddess had emerged. It circulated widely, defended and elaborated by prominent figures such as Sir Arthur Evans, who directed excavations of the Minoan palaces on Crete, and Jane Ellen Harrison, the Cambridge classicist at the heart of the influential Ritualist school. The popularity of the Great Goddess hypothesis opened the study of ancient Greece and Rome up to methods and evidence from the burgeoning fields of archaeology, anthropology and ethnography.

Further archaeological developments in the twentieth century contributed to the enthusiasm for the Goddess hypothesis. Excavating at the Neolithic (c. 7400–6000 BCE) site of Çatalhöyük in southern Turkey, first discovered in the late 1950s, James Mellaart took as a given that inhabitants of the town had been devoted to the worship of a Great Goddess. He interpreted the material evidence, including the figurines, accordingly. Mellaart's reconstruction of a prehistoric, matriarchal, goddess-worshipping society became the template for a narrative that was elaborated by the Lithuanian-American archaeologist Marija Gimbutas. Gimbutas's increasingly popularising publications transmitted the narrative to the feminist spirituality and ecological movements that took off in the 1970s and 1980s.[31]

What a site like Çatalhöyük supplied to these movements was evidence that a mother-centred, peace-loving, spiritual society living in harmony with nature wasn't just a utopian ideal. It was a possibility within human nature that had been realised for a long stretch of human history. On Gimbutas's narrative, these prehistoric societies had been destroyed by the invasion of the Kurgans from central Asia, who brought with them a violent patriarchal culture, along with metallurgy, agricultural technology and a pantheon of male gods. In her later publications, she dated the origins of women's inequality and oppression to these invasions, much as Irigaray pegs the shift from matriarchy to patriarchy to a (less specific) historical moment. For Gimbutas, as for many feminists, ecofeminists, neopagans and Goddess worshippers, remembering these earlier utopian societies and their fall paves the way for a revolution that is both political and personal. The past becomes the road 'back to the future'.[32]

But while the Goddess has met with remarkable success beyond the confines of professional archaeology, archaeologists themselves have become increasingly sceptical of the monolithic narrative of a matriarchal or matrifocal prehistoric Europe. In fact, archaeologists working within sex and gender studies have become the most vocal critics of the theory of matriarchal prehistory.

The critique has unfolded, first, at the level of the material evidence that has often been used to provide the 'hard facts' for matriarchy unavailable from texts like the *Hymn to Demeter* or the *Oresteia*. The most contested evidence in these debates is the corpus of Paleolithic and Neolithic figurines that have been the most visible and popular symbols of prehistoric matriarchy and Goddess-worship. What feminist archaeologists have resisted most has been the narrowing of a large body of material evidence to a single interpretation: the veneration of a goddess whose female form embodies fertility and nature. They've stressed, in response, that the figurines date from a period spanning over twenty thousand years and have been found at sites widely separated in space and time. Moreover, they've insisted on the need to consider the larger material context – where figurines have been found and what objects they appear together with – as well as what we can infer about how they were used and altered by users (many figurines, for example, appear to have been deliberately broken). Finally, they've drawn attention to the large cache of zoomorphic, ambiguously anthropomorphic and male figurines, while also emphasising the differences among figurines identified as female. The figurines that have been discovered, in other words, are far from homogeneous. They are often more difficult to identify, let alone interpret, than the standard story lets on.

It would be misleading to say that every prehistoric artifact is like the famous 'duck–rabbit' illusion, where the brain simply toggles between seeing first a duck, then a rabbit in the same figure. When archaeologists question dominant interpretations of figurines, they are building on fieldwork experience in the interest of developing interpretations that are consistent with other evidence discovered on-site, interpretations that can accommodate the kinds of differences that get lost in a Gimbutas-style narrative. The continuing excavations at Çatalhöyük under the direction of Ian Hodder, for example, have revised many of Mellaart's conclusions in the face of new data.[33]

The objections raised against Gimbutas's account of prehistory have critically undermined its plausibility. Yet the evidence, as the archaeologists publishing on the topic are the first to recognise, remains open to interpretation. It's at the level of interpretation that the second prong of their critique of matriarchal prehistory and Goddess worship has developed.

When prehistoric female figurines first began to be discovered in the nineteenth century, they were identified as unambiguous symbols of fertility. The female body – and, by extension, women – was simply equated with the biological capacity for reproduction. Most feminist appropriations of these figurines have turned what was a negative valuation of women into a point of celebration. But they've done so without questioning the underlying equation of women and nature. It's precisely the strong essentialism of these interpretations that has attracted heavy criticism from archaeologists studying the materialities of sex and gender. Lynn Meskell, in particular, has drawn attention to the complicity of Goddess narratives with the sexual stereotypes that have dominated reconstructions of the prehistoric past (e.g., the 'Man the Hunter' paradigm). Meskell argues that these narratives perpetuate the very dualisms that other feminists have sought to undermine (culture versus nature, mind versus body). Women are 'thrust back into the flesh zone', bound all over again to the body, their sexuality and their emotions.[34] For anyone who thinks the old sexual stereotypes are just benign artifacts, Meskell points to the perpetuation of outmoded assumptions on the reality 'survivor' shows that continue to rivet television audiences.

The fear here isn't just that a utopian, Goddess-centred past is no utopia. It is that a blind embrace of that past can lead feminists to opt out of the messy politics of the now, a fear not limited to archaeologists. Angela Carter, for example, has dismissed the Great Goddess as 'consolatory nonsense' that keeps women from making concrete political interventions in their own lives.[35] The charge isn't entirely fair, as radical feminism and ecofeminism have been some of the most politicised wings of the feminist movement. But the question remains. What should a feminist politics look like? And what does it want from the past? By advocating a less reductive approach to gender and sex roles in prehistoric and ancient societies, Meskell and other archaeologists have admirably sought to challenge the equation of women with certain kinds of roles – including the role of sexualised object of worship – in larger social and political communities. It is worth recalling here Rosemary Joyce's observation that archaeological materialities help us *resist* reductive models by 'forc[ing] us to confront our own least interrogated assumptions.'[36]

The at times hostile response by archaeologists to feminist attempts to appropriate a matriarchal past is echoed by historians of antiquity who work primarily with texts. In an otherwise positive review of Margaret Atwood's novella *The Penelopiad*, the ancient historian Mary Beard singled out Atwood's references to 'the overthrow of a matrilineal moon-cult' in early Greece as 'complete rubbish', adding that 'most feminists I know think that matriarchy is itself a myth invented by patriarchal culture.'[37] Irigaray has also come under attack for the valorisation of maternity as the defining sign of sexual difference in her pursuit of female genealogies. Eleni Varikas has criticised Irigaray's readings of Greek mythology as a throwback to the old themes of nineteenth-century German Hellenism (origins, decline) in support of a model of sexual difference that is ultimately a trap. 'Irigaray's

"Greeks", she argues, 'do not provide . . . a field where new possible configurations of gender can be imagined and worked out'.[38]

Tina Chanter has developed a more generous reading of Irigaray's female
genealogies that finds in them the resources for a complete rethinking of
the political sphere. By insisting on the specificity of sexual difference,
Chanter argues, Irigaray's work 'opens the way for an ethics that extends
beyond sexual difference'.[39] But in Irigaray's readings of the *Oresteia* and
the Demeter–Persephone myth, it's hard to see past the conflation of the
female with the mother, the privileging of closed communities of women
and the insistence that only the recovery of female genealogies can avert
ecological disaster. These factors seem to polarise politics in the name of
sexual difference, rather than move beyond it.

Earlier we traced the emergence of narratives of prehistoric matriarchy
and goddess worship to larger developments in the nineteenth and early
twentieth centuries. The success of the Goddess movement in the early
years of the new millennium can also be explained by larger historical and
cultural forces, which include the resurgence of an ecological consciousness and the popularity of New Age spirituality.

But the critiques of allegedly essentialist readings have contexts of their
own. The most notable is the rise of gender studies as a field, with its privileging of cultural construction over biological sex, its rejection of the category 'Woman' and its emphasis on the intersection of gender with other
forms of difference, such as age, race, sexual orientation and status or class.
If the development of gender studies has shaped how we look at material
artifacts and texts, it has also directed our attention to certain kinds of
evidence, as we saw with the focus on moralising and prescriptive texts in
the previous chapter.

The influence of gender studies is also visible in the spiking interest in
Antigone. Like Demeter, Antigone has long been an icon for a feminist
politics organised around the category of women. Yet readings of Antigone
in these terms have also been challenged within feminism, and these challenges have appropriated her for their own ends. Interest in Antigone has,
in fact, accelerated as gender has gained currency as an analytical category.

The restless reinterpretations of Antigone in recent years open a window onto how gender has changed the landscape of feminism and how gender itself is changing as a focal point of interpretation.

There are many factors that account for Antigone's persistent popularity over the past decade. But one aspect relevant to our aims here may be the nature of the 'female' or 'feminine' subjectivity that she is thought to embody. Her very name (*anti-gonē*, 'anti-generation') defines her through the absence of childbearing. This hasn't kept Antigone from being read as the torchbearer of her mother's curse, the mascot of a politicised 'maternal' thinking or the figure through which to theorise a concept of 'matrixial' space.[40] But Antigone is not a mother. Indeed, her premature death, at least in Sophocles, ensures she never will be. Her suspension on the threshold of adulthood matters because the equation of women with maternity continues to be seen as *the* essentialist trap threatening to undermine the work done in the name of gender to prise sex apart from sex roles. By allowing us to sidestep a concept of maternity that seems unavoidable in the case of Demeter (who is, after all, the goddess of agriculture and the iconic mourning mother), Antigone holds out the promise of gender severed from sex. Her virginity has the feel of a blank slate. It animates her with raw potentiality and lends her resistance a sense of ideological purity. Moreover, indifferent to her fiancé, she occupies an ambiguous erotic space defined by her incestuous birth and her fierce fidelity to her father and her brother. It may be precisely because the figure of Antigone responds so well to analyses developed under the rubric of gender that she's become the subject of so much attention in recent years. What's clear is that the reception of Antigone in feminism and gender studies forces us to revisit the complicated and contested relationships between gender, the sexed body and sexuality that we've seen elsewhere in this book.

The debates around Antigone also return us to a question that I introduced earlier with respect to Cavarero's reading of the Demeter myth in terms of a 'mother-centred' philosophy of birth, namely: What is the relationship of the female or 'the feminine' to the political sphere? The *Hymn to Demeter* finds its resolution in the incorporation of Demeter into the patriarchal order. At the same time, the poem sets aside the Eleusinian Mysteries as a ritual space that seems to recall and conserve the closed mother–daughter intimacy with which the poem begins. For some readers, however, Demeter's resistance to Zeus licenses a more radical outcome in the present, one that overturns the patriarchal order in the name of a return to a matriarchal past. The dream of going 'back to the future' has, as we've seen, been popular in some feminist political movements inspired as much by the archaeology of prehistory as by Greek mythology.

Turning to Antigone, we find a particularly tight relationship between readings of a specific Greek text, in this case Sophocles' *Antigone* – although Sophocles' *Oedipus at Colonus* and Euripides' *Phoenician Women* are also sometimes brought in – and feminist political theory. Even more than Demeter, Antigone forces an interrogation of what a feminist or feminine – and these terms are not the same, as we'll see – challenge to the state aims to achieve. Should Antigone represent the integrity of a space outside or before politics? Or does she license the practice of politics in a new way? In the rest of this chapter, we'll see how Antigone has been used to stake out different positions in debates about a sexed or gendered politics. These appropriations don't just allow us to track a shift from sex to gender. They also lead us to debates about how much gender still matters to the theorisation of politics and political resistance.

Arresting Antigone

Antigone is a law unto herself (*autonomos*). Such is the judgment of the Chorus of Sophocles' tragedy (*Antigone* 821). Antigone herself says in her celebrated final lament, just before she is led offstage to the living tomb to which she's been condemned, that she has a home among neither the living nor the dead (850–2). By choosing to defy her uncle Creon, the newly appointed king of Thebes, in order to bury her treacherous brother Polyneices, she's cut short her transition from daughter to wife and, eventually, mother. She occupies, as a result, an uncertain place outside the roles conventionally designated for ancient Greek women. As the daughter of the incestuous union of Oedipus and Jocasta, she's embedded in kinship relationships entangled almost beyond recognition: her father is also her brother, her mother is also her grandmother and her brothers are also nephews and uncles. By all accounts, Antigone is a hard figure to read.

And yet despite her apparent illegibility, Antigone has been read over and again in the past two centuries with uncommon passion and dedication. For Hegel, Sophocles' *Antigone* was 'the most magnificent and satisfying work of art' of all time, its 'celestial' heroine, the 'noblest of figures that ever appeared on earth'.[41] Deep admiration for Antigone was widespread among European intellectuals, writers and artists from the late eighteenth to the early twentieth century. It's true that with the rise of psychoanalysis, attention shifted to Oedipus. George Steiner, characterising Antigone as the road not taken in the twentieth century, memorably asked in his study of the modern reception of Antigone: What would have happened if psychoanalysis had chosen the daughter rather than the father for its totemic figure?[42] A quarter of a century later, the question is no longer purely hypothetical. Antigone has reemerged from the shadows, and not just in psychoanalysis. For the past half-century, she's figured prominently in some of the most important attempts to rethink subjectivity, ethics and politics from a perspective that can no longer not, in one way or another, take gender into account.

The *Antigone*, then, is not just one of the most important texts of Western civilisation. It's a text that has proven vital to a particular historical, cultural and theoretical moment in the early twenty-first century. Before considering influential readings of the play by feminists and theorists of gender, we need to take a look at the two readings of the *Antigone* that have provoked the most resistance: that of Hegel and that of the French psychoanalyst Jacques Lacan.

Hegel: Introducing the Family and the State

It is practically impossible even today to talk about Antigone or the *Antigone* without citing Hegel. Hegel, as we just saw, had the highest praise for both the play and its heroine. But to understand the extraordinary influence of his admiration, we have to put it in its wider context. For Hegel, as Miriam Leonard has written, 'arguably inaugurated the very tradition of making an example of the Greeks for so-called "modernity"'.[43] The *Antigone*, from this perspective, becomes the example *par excellence*. Hegel's interpretation of the play is thus as much a founding text for the modern and postmodern fascination with Greece as an ideal and a point of origin as it is a starting point for modern and postmodern engagements with Sophocles' tragedy.

The Hegelian reading is, in its barest form, the diagnosis of a tragic conflict between two fundamental ethical laws in the play: one divine, one human. Antigone defends the former in the name of the family, the sphere proper to women; Creon defends the latter in the name of the state, the sphere proper to men. Each ethical principle is legitimate on its own terms. Neither can survive the conflict between them. In the end, both Creon and Antigone are destroyed along with what Hegel calls the 'ethical life' (*Sittlichkeit*) of the Greek *polis*. The annihilation of the *polis* clears the space for another, more stable phase of ethical life in Rome and, later, under Christianity.

For Hegel, then, Antigone is defined through her association with the family and her *exclusion* from the political sphere. In principle, her provocative outsider status can be extended to any excluded figure. But readers since Hegel have generally followed his lead in mapping the tension between the inside and the outside of the state onto the dynamics of sexual difference. His critics have made the tragedy's apparent gendering of the political sphere into a target of attack and revision.

It is worth noting that despite Hegel's enormous influence, he never offers a proper reading of the play in his writings. That is not to deny the significance of the *Antigone* to Hegel's thinking. It's clear that the play deeply informed his ethical and political thought. Rather, the absence of a straightforward reading reminds us that what travels under the name of Hegel is knottier and more complex than the paraphrases suggest. Though I have to offer paraphrases of my own, I'll try to draw attention to the knottiness in Hegel's remarks as a way into understanding why Hegel's Antigone has provoked such a controversial reaction over the years.

Let's start with one of the most basic points made in summaries of Hegel: his equation of women and nature as forces opposed to the state. The first thing that might come to mind here is the assumption that nature is something raw and chaotic endangering a fragile political order. In 'On the Scientific Ways of Treating Natural Law' (1802–1803) Hegel does indeed imply that the female figures of the *Oresteia* (Clytemnestra, the Furies) represent such a threat. But he shifts gears when he turns to Antigone in the *Phenomenology of Mind* (1807), where we find a more complicated idea of women's relationship to the natural world. In the *Phenomenology*, Hegel defines women first and foremost in reference to an ethical duty that arises from 'being imbued with family piety'. The sphere of action proper to the family – and, by extension, to women – is ethical precisely because it imposes order on brute nature. The highest expression of the ethical duty entrusted to the family is burial, because it ensures that the individual (man) is spared becoming a victim of natural forces after his death. Burial, in other words, affirms the dead man *as a person* at his moment of greatest corporeal vulnerability. So for Hegel, Antigone's unwavering commitment to burying her brother expresses her ethical duty most purely. Her act is undertaken in *opposition* to nature, forming an integral part of ethical life.

At the same time, when it's set over and against the human community, the family is the *natural* ethical community. Hegel writes in the *Phenomenology*:

We mentioned before that each of the opposite ways in which the ethical substance exists contains that substance in its entirety, and contains all moments of its contents. If, then, the community is that substance in the form of self-consciously realised action, the other side has the form of immediate or directly existent substance. The latter is thus, on the one hand, the inner principle [*Begriff*] or universal possibility of the ethical order in general, but, on the other hand, contains within it also the moment of self-consciousness. This moment which expresses the ethical order in this element of immediacy or mere being, which, in other words, is an immediate consciousness of self (both as regards its essence and its particular thisness) in an 'other' – and hence, is a *natural* ethical community – this is the *Family*. The family, as the inner indwelling principle of sociality operating in an unconscious way, stands opposed to its own actuality when explicitly conscious . . . as the *immediate* ethical substance, it stands over against the ethical order which shapes and preserves itself by work for universal ends; the Penates of the family stand in contrast to the universal spirit.[44]

While it's true, then, that the family is opposed to nature to the extent that it participates in ethical substance, *within* the domain of ethical substance it stands for 'natural' immediacy and the unconscious working of the ethical principle. What this means is that if spirit (*Geist*), in the words of Seyla Benhabib, 'constitutes second nature by emerging out of its substantial unity into bifurcation (*Entzweiung*), where it sets itself over and against the world', the process by which nature 'sets itself over and against the world' *cannot be realised within the family*.[45] The family, in short, stands in contrast to the state as the domain where ethics is enacted without conscious knowledge or deliberation.

Hegel maps the opposition between the family and the state onto the difference between the sexes. Given what we have seen so far, it's unsurprising that when Woman is placed as a foil to Man, she is associated with naturalness (*Natürlichkeit*), whereas he is associated with freedom and universality. The naturalness of women entails, as it does for the family, an ethical life characterised by immediacy and a lack of reflection.

For Hegel, the complementarity of male and female is best expressed in the sister–brother relationship because it is a bond uncontaminated by sexual desire, leaving them both 'free individualities with respect to each other'.[46] The sister, whose ideal representative is Antigone, thus embodies the 'feminine element' that 'foreshadows most completely the nature of ethical life [*sittliches Wesen*]'.[47] She nevertheless

. . . does not become conscious of it, and does not actualise it, because
the law of the family is her inherent implicit inward nature, which
does not lie open to the daylight of consciousness, but remains inner
feeling and the divine element exempt from actuality.[48]

By unconsciously preserving the divine law, the sister's ethical development
parallels that of the brother in the realm of human law to the extent that
'both the sexes overcome their merely natural being, and become ethically
significant'.[49] But the brother also progresses beyond the sister. For, unlike
her, he succeeds in leaving the 'immediate, rudimentary and therefore, strictly
speaking, negative ethical life of the family, in order to acquire and produce
the concrete ethical order which is conscious of itself'.[50] The brother, in
other words, manages to set himself out against the world, entering a state
of 'second nature'.

The complex role occupied by nature in Hegel's analysis goes together
with the dual function of Woman (and the family): on the one hand, she's
the necessary complement to Man (and the state) within the ethical sphere;
on the other hand, she embodies a principle that threatens to undermine
the state. It is precisely the duality of Woman that lies at the heart of the
conflict in the *Antigone*. Antigone's act is, from one perspective, justified.
In burying her brother she fulfils her ethical duty to him. But it's also intol-
erably subversive. The burial privileges particularity over the universality
claimed by the state.

Hegel argues that the instability of Antigone's act points to the instability of the ethical substance more generally in ancient Greece at this
historical moment. Given the fragility of this substance, it can be easily
upset by the winds of chance. The chance events that upset the unity *within*
the tragedy are, first, the birth of brothers with equal rights to the throne and,
eventually, the death of Polyneices, which compels Antigone to challenge
the city. But the collapse of Thebes within the *Antigone*, in enacting an
ineradicable tension between the family and the state, also signals the end
of a phase of ethical life in historical Greece. For Hegel, then, the family
and the state cannot be reconciled in the *Antigone*. Neither Antigone nor

Creon can win. Rather, the tragedy exposes the tensions and conflicts within ancient Greek ethical life that eventually destroy the city outside the confines of the theatre, from whose ashes another politico-legal system will arise.

What such a summary fails to capture is the way in which Antigone challenges not just the city but the very categories that Hegel creates to contain her. Like so many nineteenth- and twentieth-century readers, he was in awe of her. But he was also convinced of her guilt. If Oedipus commits his crime unwittingly, Antigone knows what she's doing, and her knowledge means she cannot go unpunished. The idea of Antigone as a *knowing* criminal points to what is, perhaps, the most difficult problem in Hegel's remarks on the *Antigone*. Antigone should not, according to Hegel's definition of women's ethical capacity, be conscious of what she's doing. After all, her blind performance of duty is just what excludes her from the political realm as its 'natural' Other. And yet, she articulates her defiance *within the sphere of the city*.

One way of getting around the problem is to say that Antigone acts without full consciousness of the meaning of her act. But we shouldn't sidestep the quandary so quickly. For one thing, in principle Creon, too, should have a limited grasp of his ethical action, given that he belongs to a historical period when full consciousness is not yet possible. Yet it's Antigone who represents for Hegel the lack of ethical consciousness, as Woman does in his philosophy more generally, the categorical foil to Man. Even at this historical moment, then, Hegel implies that women are out of place in the public sphere, however inchoate it may be. The implied privileging of Creon's position has been seen by feminists as symptomatic of Hegel's *a priori* assumptions about the greater value and legitimacy of the position of the male in the play.

More important still, the tension within the idea of acting 'knowingly' in Hegel's analysis both of Antigone's act and of the ethical agency of women more generally calls up a larger problem that has haunted the post-Hegelian reception of the play. Is Antigone apolitical in the sense of being without a city or outside the city, incapable of grasping its logic? Or is she anti-political, acting against the city from within as a subversive insider capable of assuming power? These questions have been central to the debates that have sprung up within feminism in response to Hegel's sexing of the opposition between the family and the state. What does Antigone tell us about the relationship of women to the state? Do women have a place there? On what terms? Or are they permanent outsiders? Is it, in fact, better – more pure, more ethical or simply more praiseworthy – to be outside the system rather than inside it?

These questions have been posed without Hegel being directly engaged, as we'll see below. But some of the most robust feminist engagements with Antigone have taken Hegel's remarks on the *Antigone* as a starting point, with the result that they have been as much about Hegel as about Antigone. I cannot go into feminist debates about Hegel at any length here. Rather, I want to look briefly at how Sophocles' play has been strategically deployed both to critique Hegel and develop another theoretical model for understanding the relationship of women to the state.

The strategic use of Sophocles is especially evident in Patricia Mills' pioneering critique of Hegel's views on the *Antigone*. Besides identifying weaknesses in Hegel's arguments, Mills claims that he fails to consider Sophocles' play in its entirety. The gaps left by his 'oversimplification' create space for a more complex analysis of the play.[51] Mills goes on to draw on the tragedy itself in order to contest Hegel's broader views on women. On her reading, Antigone is indeed conscious of what she's doing, against Hegel's claim that she acts unconsciously, and Mills cites a line from the Chorus for support. But Antigone, from Mills' perspective, never admits guilt. Hers is 'a noble stance, consciously taken'.[52] She thus transcends the limited ethical position accorded to women by Hegel and enters the political realm. Her position there, as her suicide shows, is unstable. Nevertheless, precisely because Antigone embodies the tragic conflict between particularity and universality, she anticipates, Mills argues, the recent history of political protests undertaken by women:

> While embodying the tragic conflict between particular and universal,
> Antigone represents the history of the revolt of women who act in

the public sphere on behalf of the private sphere, the sphere of inaction. She is the precursor of the women who, in the recent past, proclaimed the personal as political ... In criticising Hegel's interpretation of the *Antigone* we begin to see another story in Western philosophy – one other than that of Hegelian reconciliation: the revolt of the particular against subsumption under a universal schema.[53]

By revisiting the *Antigone*, then, we find another story in the Western tradition that challenges the Hegelian dialectic and traces contemporary feminist protests to ancient precedents.

Mills critiques Hegel by offering a reading that claims greater fidelity to the ancient text, appropriating the play to support her own vision of women's relationship to politics. The potential of Antigone is *realised* through the critic's appropriation of Sophocles' tragedy as an intervention in the present. The idea of the play as an untapped and subversive reservoir of meaning is also employed by Jacques Lacan in his reading of the play, itself framed as a critique of Hegel. Lacan also opens up another angle on Antigone as the sign of a revolt against the social order, one that has encouraged further reflection on whether she rejects that order *qua* woman or simply occupies a 'feminine' position of resistance.

Lacan: Antigone's Desire

For Lacan's thoughts on Antigone, we have to turn to the remarks on the play that he delivered as part of his weekly seminar in Paris in 1959–60, which were subsequently published on the basis of transcriptions. Lacan invested his reading with a good deal of significance, making the play the cornerstone of what he called the 'ethics of psychoanalysis'. Noting the overwhelming influence of Hegel's views on the *Antigone*, he rejects outright the Hegelian model of a 'conflict of discourses'.[54] Not unlike Mills, he justifies his rejection in part by claiming, at the conclusion of his reading, that his own interpretation is more faithful to the 'Sophoclean message':

Involved here is nothing more nor less than the reinterpretation of the Sophoclean message. You can certainly resist this resharpening of the text's high points, but if you decide to reread Sophocles, you will perceive the distance we have travelled. Even if I am challenged on a given point – for I don't exclude the possibility that I, too, on occasion may misinterpret something – I believe I have dissipated the all-encompassing nonsense in which Sophocles is carefully preserved by a certain tradition.[55]

The tragedy, in other words, is a locus of truth that has been obscured by a history of *misreadings* that Lacan's own reading aims to sweep aside.

Lacan is adamant that, contra Hegel, the tragedy is not about competing views of the good. Indeed, the interpretation he develops virtually excludes Creon, except as the anaemic spokesman of morality. It is, rather, Antigone in her beauty and 'her unbearable splendour' who fascinates him and, he argues, all those who witness her suspended in a zone between life and death: the Chorus and the spectators of the play. What makes Antigone so fascinating is her implacable desire. The entire tragedy, Lacan argues, is organised around the revelation of this desire during Antigone's last appearance onstage before she leaves to be entombed alive. Everything that comes before this revelation – the 'action' of the tragedy – is nothing but preparation for this moment. For the startling disclosure of Antigone's unbearable beauty, in 'forc[ing] you to close your eyes at the very moment you look at it', produces a cathartic effect on the spectators.[56]

How does Lacan characterise Antigone's desire? It has nothing to do with ethical duty or fidelity to sacred or divine law or a respect for the earth. It doesn't have to do with what she thinks is right. It makes little sense from the perspective of conventional morality and the desire to do good. It is, rather, a desire as singular as it is absolute, binding her to the recognition of her brother Polyneices in his most basic being. Antigone's desire defines her, too, not least of all because it arises out of her and her brother's common origin in the tainted womb of Jocasta. But because her desire is so pure and uncompromising, so impossible for her to betray, it bears witness to subjectivity at its most involuntary, impersonal and universal.

Lacan defends his reading of Antigone's desire by focusing on her final justification of her act in a passage that has proved to be the most controversial of the play:

> For never, not even if I had been a mother of children, nor if I had a dead husband rotting away, would I have assumed this labour against the will of the citizens. In deference to what principle do I say these things? If a husband had died, there might have been another, and a child from another man, if I had lost this one. But with my mother and father hidden in Hades, no brother could ever be born again.
>
> (Sophocles, *Antigone* 905–12)

Antigone's reasoning here is puzzling. Goethe was so disappointed by her arguments that he famously hoped a future philologist would succeed in dismissing the lines as spurious. Much of the problem lies in the fact that any justification of Antigone that refers to unwritten laws and her sense of ethical duty to her dead kin founders on the stark singularity of her commitment to her brother. But it's precisely this singularity that Lacan seizes on to capture an ethics *beyond logic*. For Antigone's reasoning, he argues, collapses into a tautology: 'My brother is what he is, and it's because he is what he is and only he can be what he is, that I move forward to the fatal limit'.[57]

Lacan explains the tautology in terms of what he calls the 'signifying cut'. By this he means the splitting of the self that defines our existence within the symbolic order as it's enacted through language. It's at this moment that pure Being, 'the ineffaceable character of what is', is fixed by the signifier of the proper name 'in spite of the flood of possible transformations'.[58] What Antigone's tautological language indicates, then, is her honouring of the very emergence of Polyneices within language. Her desire aims for but never reaches the pure 'what is' of her brother, separated out from the historical details of his life. For Polyneices, these details encompass nothing less than his incestuous origins, his treacherous attack on Thebes and the murder of his brother. None of this matters to Antigone. Her position 'represents the radical limit that affirms the unique value of his being without reference to any content, to whatever good or evil Polyneices may have done, or to whatever he may be subjected to'.[59]

At the same time, by affirming Polyneices' being *as such*, Antigone assumes the burden of his crime. Indeed, she takes on the *atē*, a word that means both the 'daemonic drive towards ruin' and 'ruin' itself, of her whole polluted family. She is 'the guardian of the being of the criminal as such'.[60] Lacan thus locates Antigone in a space he defines as 'beyond *atē*', beyond the limits of human life that can be crossed only temporarily and exceptionally. By occupying this position, Antigone is, in essence, embracing death. Her fatal desire creates the beauty that so arrests us. The beauty of Antigone gives rise, in turn, to an ethics located beyond the law of the good and beyond the human on the threshold of the symbolic order.

What does any of this have to do with gender? Little, it might seem at first glance. The dynamics of sexual difference so active in Hegel's understanding of the text seem to stall without Creon as a countering force. But, in fact, 'the feminine' does remain in play through the trope of transgression. The domain fleetingly inhabited by Antigone stands in contrast to the space occupied by Creon and the Chorus and, for Lacan as for Hegel, the distance between these two worlds corresponds to the split created by sexual difference. The world of Antigone, as we've seen, is characterised as transgressive in the literal sense of 'going beyond'. Antigone is transgressive, too, because she takes on the ostensibly criminal desire of the mother. Her position casts her as a perfect representation of what Lacan characterises as feminine desire, defined by its excesses and its evasion of the masculine – or, more specifically, the paternal – law. The gendering of this space 'beyond the law' brings us back to Hegel's exiling of women from the political and social order, raising the question of just how much Lacan has unburdened himself of Hegel's influence.

We can identify at least some important differences between Hegel and Lacan. If Hegel casts Woman as the 'everlasting irony of the community', who contaminates the state with her private and particular ends, Lacan sees Antigone as incarnating pure desire as the most universal of ethical positions, as Slavoj Žižek, one of Lacan's most influential contemporary interpreters, has argued.[61] The ethical defined as such, however, is not political space. Then again, this is precisely why Lacan, in his anti-Hegelianism, finds it so attractive.

It is possible, of course, to follow Lacan on this point, so that the challenge Antigone poses to the normative social order acquires the legitimacy that Hegel grants to masculine political space. Such a strategy has been developed by the theorist Cecilia Sjöholm. Sjöholm argues that the Lacanian Antigone is a crucial figure for ethics because, insofar as she represents a breach in the ethical domain, she creates a 'feminine' alternative to the Oedipal identification with the law:

> Antigone is part of our ethical sensibility not because she can do what she likes, without submitting her desire to norms and rules. She is part of our ethical sensibility because she touches the void inherent in any normative order . . . In this way she reveals the subject's resistance to normalisation, which is at the core of Lacan's ethics, a resistance to be found in that part of the subject that is foreclosed in any social and normative order.[62]

For Sjöholm, the ethics of Antigone, the 'ethics of the real', can never be coopted by the symbolic. It is, rather, always unsettling the social fabric and its ethical norms. Its capacity for disruption is what gives it its 'revelatory' power, which 'allow[s] a theorization of desire that is philosophically rich' and helps us come to terms with how the social realm itself functions.[63]

By appropriating Lacan's disruptive feminine desire, Sjöholm aims to neutralise two elements in the Lacanian paradigm that seem to perpetuate Hegel's isolation of women within the family and the natural ethical order it represents. On the one hand, Sjöholm insists that she's not interested in 'the feminine' as the excluded or constitutive outside vis-à-vis the social and symbolic realm. Rather, she sees Antigone as a point of rupture *within* the system itself, identified in abstract terms with the resistance to a normative order. On the other hand, Sjöholm rejects an essentialist reading that would suggest women have a special purchase on this force of resistance. Rather, 'the feminine' is a strategic position that can be occupied by anyone.

Not everyone has been convinced that Lacan's 'excluded' Antigone is so different from Hegel's. I want to turn now to one of the most influential challenges to both the Hegelian and Lacanian readings. In her essay 'The Eternal Irony of the Community', first published in *Speculum of the Other Woman*, Luce Irigaray sets out to show how Hegel – and, following him, Lacan – entraps Antigone in a logic that necessarily opposes her to a universalising ethics and an ideal political community. Yet, as Sjöholm will do some thirty years later via Lacan, Irigaray works to reclaim the denigrated terms of the Hegelian system. At the same time, from her perspective these terms aren't structural positions in relationship to a norm but rather, in keeping with her philosophical project as we've seen it at work elsewhere, positions allied with the mother and with nature. Once we've taken a look at Irigaray's strategic mimicry of Hegel, we'll briefly consider her more recent attempts to recast Antigone as a political figure defined by her sex, before coming back to the question of what it means to designate a position, whether inside or outside politics, as 'female' or 'feminine'.

Irigaray: Reclaiming Antigone

Irigaray's approach to reading Hegel is much like her approach to Plato. She aims to expose the excess of meaning in Hegel's own texts that troubles the relationship he describes between Woman and nature and between Woman and the family. Her point of departure in 'The Eternal Irony of the Community' is the obligation of women to bury dead kin. Recall that, for Hegel, burial is how the woman protects the man from being reduced to a mere body after death and affirms the universal essence of his self. Taking her cue from Hegel, Irigaray characterises the woman as 'the guardian of the blood tie'. She comes back to the idea at the end of the essay:

Woman is the guardian of the blood. But as both she and it have had to use their substance to nourish the universal consciousness of self, it is in the form of bloodless shadows – of unconscious fantasies – that they maintain an underground subsistence. Powerless on earth, she remains the very ground in which manifest mind secretly sets its roots and draws its strength. And self-certainty – in masculinity, in community, in government – owes the truth of its word and of the oath that binds men together to that substance common to all, repressed, unconscious and dumb, washed in the waters of oblivion. This enables us to understand why femininity consists essentially in laying the dead man back in the womb of the earth, and giving him eternal life.[64]

By recasting the duty of burial as the sacrifice of maternalised substance, Irigaray undercuts Hegel's assertion that the ethical position of the woman simply complements that of the man.

Irigaray's concluding remarks are representative of her efforts throughout the essay to coax out the asymmetry haunting Hegel's relationship of sexual difference as it is expressed through the harmonious relationship of the brother and the sister. Despite Hegel's description of this relationship as one of mutual recognition, the act of recognition, Irigaray argues, is actually a debt incurred by the sister. After all, unlike the sister, the brother doesn't need to be recognised as a self within the family, since recognition is precisely what he gets from the political community. The sister, then, cannot reciprocate the act of recognition that her brother performs for her. The only way for her to pay back this debt is by 'devoting herself to his cult after death', an act of devotion that costs Antigone her life.[65] But far from being anomalous, Antigone's sacrifice point to a larger, invisible sacrifice performed by *all* women, namely, the sacrifice of substance that makes it possible for men 'to nourish the universal consciousness of self'. What this means for Irigaray is that the debt is owed not *by* the sister but *to* the sister and the blood she and, in a different way, the mother represent. The debt is owed, in other words, to the sex that effaces itself to reflect the autonomous self of the brother and the son as a kind of 'living mirror'; the sex that gives itself for the subsistence of society; the sex that forgets itself so that the soul of man and the community will not be lost to the forces of dumb nature.

Irigaray also criticises, as Mills does, Hegel's designation of female ethical agency as unconscious (a word she invests with its full psychoanalytic sense). The problem is not just that women, lacking self-consciousness, are shut out of history. For Irigaray, the tension between Hegel's claim that women are unconscious agents and his insistence on Antigone's guilt is symptomatic of

> *an amazing vicious circle in a single syllogistic system.* Whereby the unconscious, while remaining unconscious, is yet supposed to know the laws of a consciousness – which is permitted to remain ignorant of it – and will become even more repressed as a result of failing to respect those laws.[66]

While Irigaray's words apply most obviously to Hegel's remarks on the *Antigone*, she aims her critique beyond the scope of the play. For she detects in Hegel's writings a system that conceals behind the gendering of consciousness a broader class of divisions: men lie on the side of the state, history and Spirit; women lie on the side of a nature that is both the unacknowledged support and the vilified enemy of human law.

Given this division, Irigaray concludes, the Hegelian system cannot deliver the complementary model of sexual difference that it promises. In her more recent work, Irigaray has worked to develop the model that eludes Hegel. She accepts the terms of sexual difference. But she has vigorously resisted the binary between nature and culture, instead advocating a 'third world' that belongs to neither men nor women 'but is generated by the two with respect for their difference(s)'.[67] Even more important for our purposes here, she has described Antigone not as an outsider to politics but as a figure of political potentiality:

According to the most frequent interpretations – mythical, metaphor-ical and ahistorical interpretations, as well as those that denote an eternal feminine – Antigone is a young woman who opposes polit-ical power, despising governors and governments . . . Antigone wants to destroy civil order for the sake of a rather suicidal familial and reli-gious pathos, which only her innocent, virginal youth can excuse, or perhaps even make attractive . . . Antigone is nothing like that. She is young, true. But she is neither an anarchist nor suicidal, nor uncon-cerned with governing . . . It suits a great many people to say that women are not in government because they do not want to govern – but Antigone governs as far as she is permitted to do so.[68]

The values that this politicised Antigone stands for – 'the values of life, of generation, of growth' – recall those that define Irigaray's female genealo-gies against a destructive masculine order seeking to dominate the natural world.[69] Antigone, in other words, belongs to the same line of descent that Irigaray traces to Demeter and Persephone. Yet she stands here less for the utopian past than for a workable future: Antigone wants to govern and, indeed, 'governs as far as she is permitted to do so'.

Irigaray's appropriation of Antigone as a political figure stands in contrast to the radical outsider in Hegel and Lacan and recalls Mills' positioning of Antigone at the head of a long line of women who have launched attacks on the universalising status quo in the West. Yet if there's a widespread sense that Antigone might have something to say on behalf of a feminist politics, there's little agreement as to what it is. What does Antigone stand for?

Mills, we can recall, identifies Antigone with particularity against univer-sality, assimilating this to 'the personal' as the basis of the political. By this, however, she doesn't mean that Antigone should be confined to representing the family. Rather, Antigone's movement outside of the family into Creon's space exposes the impossibility of containing women within the household, pointing to the need to 'allow for women's experience and participation outside the sphere of the family'.[70]

Contrast Jean Bethke Elshtain's call to contemporary women in a 1982 article to become 'Antigone's daughters' by resisting total absorption into the modern state and 'giving voice to familial and social imperatives and duties'.[71] Elshtain doesn't advocate that women remain in the family as a private sphere. Rather, she argues that a feminist politics should be organised around female subjects who speak publicly from a perspective 'that flows from their experiences in their everyday bodily and material world', experiences of which motherhood is paradigmatic.[72] What Elshtain calls, after Sara Ruddick, 'maternal thinking' recalls Cavarero's defense of a 'mother-centred philosophy of birth' and Irigaray's alignment of Antigone with the values of life, growth and generation.[73] The problem with such a position, as Mary Dietz and others have argued, is that it 'reinforc[es] a one-dimensional view of women as creatures of the family'.[74] Dietz's own interpretation of Antigone reclaims her as a political actor who defends 'the customs and traditions of a collective civil life, an entire political ethos'; her burial of her brother is 'rooted in a devotion to the gods and to the ways and laws of her city'.[75] For Dietz, Antigone speaks *as a citizen* and, in so doing, she models the potential that women have as citizens that a feminist political consciousness must draw on.

The competing readings of the *Antigone* offered by Elshtain and Dietz represent two sides of a larger debate about the relationship of women to the state that dominated the 1980s. The problems central to this debate, such as the relationship between particularity and universalism within the domain of politics, have not gone away. Nor have people stopped seeing Antigone as the figurehead of a female and especially maternal form of protest against the state. Witness the characterisation of Cindy Sheehan, the mother of a soldier killed in Iraq who camped out in front of George W. Bush's ranch in Texas to protest his war policy, as an 'American Antigone'.[76]

But in the 1990s, the terms of the debate began to change, largely under the influence of gender studies. On the one hand, as we saw in Cecelia Sjöholm's reading of Lacan (itself a product of the rise of gender studies), the question posed by Antigone moves from being one of women as political agents to become one of 'the feminine' as a position of resistance vis-à-vis the political or social order. Such a shift sets the stage, in turn, for appropriations of Antigone that bring gender together with other categories or set it aside altogether in theorising positions of political resistance. On the other hand, the very nature of what it means to be inside or outside the political realm is subjected to interrogation in the wake of poststructuralist critiques of binary thinking.

Each of these developments can be seen in Judith Butler's influential reading of Sophocles' tragedy developed in *Antigone's Claim* (2000). Butler not only prioritises gender over the category of women, much as we saw her do in her reading of the *Timaeus*. She also subordinates gender to a larger discussion of kinship. At the same time, Butler embarks on an ambitious rethinking of what it means to locate Antigone outside political or normative social space. Her reading is especially important because of the critical role that it's played in the burgeoning of *Antigone* studies in the early twenty-first century.

Butler and Beyond: The Future of Gender

The story that Butler tells in the opening pages of *Antigone's Claim* goes something like this. She set out to read Antigone as a sign of feminine resistance to the state, but ended up in a rather different place. Antigone emerges through Butler's reading as 'not quite a queer heroine', paving the way for 'post-gender' readings of the play, even as gender remains a significant element in Butler's interpretation.[77] Antigone's transformation in Butler's hands comes about through her focus on kinship and the social norms that kinship systems underwrite, especially heteronormativity – that is, the assumption that heterosexuality is the only expression of human sexuality that qualifies as natural. The norms of kinship have been taken by most of the major thinkers of modernity – including Hegel and Lacan, as well as Lévi-Strauss, the French anthropologist who pioneered the application of structuralism to the social sphere – to be incontestable. They lie outside politics as a sphere of universality (Hegel) or the rules that stand 'at the threshold of culture' (Lévi-Strauss) or the symbolic order, which is overseen by the Law that governs desire according to Oedipal norms (Lacan, drawing on Lévi-Strauss). The assumption that kinship norms are given is precisely what Butler aims to undermine by rethinking the figure of Antigone.

One reason that Antigone is useful for Butler's theoretical project is because, as we've seen, she stands *outside* the system that condemns her. At the same time, Antigone represents categorical chaos. She embodies the principles of kinship gone awry, while through her 'masculine' defiance of the state, she perverts categories of gender. Butler's strategy hinges on her decision to unleash the confusions that Antigone incarnates into the normative order by contesting the traditional outsider status of Sophocles' heroine. In other words, by destabilising the relationship between inside and outside, Butler allows the non-normative kinship relationships that define Antigone and her subversive gender identity to infiltrate the political and the symbolic spheres, disrupting the norms that structure them. The power of Antigone in the guise of Butler's 'almost queer' heroine thus lies in her ability to force the recognition of new models of kinship: families headed by same-sex couples; African-American urban kinship structures, where an absent father may be replaced by a network of female relatives; the buddy systems that have developed, especially in the gay community, around the care of those living with HIV/AIDS.[78] Butler, in short, uses Antigone to make the argument that the family – understood, against Hegel, Freud and Lévi-Strauss, as a framework of intimate relations – is not outside or antithetical to politics.

Butler at one point describes Antigone as a problem ('a certain heterosexual fatality') that 'remains to be read'.[79] Her phrasing suggests that she's interested in returning not just to Antigone the character but to *Antigone* the text. And, in fact, she does repeatedly return to Sophocles' play over the course of the book as a resource for developing a politics of kinship. Moreover, Butler's departures from Hegel, Lévi-Strauss and Lacan are often couched in terms of divergent readings of the play, a strategy that we've seen before. Her central accusation against Hegel and Lacan – and, less fairly, Irigaray and Mills – is that they all see Antigone as a figure 'who articulates a prepolitical opposition to politics, representing *kinship as the sphere that conditions the possibility of politics without ever entering into it*.[80] By rereading the play, Butler argues, we can identify the blind spots in these Hegelian interpretations: 'Sophocles' text makes clear that the two' – that is, Antigone and Creon – 'are metaphorically implicated in one another in ways that suggest that there is, in fact, no simple opposition between the two'.[81] She thus approaches the text as a committed deconstructionist, in search of the resources it holds for dismantling a theoretical apparatus structured around binaries and two in particular: the binary between man and woman and the binary between inside and outside.

Let's take a look at an example. One of Butler's major arguments against Hegel is that Antigone's burial of Polyneices is an *aberrant* performance of kinship, rather than the paradigmatic example of the ethical duty of women towards dead relatives. That is, much like the drag queen whose performance undercuts gender norms through subversive mimicry, Antigone exposes the contingency and instability of kinship norms through her act.

Butler defends her reading by zeroing in on a passage from the *Oedipus at Colonus*, written by Sophocles at the end of his life. After years of wandering as a beggar and an outcast, Oedipus is preparing to die. He says to Antigone, who has been his companion during these years, and Ismene: 'For there is no way to have love from someone more than you have had from this man, whose absence you will suffer for the rest of your lives' (*Oedipus at Colonus*, 1617–19). Butler reads these words not just as the father's incestuous demand for loyalty but also as a curse: Antigone must love and honour only the dead man.

But which dead man is Oedipus talking about? From Antigone's perspective, Oedipus speaks not just as a father but also as a brother, born from the same womb. But then why do his words matter more than those of her other brother, Polyneices, who also makes a demand on her in the *Oedipus at Colonus* – namely, to bury his body if he dies at Thebes? Antigone does fulfil Oedipus's demand, Butler argues, but 'promiscuously'. For she responds to his command to love the dead man by honouring Polyneices, thereby perverting the meaning of the command. In fact, at the very moment Oedipus speaks, the curse has *already* been promiscuously realised. For the

Oedipus at Colonus, despite treating events that happen before those in the *Antigone*, was written and performed decades after the *Antigone* was first staged. The violation of the curse – that is, Antigone's burial of her brother – thus seems to precede Oedipus's articulation of it. The curse's 'uncertain temporality', on Butler's reading, destabilises it further.[82]

Antigone's perverse fulfilment of Oedipus's curse points to ambiguities that trouble the very source of paternal authority. Butler, leaping from Sophocles to Freud, sees in Antigone's performance a disruption of the norms of kinship themselves, which are, in fact, underwritten by Oedipus within Freudian psychoanalysis. That is to say, the wayward fate of Oedipus's curse suggests that the very 'curse' of kinship norms can be realised differently. What looks like a sign of tragic inevitability turns out to signal utopian possibilities that converge on Antigone:

> If kinship is the precondition of the human, then Antigone is the occasion for a new field of the human, achieved through political catachresis, the one that happens when the less than human speaks as human, when gender is displaced, and kinship founders on its own founding laws.[83]

The figure of catachresis – that is, the borrowing of a word or a discourse to say what otherwise cannot be expressed – reminds us that Butler's Antigone never fully belongs to the political and symbolic order. She is, rather, the outside that is always already inside: a very Butlerian heroine, silhouetted against the horizon of political potentiality.

Butler's reading is an excellent example of a more general shift towards interpreting Antigone and the *Antigone* in terms of gender rather than sexual difference. These developments have appropriated and reframed the debate about women and the state without departing from a politics committed to social change. The transition from sex to gender in the reception of Antigone has paved the way, in turn, for analyses in which the category of gender continues to exercise critical force without monopolising the positions from which social and political norms are challenged.

Consider, for example, the series of readings of the *Antigone* that the political theorist Bonnie Honig has been developing over the past several years.[84] These readings continue to theorise the political from a gendered perspective while mobilising a vocabulary that is larger than gender. In one recent article, Honig reclaims the figure of Ismene, who is almost uniformly dismissed as the quiescent or passive sister, as a political agent. Rereading the play closely, she argues that it is, in fact, Ismene who undertakes the mysterious first burial of Polyneices in the play, which alerts Creon to the violation of his edict and leads to the capture of Antigone, apprehended as she performs a second burial. Ismene ends up being a major actor in the play, working in concert with her sister but also, more subtly, as her rival. Honig concludes by using her reading to conceptualise a politics of sisterhood, both cooperative and competitive, in terms of what she calls 'sororal agency'.[85]

Yet Honig doesn't privilege sorority as an essential site of political action. Rather, she takes the relationship between Antigone and Ismene as an opportunity to think through political agency under near impossible conditions and to define such agency through the relationship between different modalities of acting, one sacrificial and heroic (Antigone), the other anti-heroic and worldly (Ismene). If these positions are gendered, it's because they emerge within a context, both dramatic and historical, where constraints on political action are imposed according to sex. But in principle, they're not just available to women. Any marginalised figure could claim the position of Antigone or Ismene. Honig thus situates her reading within the feminist tradition of theorising political resistance, reform and revolution without assuming an ahistorical female subject of politics.

Elsewhere, Honig takes a more severe view of feminist characterisations of Antigone's critical potential in terms of her 'maternal' valuing of mortality and particularity.[86] Much as Dietz had argued over twenty-five years earlier in her critique of Elshtain, Honig objects that such strategies end up reinstating another universalism in their reliance on the timeless figure of the mother. She advocates instead adopting Antigone as a figure through which political theory can develop an alternative to humanism and anti-humanism, which she calls 'agonistic humanism'. Returning to Antigone's infamous claim that she would not have risked everything for a husband or a child, Honig sets gender aside to read the statement as a political act that exploits the strategies of parody, mimicry and citation to intervene in fifth-century BCE democratic politics in such a way as 'to make a new kind of sense'.[87] Here, as in the article on Ismene, Antigone's creative intervention depends on a subject position that is historically contingent rather than essentially female or feminine. The lessons that she has to teach both ancient and contemporary democratic culture about value and loss are bound neither to sex nor to gender. Moreover, these lessons are political lessons, and Antigone herself is a political actor rather than a figure defined through her exclusion from the public realm.

The critical theorist Tina Chanter has also recently revisited Antigone as a figure whose capacity to stimulate our thinking on contemporary political issues goes beyond gender. Chanter forcefully rejects Lacanian readings of the tragedy that, she argues, see Antigone only as a monstrous outsider in order to reclaim the political agency of Sophocles' hero. Like Honig, she grounds the political nature of Antigone's act in her justification of the burial as a responsibility that she owes her brother alone. Following a reading of the speech developed by Mary Beth Mader, Chanter argues that Antigone's claim makes perfect sense as an attempt to reinstate proper kinship relations (sister–brother) in place of the incestuous tangle she's inherited.[88] Antigone thus appeals to an intelligible logic that her contemporary readers have simply refused to parse. From this Chanter concludes, in an echo of Irigaray's claim that Antigone 'governs as far as she is permitted to do so', that Antigone 'proves herself in death to have had the potential to be a more effective political leader than Creon could ever be'.[89] Antigone here becomes the exemplary political actor, the very antithesis of the apolitical or antipolitical rebel.

Chanter, working within a feminist tradition of interpretation, continues to understand Antigone through her gender. Like Honig, however, she emphasises the *historical* nature of the gender conventions that define Antigone both in Sophocles' play and in its reception and, by extension, the historical contingency of the position from which she challenges

Creon. The emphasis on contingency allows Chanter to open up another way of interpreting Antigone's position:

> Antigone's defiance of these conventions constitutes an intervention that can be read beyond the specificity of a particular tradition that discriminates on the basis of gender: Antigone calls attention to the blindness and hypocrisy of a polity that defines its membership by precluding as worthy of full political participation those on whom it nonetheless remains dependent materially and psychically.[90]

Antigone's defiance, that is, becomes the heritage not just of women but of *anyone* who has been excluded from acting on equal terms in the political sphere. Chanter goes on to contextualise the shifting nature of what Antigone stands for in terms of the very successes achieved by feminist and gender-sensitive interpretations of the play. It's precisely because of these successes, she argues, that 'the political legacy Antigone bequeaths has become more variegated'.[91]

For both Honig and Chanter, the broadening of Antigone's identity beyond gender goes hand in hand with a strategy to reassert, in the face of the Hegelian and Lacanian readings, her viability as a political agent, an agent whose challenge to Creon is articulated in a shared public domain and, indeed, promises to transform it. Their readings uphold the idea that 'a specific ideology of gender is fundamental to any reading of Antigone', as the classicist Peter Burian has argued in a recent interpretation of the play that also appeals to the political intelligibility of Antigone's defiance in the face of depoliticised psychoanalytic and poststructuralist readings.[92] But they don't want to define Antigone by her gender.

What we see in these recent readings, then, is a self-conscious departure from the rigid parallelism of the old Hegelian binaries – family and state (or private and public) aligned with female and male – as well as Lacan's designation of the space outside the law as categorically feminine. By moving Antigone firmly into the political sphere and contesting the idea that there is something essentially female or feminine about her act, these critics trouble the Hegelian binaries while continuing to recognise that Antigone's public role is anomalous for a woman in classical Athens, as the characters in the tragedy themselves emphasise. These readings part ways, then, too, with feminists such as Elshtain and Irigaray, who, while claiming political agency for Antigone, have designated that agency as female or maternal. Honig, Chanter and Burian don't deny that Antigone acts on behalf of her kin and in the name of burial. But they shift attention from those details, so central to the Hegelian reception of the play, in order to frame Antigone's commitments in terms of 'agonistic humanism', political resistance and civil disobedience – in short, in terms of her confrontation with Creon. Her political identity is thus defined in terms of her relationships to other actors as much as it is in terms of the values she upholds. Those values are redefined in ways less burdened by longstanding representations of sexual difference.

The arc of Antigone's reception has entered territory that looks very different from the landscape of those who see traces of a lost matriarchy in the myth of Demeter and Persephone or Neolithic figurines. Among the readers of the *Antigone*, the shift from sex to gender increasingly seems to point towards readings that no longer privilege gender at all. For proponents of prehistoric matriarchy, what matters is the essential nature of women, grounded in their capacities to give birth and nurture life and their affinities with the earth. Moreover, in each world, the past is used differently to imagine political and social communities of the future. Many recent interpretations of the *Antigone*, taking into account not just the play's philosophical and literary reception but the history of its performance in the last century, have laid stress on Antigone as an icon of political resistance. By contrast, the historian Cynthia Eller has argued that one reason stories about a lost matriarchy are so popular is because they offer a social agenda 'that is not nearly so beset with failure and frustration as political activism'. These stories, she goes on, take

a situation that invites despair – patriarchy is here, it's always been here, it's inevitable – and transforms it into a surpassing optimism:

patriarchy is recent and fallible, it was preceded by something much better, and it can be overthrown in the near future.[93]

If, then, one path of reception that developed at the intersection of antiquity and feminism has largely displaced women, the other has continued to keep them absolutely central.

The divergence of these paths offers a different version of the split we've seen in engagements with 'the ancients' over the course of this book. Here, rather than representing two variant models of the past ('same' or 'other'), the opposition maps onto the binary between sex (and sexuality) and gender. Nevertheless, in this case, too, what we actually find in our ancient evidence is more complicated, and these complications can be useful in helping us uncover our motivations for focusing on what we do when we turn to antiquity. Those who have 'unsexed' Antigone by contrasting the determining factor of gender in the past with the fluidity of identity today might reflect more on what it is about Antigone that makes it easy to appropriate her as an icon for a politics 'beyond gender' – namely, her rejection of adult sexuality and maternity. Could a figure like Demeter ever be disentangled from sexual difference and female genealogies to make a different, non-gendered kind of political sense? If not, what does that tell us about current assumptions about the proper relationship of sexuality or parenthood to politics and our political identities? About our twenty-first century love affair with youth? About the desire for ideological purity among progressives weary of compromise and backsliding?

Moreover, we have to be careful about turning the myths of Demeter and Antigone into tales about women in the ancient world or Woman *tout court* because their identities are so bound up with other categories and specificities. It's impossible to forget, for one thing, that Demeter is a goddess and Antigone is a mere mortal. For another, while Antigone might be classed as female by Creon or Ismene, we shouldn't overlook the fact that she herself never claims to speak on behalf of her sex, choosing instead to situate herself in relationship to the gods, her father and her brother. That these figures are female seems both more and less significant in classical Greece than it does in the first decades of the twenty-first century, after some three decades of emphasising the contingency of gender, on the one hand, and prioritising it as a category of analysis, on the other.

All of this reminds us that the interpretation of the past for the present is far from straightforward. How ancient Greek texts have shaped our thinking about the gendering of politics is inseparable from the contemporary politics of gender. A decade into the new millennium, we're facing an increasingly urgent degradation of the planet and our bodies by forces that feminists have traditionally tarred as the byproducts of patriarchal values and cultures. That larger context can help explain the persistent popular appeal of a matriarchal past. At the same time, especially within academic feminism and the fields of gender and sexuality studies, scholars are asking whether gender continues to matter to the extent that it did several decades ago, whether, as Vanda Zajko elegantly writes,

> a discourse that prioritises and theorises gender difference over and above any other persists in having the capacity to generate debate and provide intellectual sustenance for those inhabiting a world where, for some at least, the possibilities for identification are multiple and multiplying.[94]

The analytical category of gender has a life of its own, dependent not simply on what it can help us see in ancient cultures and in our own but on changing views regarding the 'intellectual sustenance' and the critical potential that it can offer.

But recent debates about the relationship between gender and politics don't just influence what sense we make of evidence from antiquity. These debates have also been shaped in far-reaching ways, as we've seen, by readings of ancient texts and artifacts that stretch back to Hegel and Bachofen. Indeed, in this chapter more than any other we can see how the very history of using the ancients to map sexual difference onto the political realm, from the exemplarity of Hegel's Antigone as Woman to nineteenth-century theories of a nature- and body-centred matriarchy in prehistory, has haunted contemporary debates in feminism and gender studies.

Is such a legacy crippling? The political theorist Catherine Holland suggests it might be. She writes that the 'strategic reinstatement of the past', insofar as it's undertaken within the confines of the Western tradition, 'does not serve feminism well, for it overcommits feminists to a backward-looking and reclamationist rather than a transformative imagination'.[95]

Do the requirements of a 'transformative imagination' demand that we break off with the Greeks altogether? Holland's main point is that, too often, the return to ancient texts as the ground of a contemporary feminist politics has found only the common ground we share with these texts. But this doesn't lead her to reject the early Western tradition as a resource for theorists and activists interested in politics today: far from it. Holland goes on to offer her *own* reading of the *Antigone* that uses Antigone to underwrite and explicate her preferred method of engaging the past. Antigone, in other words, comes to stand not just for a lesson from the past but for a way of reading the past. Holland's method draws on the spirit of Friedrich Nietzsche's concept of the past as 'untimely', which I introduced at the end of the first chapter, in order to approach history as the source of unexpected disruptions capable of pushing the present in genuinely new directions. To unleash the potential of the past, Holland argues, we need to respect its differences. I couldn't agree more.

What does this mean for gender in negotiations of the political at the intersection of the Greek past and the global present? My own position is that stories of a lost matriarchy are too monolithic and too utopian to do justice to history's capacity to disrupt our assumptions, to say nothing of the constraints imposed by the vision of female nature that they rely on. If we turn to the *Antigone*, recent trends in interpretations of the play have been persuasive in suggesting that at this particular historical and intellectual moment, the disruptive potential of Sophocles' play can be set in motion more effectively by expanding our focus beyond gender.

I would question further whether the *Antigone* itself, or at least the stripped down paraphrases of the play that tend to circulate, has become too familiar to carry the charge it once did. Antigone should make us *uncomfortable* – on this point at least, Lacan was right. The classicist Mark Griffith has provocatively argued that it's precisely because Antigone would have been such a shock to the original – predominantly if not exclusively male – audience that Sophocles had to usher her offstage two thirds of the way through the tragedy.[96] As critics, we should hesitate before assuming that Antigone says what we'd like her to say, appropriating her outsider status to authenticate our own convictions. We might pause, too, before turning Creon into a one-dimensional enemy akin to the men in suits of contemporary conspiracy movies. For if we take a closer look at the complexities and ambiguities of Sophocles' tragedy, we would quickly see that they undermine any reading that simply idealises Antigone, even if events unfold in such a way as to magnify Creon's culpability.

Despite the excitement generated by contemporary readings of the *Antigone*, then, there's a risk that the 'Antigone industry' will turn Antigone into little more than a name that confers cultural cachet or ancient authority on what we think we already know, rather than a figure of strangeness and difficulty that resists appropriation. The familiarity of Antigone these days may mean that the broadening of our vocabulary beyond gender requires a broadening, too, of our ancient corpus of material (to include other tragedies, other genres, Rome as well as Greece) to revitalise contemporary debates about the political.

Still, the reception of Antigone, like myths of a matriarchal prehistory, makes it clear that the history of interpretation acts through accretion as much as through innovation. It's not simply a question of inaugurating new strategies of analysis or of breaking free, once and for all, from the ancients. What we've seen in this chapter is the extent to which the contemporary language of politics and power, whether in academic theory or in popular anti-patriarchy movements, is entangled in the early modern reception of ancient texts and the rise of archaeology and anthropology in the nineteenth century. The debates within feminism and gender studies, for better or worse, have perpetuated the privilege of a handful of ancient texts and material artifacts, which are now inextricably woven into current debates about the gendering of the political. Despite our longing to start from a blank slate, the only way to move these debates forward, I believe, is to understand how they've developed. Even if we've only scratched the surface of the story in this chapter, we've nevertheless glimpsed how important figures like Antigone, Demeter and Clytemnestra have been to contemporary attempts to map the boundaries of politics and how important they remain to efforts to imagine our political future.

CONCLUSION

I began this book by pointing out that gender seems to be everywhere these days. The ancient Greeks and Romans, too, still loom remarkably large in the popular imagination, from *Troy* to HBO's 'Rome' miniseries. But the role that classical antiquity has played in shaping the contemporary landscape of sex and gender hasn't been sufficiently acknowledged or understood. What I hope to have shown over the course of this book is just how deeply embedded classical antiquity has been in the theories and debates that have defined gender studies as a field and just how important ancient texts and artifacts have been to our struggles to mould, articulate and contest our own sexed and gendered identities. From the use of ancient medical texts to destabilise sexual dimorphism to wrangling over the language of Plato in a Colorado courtroom to heated debates over what kind of future figures like Demeter or Antigone should inspire us to pursue, the ancients have been an integral part of how we talk to each other about gender, sex, sexuality and sexual difference, reassuring us, baffling us and needling us.

It isn't enough, though, to point out that classical antiquity has been fundamental to the birth and growth of gender studies. I have aimed as well to uncover some of the most influential strategies for using the ancients to advance contemporary conversations. These strategies, as we've seen, fall into roughly two camps, one that looks primarily to the continuities between the ancients and the moderns, one that focuses instead on ruptures and discontinuities, most commonly framed in terms of a gulf between the premodern and the modern. To some degree, the dynamics of sameness

181

and difference are inseparable from our efforts to define ourselves in relationship to the past. But, as I've tried to show, the language of same and
other is always in danger of making things seem too simple. Such language
risks compromising the potential of ancient Greece and Rome to destabilise
and energise our own thinking by shoring up and legitimating stale binaries
and failing to do justice to historical difference. It might seem futile in a
world where history seems to matter less and less to insist that we need to
attend to the details and 'plotless' stories, to develop more sophisticated
models of reception capable of balancing areas of resonances with areas of
unfamiliarity. But for the practice of history to generate 'untimely' interventions in the present, one needs to take care and respect historical
difference. At the same time, those dedicated to the study of the past need
to recognise the urgency of their task by learning to speak to the present
in a language that demands attention.

Throughout this book, we've seen that the contemporary concept of
gender is bound up in complicated ways with the concepts of sex and sexuality. The material we've surveyed from classical antiquity has clustered
these concepts together in familiar ways. But it's also yielded up unfamiliar
configurations that challenge deep-seated assumptions. Consider, for
example, how ancient Greco-Roman medical writing and popular texts alike
embed both sex, understood primarily in terms of genitalia and reproductive capacity, and gender in the physical body while recognising how that
body can change under certain conditions and in response to certain
practices. The domains that we would identify as nature and culture overlap
here in manifold ways, putting pressure on how we ourselves draw the line
between them. Or consider the very different way of thinking sexuality and
gender together in Greece and Rome, where what we define as same-sex
erotic behaviour was parsed according to the categories of active and passive,
masculine and feminine, free and slave. The definition of masculinity that
has dominated research on the sexed brain – namely, that to be masculine
is to desire women – simply doesn't make sense in antiquity. And yet, in
our ancient sources gender is inextricable from sexuality, and sexuality from
power, challenging us to reflect on how these associations persist in our

own thinking about sex, power, social norms and domination. Or consider, finally, the ways in which gender participates in more specific identities in antiquity, identities complicated by status (including the status of being human), age, kinship and lineage, as well as the ways in which it refracts light differently according to the circumstances under which it becomes salient. Sex and sexuality still matter here, of course, as they do for us. But antiquity can also help us think of gender as a factor that comes in and out of focus under different conditions, appearing in and disappearing from a range of configurations that have a purchase on how we define ourselves and how we exercise social and political agency.

The very idea of the history of ideas is something of a conundrum. What does it mean for an idea to have a history? Is it the same idea at the beginning and the end? How should we define an idea or a concept anyway? In the introduction, I claimed that our concept of gender, defined through its opposition to sex and cultivated across a range of fields influenced by second-wave feminism, post-structuralism and cultural theory, emerged only recently. Yet our Greek and Roman sources have a lot to say about related ideas. As we've seen over the course of this book, they've proven one of the most significant resources for the contemporary conceptualisation of gender. The potential to learn from them further has not yet been exhausted.

SOME SUGGESTIONS FOR FURTHER READING

INTRODUCTION

For a general overview of gender, see, for example, David Glover and Cora Kaplan, *Genders* (London: Routledge, 2000); Claire Colebrook, *Gender* (Basingstoke: Palgrave Macmillan, 2004); Tina Chanter, *Gender: Key Concepts in Philosophy* (London: Continuum, 2007); Harriet Bradley, *Gender* (Cambridge: Polity, 2007); Momin Rahman and Stevi Jackson, *Gender and Sexuality* (Cambridge: Polity, 2010).

For surveys of the ancient Greek and Roman material, see Sue Blundell, *Women in Ancient Greece* (London: British Museum Press, 1995); Laura K. McClure (ed.), *Sexuality and Gender in the Classical World: Readings and Sources* (Malden, Mass.: Blackwell, 2002); Thomas K. Hubbard (ed.), *Homosexuality in Greece and Rome: A Sourcebook of Basic Documents* (Berkeley: University of California Press, 2003); Mary R. Lefkowitz and Maureen B. Fant, *Women's Life in Greece and Rome: A Source Book in Translation*, 3rd ed. (Baltimore: The Johns Hopkins University Press, 2005); Marilyn B. Skinner, *Sexuality in Greek and Roman Culture* (Malden, Mass.: Blackwell, 2005); Kirk Ormand, *Controlling Desires: Sexuality in Ancient Greece and Rome* (Westport, Conn.: Praeger, 2009).

On the emergence of 'gender identity' in the middle of the twentieth century, see Joanne Meyerowitz, *How Sex Changed: A History of*

Transsexuality in the United States (Cambridge, Mass.: Harvard University Press, 2002), esp. pp. 98–129.

The best account of the 'sex/gender system' remains Gayle Rubin, 'The Traffic in Women: Notes on the "Political Economy" of Sex', in Rayna R. Reiter (ed.), *Toward an Anthropology of Women* (New York: Monthly Review Press, 1975), pp. 157–210.

On the background to the debate about the status of ancient women, see Josine Blok, 'Sexual Asymmetry: A Historiographical Essay', in Josine Blok and Peter Mason (eds.), *Sexual Asymmetry: Studies in Ancient Society* (Amsterdam: Gieben, 1987), pp. 1–57; Marilyn A. Katz, 'Ideology and "The Status of Women" in Ancient Greece', in Richard Hawley and Barbara Levick (eds.), *Women in Antiquity: New Assessments* (London: Routledge, 1995), pp. 21–43, first published in *History and Theory* 31 (1992), pp. 70–97. On the impact of feminism on Classics as a field, see Barbara F. McManus, *Classics and Feminism: Gendering the Classics* (New York: Twayne, 1997).

For concerns about gender studies from a feminist perspective within ancient history, see Nancy Sorkin Rabinowitz, introduction to Nancy Sorkin Rabinowitz and Amy Richlin (eds.), *Feminist Theory and the Classics* (New York: Routledge, 1993), pp. 1–20; Alison Sharrock, 'Re(ge)ndering Gender(ed) Studies', *Gender and History* 9 (1997), pp. 603–14. The critique of feminist studies focused on male-authored texts is most associated with Phyllis Culham, 'Decentering the Text: The Case of Ovid', *Helios* 17 (1990), pp. 161–70. For recent reflections on the tension between gender and women in the study of antiquity, see Genevieve Liveley, 'Surfing the Third Wave?: Postfeminism and the Hermeneutics of Reception', in Charles Martindale and Richard F. Thomas (eds.), *Classics and the Uses of Reception* (Malden, Mass.: Blackwell, 2006), pp. 55–66, and Vanda Zajko, '"What Difference Was Made"?: Feminist Models of Reception', in Lorna Hardwick and Christopher Stray (eds.), *A Companion to Classical Receptions* (Malden, Mass.: Blackwell, 2008), pp. 195–206.

For the work of Joan Wallach Scott on gender, see, in addition to her groundbreaking article 'Gender: A Useful Category of Historical Analysis', *American Historical Review* 91 (1986), pp. 1053–75 (reprinted in Joan Wallach Scott, *Gender and the Politics of History* [New York: Columbia University Press, 1988; rev. ed., 1999], pp. 28–51), the preface to the revised edition of *Gender and the Politics of History*; Joan Wallach Scott, 'Unanswered Questions', *American Historical Review* 113 (2008), pp. 1422–9; and Joan Wallach Scott, 'Gender: Still a Useful Category of Analysis?' *Diogenes* 57 (2010), pp. 7–14, where Scott defends the need to study gender rather than 'women'. For the impact of Scott's work, see Joanne Meyerowitz, 'A History of "Gender"', *American Historical Review* 113 (2008), pp. 1346–56.

On the relationship of grammatical gender and biological sex, especially in Latin, see Anthony Corbeill, '*Genus quid est*?: Roman Scholars on Grammatical Gender and Biological Sex', *Transactions of the American Philological Association* 138 (2008), pp. 75–105.

CHAPTER I

On structuralist approaches to myth, see Eric Csapo, *Theories of Mythology* (Malden, Mass.: Blackwell, 2005), pp. 181–261. Vernant's work on the masculine/feminine binary in Greek myth is exemplified by his 'Hestia–Hermes: The Religious Expression of Space and Movement in Ancient Greece', in Jean-Pierre Vernant, *Myth and Thought Among the Greeks*. Trans. Janet Lloyd (New York: Zone, 2006), pp. 157–96. Some of the most important essays representative of postwar French thought are collected in Gregory Nagy, Laura Slatkin and Nicole Loraux (eds.), *Antiquities: Postwar French Thought*, Volume 3 (New York: New Press, 2001). See also the collected essays in Froma I. Zeitlin, *Playing the Other: Gender and Society in Classical Greek Literature* (Chicago: University of Chicago Press, 1996). For the afterlife of Pandora's jar in Western art and literature, see Dora Panofsky and Erwin Panofsky, *Pandora's Box: The Changing Aspects of a Mythical Symbol* (New York: Pantheon Books, 1956).

For issues of gender and the sexed body in ancient Greco-Roman medical and biological writing, the following books provide sophisticated and useful overviews: Lesley Dean-Jones, *Women's Bodies in Classical Greek Science* (Oxford: Oxford University Press, 1994); Rebecca Flemming, *Medicine and the Making of Roman Women: Gender, Nature and Authority from Celsus to Galen* (Oxford: Oxford University Press, 2000); Helen King, *Hippocrates' Woman: Reading the Female Body in Ancient Greece* (London: Routledge, 1998). Also valuable is Ann Ellis Hanson, 'Conception, Gestation, and the Origin of Female Nature in the *Corpus Hippocraticum*', *Helios* 19 (1992), pp. 31–71, and Jean-Baptiste Bonnard, 'La construction des genres dans la Collection hippocratique', in Violaine Sebillotte Cuchet, et al. (eds.), *Problèmes du genre* (Paris: Publications de la Sorbonne, 2007), pp. 159–70. On the wandering womb, see now Christopher A. Faraone, 'Magical and Medical Approaches to the Wandering Womb in the Ancient Greek World', *Classical Antiquity* 30 (2011), pp. 1–32.

On the influence of ancient medical and philosophical writers, especially Galen and Aristotle, on sexual difference in medieval medicine, see Joan Cadden, *Meanings of Sex Difference in the Middle Ages: Medicine, Science, and Culture* (Cambridge: Cambridge University Press, 1993). For the influence of Galen on later medicine in general terms, see Oswei Temkin, *Galenism: Rise and Decline of a Medical Philosophy* (Ithaca: Cornell University Press, 1973).

For Aristotle's views on sexual difference, see Marguerite Deslauriers, 'Sex and Essence in Aristotle's Metaphysics and Biology', in Cynthia Freeland (ed.), *Feminist Interpretations of Aristotle* (University Park, Pa.: Pennsylvania State University Press, 1998), pp. 138–67. The entire volume is worth consulting as it contains a number of useful interventions in the debate about Aristotle and feminism. The two sides of the debate about whether Aristotle was blinded by his prejudices in his views on female biology or justified in his observations by relatively sound scientific principles are well represented by G. E. R. Lloyd, *Science, Folklore and Ideology: Studies in the Life Sciences in Ancient Greece* (Cambridge: Cambridge University Press, 1983) and Robert Mayhew, *The Female in Aristotle's Biology: Reason or Rationalization* (Chicago: University of Chicago Press, 2004), respectively.

Many historians of ancient medicine have been uncomfortable with Laqueur's reading of the ancient Greek evidence. For two cogent objections, see Flemming, *Medicine and the Making of Roman Women*, pp. 3–28, and Helen King, 'The Mathematics of Sex: One to Two, or Two to One'? in *Studies in Medieval and Renaissance History*, ser. 3, 2 (2005), pp. 47–58. The review by Katharine Park and Robert A. Nye, 'Destiny is Anatomy', *The New Republic*, 18 Feb. 1991, pp. 53–7, remains one of the fullest critiques of Laqueur's book. For other objections to Laqueur's model, see nn. 29–30 to the text. For its reception among early modern scholars, see Karen Harvey, 'The Century of Sex?: Gender, Bodies, and Sexuality in the Long Eighteenth Century', *The Historical Journal* 45 (2002), pp. 899–916.

On myths of autochthony, see especially two books by Nicole Loraux: *The Children of Athena: Athenian Ideas about Citizenship and the Division Between the Sexes*. Trans. Caroline Levine (Princeton: Princeton University Press, 1993); *Born of the Earth: Myth and Politics in Athens*. Trans. Selina Stewart (Ithaca: Cornell University Press, 2000). For the association of woman and the body in antiquity, see Page duBois, *Sowing the Body: Psychoanalysis and Ancient Representations of Women* (Chicago: University of Chicago Press, 1988).

On Irigaray's relationship to classical antiquity, see Miriam Leonard, 'Irigaray's Cave: Feminist Theory and the Politics of French Classicism', *Ramus* 28 (1999), pp. 152–68, and the essays in Elena Tzelepis and Athena Athanasiou (eds.) *Rewriting Difference: Luce Irigaray and 'The Greeks'* (Buffalo: State University of New York Press, 2010).

On the New Materialism, see Myra J. Hird, 'Feminist Matters: New Materialist Considerations of Sexual Difference', *Feminist Theory* 5 (2004), pp. 223–32, and *Sex, Gender and Science* (Basingstoke: Palgrave Macmillan, 2004). See also Diana Coole and Samantha Frost (eds.), *New Materialisms: Ontology, Agency, and Politics* (Durham: Duke University Press, 2010). For criticisms of the movement's premise, see Sara Ahmed, 'Imaginary Prohibitions: Some Preliminary Remarks on the Founding Gestures of the "New Materialism"', *European Journal of Women's Studies* 15 (2008), pp. 23–39, at p. 24, and the response by Noela Davis, 'New Materialism and Feminism's Anti-Biologism: A Response to Sara Ahmed', *European Journal of Women's Studies* 16 (2009), pp. 67–80. For representative work, see esp. Karen Barad, *Meeting the Universe Halfway: Quantum Physics and the Entanglement of Matter and Meaning* (Durham: Duke University Press, 2007) and Elizabeth A. Wilson, *Psychosomatic: Feminism and the Neurological Body* (Durham: Duke University Press, 2004).

For earlier feminist work on biology and science more generally, see Lynda Birke, 'Biological Sciences', in Alison M. Jaggar and Iris Marion Young (eds.), *A Companion to Feminist Philosophy* (Malden, Mass.: Blackwell, 1998), pp. 194–203, with further bibliography.

CHAPTER II

Christiane Sourvinou-Inwood offers an exhaustive account of the Hermaphroditus and Salmacis myth in 'Hermaphroditos and Salmakis: The Voice of Halikarnassos', in Signe Isager and Poul Pedersen (eds.), *The Salmakis Inscription and Hellenistic Halikarnassos* (Odense: University Press of Southern Denmark, 2004), pp. 59–84. For a more general account of the figure of the hermaphrodite in antiquity, see Luc Brisson, *Sexual Ambivalence: Androgyny and Hermaphroditism in Graeco-Roman Antiquity.* Trans. Janet Lloyd (Berkeley: University of California Press, 2002).

The best way to get acquainted with the main lines of response to Foucault's work on antiquity is to read through David H. J. Larmour, Paul Allen Miller and Charles Platter (eds.), *Rethinking Sexuality: Foucault and Classical Antiquity* (Princeton: Princeton University Press, 1998).

The 'constructivist' position on sexuality is perhaps more accurately associated with the historian Jeffrey Weeks: see, for example, his *Sex, Politics and Society: The Regulation of Sexuality Since 1800* (London: Longman, 1981; 2nd ed. 1989). Weeks discusses the relationship between his own work and that of Foucault in 'Uses and Abuses of Michel Foucault', in *Against Nature: Essays on History, Sexuality and Identity* (London: Rivers Oram Press, 1991), pp. 157–69. The 'essentialist' position tends to be represented by John Boswell, *Christianity, Social Tolerance, and Homosexuality: Gay People in Western Europe from the Beginning of the Christian Era to the Fourteenth Century* (Chicago: University of Chicago Press, 1980), but, as I point out in the text, there is more overlap between the two positions than the polemical formulations suggest.

For the 'Foucauldian' approach to ancient sexuality, three texts are landmarks: David M. Halperin, *One Hundred Years of Homosexuality: And Other Essays on Greek Love* (London: Routledge, 1990); David M. Halperin, John J. Winkler and Froma I. Zeitlin (eds.), *Before Sexuality: The Construction of Erotic Experience in the Ancient Greek World* (Princeton: Princeton University Press, 1990); and John J. Winkler, *The Constraints of Desire: The Anthropology of Sex and Gender in Ancient Greece* (New York: Routledge, 1990). Halperin's collection of essays, *How to Do the History of Homosexuality* (Chicago: University of Chicago Press, 2002), offers a more nuanced account of his position. Dover's *Greek Homosexuality* (Cambridge, Mass.: Harvard University Press, 1978) remains fundamental, as does Craig Williams' *Roman Homosexuality*, 2nd ed. (New York: Oxford University Press, 2010).

For an alternative reading of the Greek evidence on male same-sex desire, see James Davidson, *The Greeks and Greek Love: A Radical Reappraisal of*

Homosexuality in Ancient Greece (London: Weidenfeld and Nicolson, 2007). For a reappraisal of the regulation of sexuality in classical Athens, see David Cohen, *Law, Sexuality and Society: The Enforcement of Morals in Classical Athens* (Cambridge: Cambridge University Press, 1991). Cohen offers a more pointed critique of Foucault in David Cohen and Richard Saller, 'Foucault on Sexuality in Greco-Roman Antiquity', in Jan Goldstein (ed.), *Foucault and the Writing of History* (Malden, Mass.: Blackwell, 1994), pp. 35–59.

On ancient sex and sexuality, two feminist texts are pioneering: Amy Richlin, *The Garden of Priapus: Sexuality and Aggression in Roman Humor* (New Haven: Yale University Press, 1983; rev. ed. Oxford: Oxford University Press, 1992) and Eva C. Keuls, *The Reign of the Phallus: Sexual Politics in Ancient Athens* (New York: Harper & Row, 1985). The gaps in the Foucauldian approach to ancient sexuality can be addressed as well by consulting, on female same-sex desire, Judith P. Hallett, 'Female Homoeroticism and the Denial of Roman Reality in Latin Literature', *Yale Journal of Criticism* 3 (1989), pp. 209–27; Bernadette J. Brooten, *Love Between Women: Early Christian Responses to Female Homoeroticism* (Chicago: University of Chicago Press, 1996); Sandra Boehringer, *L'homosexualité féminine dans l'Antiquité grecque et romaine* (Paris: Les Belles Lettres, 2006); and the essays in Nancy Sorkin Rabinowitz and Lisa Auanger (eds.), *Among Women: From the Homosocial to the Homoerotic in the Ancient World* (Austin, Tx.: University of Texas Press, 2002). For the shortcomings of Foucault's paradigms in relationship to non-prescriptive texts, see Simon Goldhill, *Foucault's Virginity: Ancient Erotic Fiction and the History of Sexuality* (Cambridge: Cambridge University Press, 1995). For a greater emphasis on desire, see Anne Carson, *Eros the Bittersweet* (Princeton: Princeton University Press, 1985); Froma I. Zeitlin, 'Reflections on Erotic Desire in Archaic and Classical Greece', in James I. Porter (ed.), *Constructions of the Classical Body* (Ann Arbor: University of Michigan Press, 1999), pp. 50–76; and Giulia Sissa, *Sex and Sensuality in the Ancient World*. Trans. George Staunton (New Haven: Yale University Press, 2008).

The essays in Judith P. Hallett and Marilyn B. Skinner (eds.), *Roman Sexualities* (Princeton: Princeton University Press, 1997) help correct the overemphasis on Greek texts in the more 'Foucauldian' work.

The study of ancient masculinity has exploded over the past fifteen years. Maud W. Gleason, *Making Men: Sophists and Self-Presentation in Ancient Rome* (Princeton: Princeton University Press, 1995) is a pioneer in the field. See also Karen Bassi, *Acting Like Men: Gender, Drama, and Nostalgia in Ancient Greece* (Ann Arbor, University of Michigan Press, 1998); Erik Gunderson, *Staging Masculinity: The Rhetoric of Performance in the Roman World* (Ann Arbor: University of Michigan Press, 2000); Myles McDonnell, *Roman Manliness: 'Virtus' and the Roman Republic* (Cambridge: Cambridge University Press, 2006); Joseph Roisman, *The Rhetoric of Manhood: Masculinity in the Attic Orators* (Berkeley: University of California Press, 2005). Also useful are the essays in Lin Foxhall and John Salmon (eds.), *Thinking Men: Masculinity and Its Self-Representation in the Classical Tradition* (London: Routledge, 1998) and Lin Foxhall and John Salmon (eds.), *When Men Were Men: Masculinity, Power and Identity in Classical Antiquity* (London: Routledge, 1998).

CHAPTER III

For an introduction to gender in the study of classical mythology, see Lillian E. Doherty, *Gender and the Interpretation of Classical Myth* (London: Duckworth, 2001) and Vanda Zajko, 'Women and Greek Myth', in Roger D. Woodard (ed.), *The Cambridge Companion to Greek Mythology* (Cambridge: Cambridge University Press, 2007), pp. 387–406. More specialised studies can be found in Vanda Zajko and Miriam Leonard (eds.), *Laughing with Medusa: Classical Myth and Feminist Thought* (Oxford: Oxford University Press, 2006).

On the intersection of gender and ancient political thought, Arlene W. Saxonhouse, *Fear of Diversity: The Birth of Political Science in Ancient Greek*

Thought (Chicago: University of Chicago Press, 1992) remains important. Miriam Leonard, *Athens in Paris: Ancient Greece and the Political in Post-War French Thought* (Oxford: Oxford University Press, 2005) establishes the importance of antiquity to post-structuralist thinking about the political more generally.

On the *Homeric Hymn to Demeter*, Helene P. Foley, *The Homeric Hymn to Demeter* (Princeton: Princeton University Press, 1994) is an excellent resource for both specialists and non-specialists. See also Ann Suter, *The Narcissus and the Pomegranate: An Archaeology of the Homeric Hymn to Demeter* (Ann Arbor: University of Michigan Press, 2002). For the reception of the myth over the past century-and-a-half, see Susan Gubar, 'Mother, Maiden and the Marriage of Death: Women Writers and an Ancient Myth', *Women's Studies* 6 (1979), pp. 301–15; Andrew Radford, *The Lost Girls: Demeter–Persephone and the Literary Imagination, 1850–1930* (Amsterdam: Rodopi, 2007); Tracey L. Walters, *African American Literature and the Classicist Tradition: Black Women Writers from Wheatley to Morrison* (New York: Palgrave MacMillan, 2007).

The narrative of a matriarchal Çatalhöyük is outlined in James Mellaart, *The Neolithic of the Near East* (London: Thames and Hudson, 1975). For the work of Marija Gimbutas, see her *Goddesses and Gods of Old Europe*, rev. ed. (Berkeley: University of California Press, 1982); *The Language of the Goddess: Unearthing the Hidden Symbols of Western Civilization* (London: Thames and Hudson, 1989); and *The Civilization of the Goddess: The World of Old Europe* (San Francisco: HarperCollins, 1991). For an influential feminist adaptation of Gimbutas's ideas, see Riane Eisler, *The Chalice and the Blade: Our History, Our Future* (San Francisco: Harper and Row, 1987). In the 1990s, the critique of theories of prehistoric matriarchy by archaeologists working in feminism and gender studies took off. See, in particular, Margaret W. Conkey and Ruth E. Tringham, 'Archaeology and the Goddess: Exploring the Contours of Feminist Archaeology', in Domna C. Stanton and Abigail J. Stewart (eds.), *Feminisms in the Academy* (Ann Arbor:

University of Michigan Press, 1995), pp. 199–245; Lynn Meskell, 'Goddesses, Gimbutas and "New Age" Archaeology', *Antiquity* 69 (1995), pp. 74–86, and 'Denaturalizing Gender in Prehistory', in Susan McKinnon and Sydel Silverman (eds.), *Complexities: Beyond Nature and Nurture* (Chicago: University of Chicago Press, 2005), pp. 157–75; Ruth Tringham and Margaret Conkey, 'Rethinking Figurines: A Critical View from Archaeology of Gimbutas, the "Goddess" and Popular Culture', in Lucy Goodison and Christine Morris (eds.), *Ancient Goddesses: The Myths and the Evidence* (London: The British Museum Press, 1998), pp. 22–45. See also Cynthia Eller, *The Myth of Matriarchal Prehistory: Why an Invented Past Won't Give Women a Future* (Boston: Beacon Press, 2000). For an excellent and highly readable survey of the current state of thinking on gender in archaeology, see Rosemary A. Joyce, *Ancient Bodies, Ancient Lives: Sex, Gender and Archaeology* (New York: Thames and Hudson, 2008).

For Hegel's reception of the *Antigone* and its subsequent influence, Martin Donougho, 'The Woman in White: On the Reception of Hegel's "Antigone"', *Owl of Minerva* 21 (1989), pp. 65–89 is very valuable. The classic feminist responses are Patricia J. Mills, 'Hegel's *Antigone*', *Owl of Minerva* 17 (1986), pp. 131–52, and Heidi M. Ravven, 'Has Hegel Anything to Say to Feminists?' *Owl of Minerva* 19 (1988), pp. 149–68, reprinted in Patricia J. Mills (ed.), *Feminist Interpretations of G. W. F. Hegel* (University Park, Pa.: The Pennsylvania State University Press, 1996), pp. 225–52, with a new postscript. Mills and Ravven respond to their critics and restate their arguments in Patricia J. Mills, '"Hegel's *Antigone*" Redux: Woman in Four Parts', *Owl of Minerva* 33 (2002), pp. 205–21 and Heidi M. Ravven, 'Further Thoughts on Hegel and Feminism: A Response to Philip J. Kain and Nadine Changfoot', *Owl of Minerva* 33 (2002), pp. 223–31. Also useful is Seyla Benhabib, 'On Hegel, Women and Irony', in *Situating the Self: Gender, Community and Postmodernism in Contemporary Ethics* (Cambridge: Polity Press, 1992), pp. 242–59.

On 'maternal thinking' and the feminist debate about women, the family, and the state as it has unfolded around the figure of Antigone, see Jean

Bethke Elshtain, 'Antigone's Daughters: Reflections on Female Identity and the State', *Democracy* 2 (1982), pp. 46–59, and her restatement of her position in 'Antigone's Daughters Reconsidered: Continuing Reflections on Women, Politics, and Power', in Stephen K. White (ed.), *Life-World and Politics: Between Modernity and Postmodernity* (Notre Dame: University of Notre Dame, 1989), pp. 222–35. For critiques, see Mary G. Dietz, 'Citizenship with a Feminist Face: The Problem with Maternal Thinking', *Political Theory* 13 (1985), pp. 19–37, and Valerie A. Hartouni, 'Antigone's Dilemma: A Problem in Political Membership', *Hypatia* 1 (1986), pp. 3–20. For the attempt to develop a third way between the two positions, see Linda M. G. Zerilli, 'Machiavelli's Sisters: Women and "The Conversation" of Political Theory', *Political Theory* 19 (1991), pp. 252–76.

There is a vast bibliography on Antigone. Four collections – two special issues and an edited volume – devoted to her have recently appeared and offer a useful overview of the current state of the field. See *Helios*, vol. 33, supplement, 2006; *Mosaic*, vol. 41.3, 2008, especially Keri Walsh's essay 'Antigone Now' at pp. 1–13; and S. E. Wilmer and Audronė Žukauskaitė (eds.), *Interrogating Antigone in Postmodern Philosophy and Criticism* (New York: Oxford University Press, 2010). The fourth volume covers the performance tradition of *Antigone*: Erin B. Mee and Helene P. Foley (eds.), *Antigone on the Contemporary World Stage* (New York: Oxford University Press, 2011). On that tradition, see also Barbara Goff and Michael Simpson, *Crossroads in the Black Aegean: Oedipus, Antigone and Dramas of the African Diaspora* (Oxford: Oxford University Press, 2007) and the essays in Part IV of Wilmer and Žukauskaitė, *Interrogating Antigone*. For the earlier reception of the Antigone myth, George Steiner, *Antigones: How the Antigone Legend Has Endured in Western Literature, Art and Thought* (Oxford: Oxford University Press, 1986) remains valuable. Some of the most important feminist treatments of Antigone are gathered in Fanny Söderbäck (ed.), *Feminist Readings of Antigone* (Albany: State University of New York Press, 2010). See finally, Bonnie Honig, *Antigone, Interrupted* (Cambridge: Cambridge University Press, Forthcoming), which promises to reinvigorate the debate around Antigone once again.

NOTES

Introduction

1 Simone de Beauvoir, *The Second Sex*. Trans. Constance Borde and Sheila Malovany-Chevallier (New York: Knopf, 2009), p. 283. The book was originally published as *Le deuxième sexe* (Paris: Gallimard, 1949).

2 Kate Millett, *Sexual Politics* (Garden City, N.Y.: Doubleday, 1970), p. 29 (emphasis in original).

3 The papers from the 1973 *Arethusa* issue, as well as from a second double issue of *Arethusa* in 1978 (also devoted to women in antiquity) were subsequently published as John Peradotto and J. P. Sullivan (eds.), *Women in the Ancient World: The 'Arethusa' Papers* (Albany: State University of New York Press, 1984).

4 Sarah B. Pomeroy, *Goddesses, Whores, Wives, and Slaves: Women in Classical Antiquity* (New York: Schocken Books, 1975).

5 'Seamier legacies': John Peradotto and J. P. Sullivan, introduction to Peradotto and Sullivan, *Women in the Ancient World*, p. 1.

6 Joan Wallach Scott, 'Gender: A Useful Category of Historical Analysis', *American Historical Review* 91 (1986), pp. 1053–75, reprinted in Joan Wallach Scott, *Gender and the Politics of History* (New York: Columbia University Press, 1988; rev. ed., 1999), pp. 28–51.

7 Michael Squire, *The Art of the Body: Antiquity and Its Legacy* (London: I.B.Tauris, 2011).

Chapter I

1 See Winfried Schleiner, 'Early Modern Controversies about the One-Sex Model', *Renaissance Quarterly* 53 (2000), pp. 180–91, at pp. 185–7; Helen King, 'Barbes, sang et genre: afficher la différence dans le monde antique', in Jérôme Wilgaux and Véronique Dasen (eds.), *Langages et métaphores du corps dans le monde antique* (Rennes: Presses universitaires de Rennes, 2008), pp. 153–68, at pp. 163–5. I thank Helen King for bringing the reception of the story to my attention.

2 Judith Butler, *Bodies that Matter: On the Discursive Limits of 'Sex'* (New York: Routledge, 1993), p. 49.

3 Jean-Pierre Vernant, 'The Myth of Prometheus in Hesiod', in *Myth and Society in Ancient Greece*. Trans. Janet Lloyd (New York: Zone, 1988), pp. 183–201, at p. 193.

4 Ibid., p. 199.

5 Nicole Loraux, *The Children of Athena: Athenian Ideas about Citizenship and the Division between the Sexes*. Trans. Caroline Levine (Princeton: Princeton University Press, 1993), p. 78.

6 Marilyn B. Arthur [later, Katz], 'The Dream of a World without Women: Poetics and the Circles of Order in the *Theogony* Prooemium', *Arethusa* 16 (1983), pp. 97–116, at p. 112.

7 Froma I. Zeitlin, *Playing the Other: Gender and Society in Classical Greek Literature* (Chicago: University of Chicago Press, 1996), p. 53.

8 Ibid., p. 56.

9 Ibid., p. 83.

10 See, for example, Marilyn B. Arthur [later, Katz], 'Cultural Strategies in Hesiod's *Theogony*: Law, Family, Society', *Arethusa* 15 (1982), pp. 63–82, at p. 67.

11 See esp. Loraux, *Children of Athena*.

12 Josine H. Blok, 'Becoming Citizens: Some Notes on the Semantics of "Citizen" in Archaic Greece and Classical Athens', *Klio* 87 (2005), pp. 7–40; Josine H. Blok, 'Perikles' Citizenship Law: A New Perspective', *Historia* 58 (2009), pp. 141–70; Josine H. Blok, 'Citizenship, the Citizen Body and its Assemblies', in H. Beck (ed.), *A Companion to Ancient Greek Government* (Malden, Mass.: Blackwell, Forthcoming).

13 Joan Breton Connelly, *Portrait of a Priestess: Women and Ritual in Ancient Greece* (Princeton: Princeton University Press, 2007).

14 See Rosemary A. Joyce, *Ancient Bodies, Ancient Lives: Sex, Gender and Archaeology* (New York: Thames and Hudson, 2008), pp. 41–2.

15 Kate Gilhuly, *The Feminine Matrix of Sex and Gender in Classical Athens* (Cambridge: Cambridge University Press, 2009).

16 Mark Griffith, 'Antigone and Her Sister(s): Embodying Women in Greek Tragedy', in André Lardinois and Laura McClure (eds.), *Making Silence Speak: Women's Voices in Greek Literature and Society* (Princeton: Princeton University Press, 2001), pp. 117–36, at p. 136.

17 Violaine Sebillotte Cuchet, 'Les antiquistes et le genre', in Violaine Sebillotte Cuchet et al. (eds.), *Problèmes du genre* (Paris: Publications de la Sorbonne, 2007), pp. 11–26.

18 Joyce, *Ancient Bodies, Ancient Lives*, p. 130.

19 Thomas Laqueur, *Making Sex: Body and Gender from the Greeks to Freud* (Cambridge, Mass.: Harvard University Press, 1990).

20 Brooke Holmes, *The Symptom and the Subject: The Emergence of the Physical Body in Ancient Greece* (Princeton: Princeton University Press, 2010).

21 Parmenides: Aristotle, *Parts of Animals* 648a29–30; Empedocles: Fr. B65 in Hermann Diels (ed.), *Die Fragmente der Vorsokratiker*, 6th ed., rev. by W. Kranz (Berlin: Weidmann, 1951–52).

22 Lesley Dean-Jones, *Women's Bodies in Classical Greek Science* (Oxford: Oxford University Press, 1994), p. 56.

23 For the use of different treatments, see Heinrich von Staden, 'Women and Dirt', *Helios* 19 (1992), pp. 7–30.

24 Helen King, 'Once Upon a Text: Hysteria from Hippocrates', in *Hippocrates' Woman: Reading the Female Body in Ancient Greece* (London: Routledge, 1998), pp. 205–46.

25 Lesley Dean-Jones, 'The Politics of Pleasure: Female Sexual Appetite in the Hippocratic Corpus', *Helios* 19 (1992), pp. 72–91, at p. 76.

26 Roger Just, 'Freedom, Slavery, and the Female Psyche', *History of Political Thought* 6 (1985), pp. 169–88, at p. 181.

27 Michel Foucault, *The History of Sexuality*, vol. 2: *The Use of Pleasure*. Trans. Robert Hurley (New York: Pantheon, 1985) and *The History of Sexuality*, vol. 3: *The Care of the Self*. Trans. Robert Hurley (New York: Pantheon, 1986).

28 Laqueur, *Making Sex*, p. 35.

29 Joan Cadden, *Meanings of Sex Difference in the Middle Ages: Medicine, Science, and Culture* (Cambridge: Cambridge University Press, 1993), p. 108; Katharine Park, 'Cadden, Laqueur, and the "One-Sex Body"', *Medieval Feminist Forum* 46 (2010), pp. 96–100. Available at: http://nrs.harvard.edu/urn-3:HUL.InstRepos:4774909 (accessed 26–08–2011). For some sixteenth-century objections to the one-sex model, see Schleiner, 'Early Modern Controversies'.

30 Park, 'Cadden, Laqueur, and the "One-Sex Body"', p. 100 [5].

31 Rebecca Flemming, *Medicine and the Making of Roman Women: Gender, Nature and Authority from Celsus to Galen* (Oxford: Oxford University Press, 2005), pp. 325–6.

32 Heinrich von Staden, '*Apud nos foediora verba*: Celsus' Reluctant Construction of the Female Body', in Guy Sabbah (ed.), *Le latin médical: la constitution d'un langage scientifique* (Saint-Étienne: Université de Saint-Étienne, 1991), pp. 271–96, at p. 296.

33 Laqueur, *Making Sex*, p. 28.

34 Cited in Katharine Park and Robert A. Nye, 'Destiny is Anatomy', *The New Republic*, 18 Feb. 1991, pp. 53–7, at p. 54. See further, on Aristotle as an advocate of strict sexual dimorphism in the early modern period, Katharine Park, 'The Rediscovery of the Clitoris: French Medicine and the Tribade, 1570–1620', in David Hillman and Carla Mazzio (eds.), *The Body in Parts: Fantasies of Corporeality in Early Modern Europe* (London: Routledge, 1996), pp. 171–93, at pp. 180–2.

35 Marguerite Deslauriers, 'Sex and Essence in Aristotle's Metaphysics and Biology', in Cynthia A. Freeland (ed.), *Feminist Interpretations of Aristotle* (University Park, Pa.: Pennsylvania State University Press, 1998), pp. 138–67.

36 Some ancient sources do recognise female-to-male transformations: see, for example, Diodorus Siculus 32.11; Livy 24.10; Pliny, *Natural History* 7.4.36. By contrast, male-to-female transformation is never presented as a real-life phenomenon (although it does occur in myth, as in the story of Tiresias, who goes from male to female and back again; see also the story of Hermaphroditus in the next chapter).

37 For this argument, see Johannes Morsink, 'Was Aristotle's Biology Sexist?' *Journal of the History of Biology* 12 (1979), pp. 83–112, at pp. 98–100; Robert Mayhew, *The Female in Aristotle's Biology: Reason or Rationalization* (Chicago: University of Chicago Press, 2004), pp. 39–41.

38 Deslauriers, 'Sex and Essence', p. 157.

39 Laqueur, *Making Sex*, p. 29.

40 Donna Haraway, '"Gender" for a Marxist Dictionary: The Sexual Politics of a Word', in *Simians, Cyborgs, and Women: The Reinvention of Nature* (New York: Routledge, 1991), pp. 127–48, at p. 134.

41 See, for example, Moira Gatens, 'A Critique of the Sex/Gender Distinction', in Judith Allen and Paul Patton (eds.), *Beyond Marxism?: Interventions After Marx* (Leichhardt: Intervention, 1983), pp. 143–60.

42 L. J. Jordanova, 'Natural Facts: A Historical Perspective on Science and Sexuality', in Carol P. MacCormack and Marilyn Strathern (eds.), *Nature, Culture and Gender* (Cambridge: Cambridge University Press, 1980), pp. 42–69.

43 Londa L. Schiebinger, *The Mind Has No Sex?: Women in the Origins of Modern Science* (Cambridge, Mass.: Harvard University Press, 1989), esp. ch. 6–8.

44 See, for example, Michael Stolberg, 'A Woman Down to Her Bones: The Anatomy of Sexual Difference in the Sixteenth and Early Seventeenth Centuries', *Isis* 94 (2003), pp. 274–99. Both Laqueur and Schiebinger defend their positions in 'Sex in the Flesh', *Isis* 94 (2003), pp. 300–306, and 'Skelettestreit', *Isis* 94 (2003), pp. 307–13, respectively.

45 Rebecca M. Jordan-Young, *Brain Storm: The Flaws in the Science of Sex Differences* (Cambridge, Mass.: Harvard University Press, 2010).

46 Anne Fausto-Sterling, *Myths of Gender: Biological Theories about Women and Men*, rev. ed. (New York: Basic Books, 1992); *Sexing the Body: Gender Politics and the Construction of Sexuality* (New York: Basic Books, 2000).

47 Anne Fausto-Sterling, 'The Five Sexes: Why Male and Female Are Not Enough', *The Sciences* 33 (1993), pp. 20–5, at p. 21.

48 Flemming, *Medicine and the Making of Roman Women*, p. 14.

49 Laqueur, *Making Sex*, p. 28.

50 Jean-Pierre Vernant, 'Hestia–Hermes: The Religious Expression of Space and Movement in Ancient Greece', in *Myth and Thought Among the Greeks*. Trans. Janet Lloyd (New York: Zone, 2006), pp. 157–96, at p. 165.

51 Page duBois, *Sowing the Body: Psychoanalysis and Ancient Representations of Women* (Chicago: University of Chicago Press, 1988).

52 Luce Irigaray, *Speculum of the Other Woman*. Trans. Gillian C. Gill (Ithaca: Cornell University Press, 1985), p. 345 (emphasis original).

53 Luce Irigaray, 'The Return', in Elena Tzelepis and Athena Athanasiou (eds.), *Rewriting Difference: Luce Irigaray and 'The Greeks'* (Albany: State University of New York Press, 2010), pp. 259–72, at p. 262. The paper was first published in Luce Irigaray and Mary Green (eds.), *Luce Irigaray: Teaching* (London: Continuum, 2008), pp. 219–30.

54 Miriam Leonard, 'Irigaray's Cave: Feminist Theory and the Politics of French Classicism', *Ramus* 28 (1999), pp. 152–68, at p. 159.

55 Irigaray, *Speculum*, p. 298.

56 Ibid., p. 161.
57 Ibid., p. 162.
58 Ibid.
59 David M. Halperin, 'Why is Diotima a Woman?', in *One Hundred Years of Homosexuality: And Other Essays on Greek Love* (London: Routledge, 1990), pp. 113–51, at p. 144. See also Gilhuly, *The Feminine Matrix*, pp. 58–97. Irigaray herself offers a rather different reading of the dialogue: 'Sorcerer Love: A Reading of Plato, *Symposium*, Diotima's Speech', in *An Ethics of Sexual Difference*. Trans. Carolyn Burke and Gillian C. Gill (Ithaca: Cornell University Press, 1993), pp. 20–33.
60 Irigaray, *Speculum*, p. 307.
61 Julia Kristeva, *Revolution in Poetic Language*. Trans. Margaret Waller (New York: Columbia University Press, 1984).
62 Butler, *Bodies that Matter*, p. 42.
63 Ibid., p. 54.
64 Judith Butler, *Gender Trouble: Feminism and the Subversion of Identity* (New York: Routledge, 1990), pp. 117–18.
65 Butler, *Bodies that Matter*, p. 28.
66 See esp. Monique Wittig, *The Straight Mind and Other Essays* (Boston: Beacon Press, 1992).
67 Butler, *Bodies that Matter*, p. 52.
68 Judith Butler, 'The Question of Social Transformation', in *Undoing Gender* (New York: Routledge, 2004), pp. 204–31, at p. 212.
69 Laqueur, *Making Sex*, p. 23.
70 Butler, *Gender Trouble*, p. 143.
71 For this tension, see Sandra Harding, 'The Instability of the Analytical Categories of Feminist Theory', *Signs* 11 (1986), pp. 645–64, and *The Science Question in Feminism* (Ithaca: Cornell University Press, 1986).
72 Karen Barad, 'Posthumanist Performativity: Toward an Understanding of How Matter Comes to Matter', *Signs* 28 (2003), pp. 801–31, at p. 809 (emphasis original). Barad is here speaking of the materiality of the body, but her argument extends to matter more generally understood. The second quote is from Elizabeth Grosz, *The Nick of Time: Politics, Evolution, and the Untimely* (Durham: Duke University Press, 2004), p. 4.
73 Gilles Deleuze, *The Logic of Sense*. Trans. Mark Lester (New York: Columbia University Press, 1990).
74 Michel Serres, *The Birth of Physics*. Trans. Jack Hawkes (Manchester: Clinamen Press, 2000).
75 Friedrich Nietzsche, *Untimely Meditations*. Trans. R. J. Hollingdale (Cambridge: Cambridge University Press, 1983), p. 60.

Chapter II

1 K. J. Dover, *Greek Homosexuality* (Cambridge, Mass.: Harvard University Press, 1978).

2 David M. Halperin, *How to Do the History of Homosexuality* (Chicago: University of Chicago Press, 2002), p. 135.

3 James Davidson, 'Dover, Foucault and Greek Homosexuality: Penetration and the Truth of Sex', *Past and Present* 170 (2001), pp. 3–51, at p. 6.

4 Ruth Mazo Karras, 'Active/Passive, Acts/Passions: Greek and Roman Sexualities', *American Historical Review* 105 (2000), pp. 1250–65, at p. 1250.

5 Marilyn B. Skinner, 'Zeus and Leda: The Sexuality Wars in Contemporary Classical Scholarship', *Thamyris* 3 (1996), pp. 103–23.

6 Eve Kosofsky Sedgwick, *Epistemology of the Closet* (Berkeley: University of California Press, 1990), p. 30. The importance of not conflating gender and sexuality has also been stressed by Gayle Rubin, 'Thinking Sex: Notes for a Radical Theory of the Politics of Sexuality', in Carole S. Vance (ed.), *Pleasure and Danger: Exploring Female Sexuality* (Boston: Routledge and Keel, 1984), pp. 267–319, esp. pp. 308–9.

7 Michel Foucault, *Discipline and Punish: The Birth of the Prison*. Trans. Alan Sheridan (New York: Pantheon, 1977), p. 31.

8 Foucault, *The History of Sexuality*, vol. 1: *An Introduction*. Trans. R. Hurley (New York: Pantheon, 1978), p. 103.

9 Michel Foucault, 'The Confession of the Flesh', in Colin Gordon (ed.), *Power/Knowledge: Selected Interviews and Other Writings 1972–1977* (New York: Pantheon, 1980), pp. 194–228, at p. 194.

10 Foucault, *The History of Sexuality*, vol. 1, p. 8.

11 Ibid., p. 154.

12 Ibid., p. 157.

13 Ibid., p. 43.

14 Pierre Hadot, *Philosophy as a Way of Life: Spiritual Exercises from Socrates to Foucault*. Trans. M. Chase (Cambridge, Mass.: Harvard University Press, 1995).

15 Foucault, *The History of Sexuality*, vol. 2, pp. 10–11.

16 Michel Foucault, 'The Ethics of the Concern of the Self as a Practice of Freedom', in Paul Rabinow (ed.), *The Essential Works of Foucault 1954–1984*, vol. 1: *Ethics: Subjectivity and Truth* (New York: The New Press, 1997), pp. 281–301 at pp. 294–5.

17 Sedgwick, *Epistemology of the Closet*, p. 48. Halperin thoughtfully responds to Sedgwick's arguments in Halperin, *How to Do the History*, pp. 10–13, pp. 109–10.

18 Bruce Thornton, 'Constructionism and Ancient Greek Sex', *Helios* 18 (1991), pp. 181–93, and 'Idolon Theatri: Foucault and the Classicists', *Classical and Modern Literature* 12 (1991), pp. 81–100.

19 John Boswell, 'Concepts, Experience and Sexuality', *differences* 2 (1990), pp. 67–87, at p. 70.

20 David M. Halperin, John J. Winkler and Froma I. Zeitlin (eds.), *Before Sexuality: The Construction of Erotic Experience in the Ancient Greek World* (Princeton: Princeton University Press, 1990). The editors leave open both the strong version of the title, where 'sexuality' refers to Foucault's modern invention, and the weak version, according to which sexuality in the loose sense of 'the interpretation of the human body's erogenous zones and sexual capacities' is culturally determined (p. 3).

21 John J. Winkler, *The Constraints of Desire: The Anthropology of Sex and Gender in Ancient Greece* (New York: Routledge, 1990), pp. 45–6.

22 Halperin, *How to Do the History of Homosexuality*, 35.

23 Maud Gleason, 'The Semiotics of Gender: Physiognomy and Self-Fashioning in the Second Century CE', in Halperin, Winkler and Zeitlin, *Before Sexuality*, pp. 389–415, at p. 411.

24 Halperin, *One Hundred Years of Homosexuality*, p. 27 (emphasis original).

25 Halperin, *How to Do the History*, p. 99.

26 Holt N. Parker, 'The Myth of the Heterosexual: Anthropology and Sexuality for Classicists', *Arethusa* 34 (2001), pp. 313–62, at pp. 323–4.

27 Craig Williams, *Roman Homosexuality*, rev. ed. (New York: Oxford University Press, 2010), p. 232.

28 Ibid., p. 239.

29 James Davidson, *The Greeks and Greek Love: A Radical Reappraisal of Homosexuality in Ancient Greece* (London: Weidenfeld and Nicolson, 2007).

30 Davidson, 'Dover, Foucault and Greek Homosexuality', pp. 22–8.

31 Ibid., p. 49.

32 Rebecca Langlands, *Sexual Morality in Ancient Rome* (Cambridge: Cambridge University Press, 2006); Williams, *Roman Homosexuality*, pp. 259–61.

33 See Amy Richlin, *The Garden of Priapus: Sexuality and Aggression in Roman Humor* (New Haven: Yale University Press, 1983; rev. ed. Oxford: Oxford University Press, 1992); Williams, *Roman Homosexuality*, pp. 183–97; Jonathan Walters, 'Invading the Roman Body: Manliness and Impenetrability in Roman Thought', in Hallett and Skinner (eds.), *Roman Sexualities* (Princeton: Princeton University Press, 1997), pp. 29–43; Holt N. Parker, 'The Teratogenic Grid', in Hallett and Skinner, *Roman Sexualities*, pp. 47–65; David Fredrick, 'Mapping Penetrability in Late Republican and Early Imperial Rome', in David Fredrick (ed.), *The Roman Gaze: Vision, Power, and the Body* (Baltimore: The Johns Hopkins University Press, 2002), pp. 236–64.

34 For Athenian evidence on taking the 'female' role, see David Cohen, 'Law, Society and Homosexuality in Classical Athens', *Past and Present* 117 (1987), pp. 3–21.

35 Giulia Sissa, *Sex and Sensuality in the Ancient World*. Trans. George Staunton (New Haven: Yale University Press, 2008).

36 Froma I. Zeitlin, 'Reflections on Erotic Desire in Archaic and Classical Greece', in James I. Porter (ed.), *Constructions of the Classical Body* (Ann Arbor: University of Michigan Press, 1999), pp. 50–76, at p. 50.

37 Lin Foxhall, 'Pandora Unbound: A Feminist Critique of Foucault's *History of Sexuality*', in David H. J. Larmour, Paul Allen Miller and Charles Platter (eds.), *Rethinking Sexuality: Foucault and Classical Antiquity* (Princeton: Princeton University Press, 1998), pp. 122–37, at p. 123.

38 Richlin, *Garden of Priapus*, p. xvi.

39 Ibid., p. xiv. See also Amy Richlin, 'Zeus and Metis: Foucault, Feminism, Classics', *Helios* 18 (1991), pp. 160–80.

40 Foxhall, 'Pandora Unbound'.

41 Ellen Greene, 'Sappho, Foucault, and Women's Erotics', *Arethusa* 29 (1996), pp. 1–14. See also Page duBois, 'The Subject in Antiquity after Foucault', in

Larmour, Miller and Platter, *Rethinking Sexuality*, pp. 85–103.

42 Amy Richlin, 'Foucault's *History of Sexuality*: A Useful Theory for Women?', in Larmour, Miller and Platter, *Rethinking Sexuality*, pp. 138–70, at pp. 152–62.

43 Hélène Cixous, 'Sorties: Out and Out: Attacks/Ways Out/Forays', in Hélène Cixous and Catherine Clément, *The Newly Born Woman*. Trans. Betsy Wing (Minneapolis: University of Minnesota Press, 1986), pp. 63–132. On cross-gender identification, see Vanda Zajko, '"Who Are We When We Read?": Keats, Klein, Cixous, and Elizabeth Cook's *Achilles*', in Vanda Zajko and Miriam Leonard (eds.), *Laughing with Medusa: Classical Myth and Feminist Thought* (Oxford: Oxford University Press, 2006), pp. 45–66.

44 Jordan-Young, *Brain Storm*, pp. 109–43.

45 Amy Richlin, 'Not Before Homosexuality: The Materiality of the *Cinaedus* and the Roman Law Against Love Between Men', *Journal of the History of Sexuality* 3 (1993), pp. 523–73.

46 Ibid., p. 528.

47 Rabun Taylor, 'Two Pathic Subcultures in Ancient Rome', *Journal of the History of Sexuality* 7 (1997), pp. 319–71.

48 Ibid., p. 320.

49 Foucault, *The History of Sexuality*, vol. 2, p. 9.

50 Halperin, *How to Do the History*, p. 15.

51 Winkler, *Constraints of Desire*, p. 126.

52 Davidson, 'Dover, Foucault and Greek Homosexuality', p. 49.

53 *Bowers v. Hardwick* 478 US 191 (1986).

54 Ibid. 196. The language of 'ancient roots' is used by Justice White at *Bowers*, 192.

55 *Bowers v. Hardwick* 478 US 197 (1986).

56 *Lawrence v. Texas* 539 US (2003) No. 02–102 6.

57 Jeffrey S. Carnes, '"Certain Intimate Conduct": Classics, Constructionism, and the Courts', in *Gender and Diversity in Place: Proceedings of the Fourth Conference on Feminism and Classics*, available at: http://www.stoa.org/diotima/essays/fc04, 2004, np (accessed 03–07–2011).

58 John Finnis, 'Law, Morality, and "Sexual Orientation"', *Notre Dame Law Review* 69 (1994), pp. 1049–76; see esp. pp. 1058–61.

59 Daniel Mendelsohn, 'The Stand: Expert Witnesses and Ancient Mysteries in a Colorado Courtroom', *Lingua Franca* 6.6 (1996), pp. 34–46, at p. 46.

60 Skinner, 'Zeus and Leda', p. 107.

61 Winkler, *Constraints of Desire*, p. 50.

62 Williams, *Roman Homosexuality*, p. 156.

63 Richard Alston, 'Arms and the Man: Soldiers, Masculinity and Power in Republican and Imperial Rome', in Lin Foxhall and John Salmon (eds.), *When Men Were Men: Masculinity, Power and Identity in Classical Antiquity* (London: Routledge, 1998), pp. 205–23.

64 Nancy Worman, *Abusive Mouths in Classical Athens* (Cambridge: Cambridge University Press, 2008).

65 Anthony Corbeill, 'Dining Deviants in Roman Political Invective', in Hallett and Skinner, *Roman Sexualities*, pp. 99–128, at p. 112.

66 Cohen, *Law, Sexuality and Society*.

67 Gleason, 'The Semiotics of Gender'. See also Maud W. Gleason, *Making Men: Sophists and Self-Presentation in Ancient Rome* (Princeton: Princeton University Press, 1995).

68 Joy Connolly, *The State of Speech: Rhetoric and Political Thought in Ancient Rome* (Princeton: Princeton University Press, 2007), p. 111.

69 Ibid., p. 126.

70 Alison Keith, *Engendering Rome: Women in Latin Epic* (Cambridge: Cambridge University Press, 2000); Amy Richlin, 'Gender and Rhetoric: Producing Manhood in the Schools', in William J. Dominik (ed.), *Roman Eloquence: Rhetoric in Society and Literature* (London: Routledge, 1997), pp. 90–110.

71 Erik Gunderson, *Staging Masculinity: The Rhetoric of Performance in the Roman World* (Ann Arbor: University of Michigan Press, 2000), pp. 67–8.

72 Butler, *Gender Trouble*, p. 173 (emphasis original).

73 Ibid.

74 Gunderson, *Staging Masculinity*, p. 69.

75 Victoria Wohl, *Love Among the Ruins: The Erotics of Democracy in Classical Athens* (Princeton: Princeton University Press, 2002), pp. 20–3 on symptomatic reading.

76 Froma I. Zeitlin, 'Playing the Other: Theater, Theatricality, and the Feminine in Greek Drama', in *Playing the Other*, pp. 341–74.

77 Kathleen McCarthy, *Slaves, Masters, and the Art of Authority in Plautine Comedy* (Princeton: Princeton University Press, 2000).

78 Marilyn Skinner, '*Ego Mulier*: The Construction of Male Sexuality in Catullus', *Helios* 20 (1993), pp. 107–30, at p. 120.

Chapter III

1 J. J. Bachofen, *An English Translation of Bachofen's Mutterrecht: A Study of the Religious and Juridical Aspects of Gynecocracy in the Ancient World*. Trans. David Partenheimer (Lewiston, N.Y.: Edwin Mellen Press, 2003).

2 Luce Irigaray, 'Body against Body: In Relation to the Mother', in *Sexes and Genealogies*. Trans. Gillian C. Gill (New York: Columbia University Press, 1993), pp. 7–21, at p. 11.

3 Adriana Cavarero, *In Spite of Plato: A Feminist Rewriting of Ancient Philosophy*. Trans. Serena Anderlini-D'Onofrio and Áine O'Healy (New York: Routledge, 1995), pp. 4–5.

4 Joan Bamberger, 'The Myth of Matriarchy: Why Men Rule in Primitive Society', in Michelle Zimbalist Rosaldo and Louise Lamphere (eds.), *Women, Culture, and Society* (Stanford: Stanford University Press, 1974), pp. 263–80, at p. 267.

5 Froma I. Zeitlin, 'The Dynamics of Misogyny: Myth and Mythmaking in Aeschylus's *Oresteia*', in *Playing the Other*, pp. 87–119, at p. 90.

6 Ibid., p. 87.

7 Christa Wolf, *Cassandra: A Novel and Four Essays*. Trans. Jan van Heurck

(New York: Farrar, Straus, Giroux, 1984), first published in German as *Kassandra: Erzählung* (Darmstadt: Luchterhand, 1983); Elizabeth Cook, 'Iphigeneia's Wedding', in Zajko and Leonard, *Laughing with Medusa*, pp. 399–410.

8 Vanda Zajko and Miriam Leonard, 'Introduction', in Zajko and Leonard, *Laughing with Medusa*, pp. 1–17, at pp. 2–3.

9 Lillian Doherty, 'Putting the Women Back into the Hesiodic *Catalogue of Women*', in Zajko and Leonard, *Laughing with Medusa*, pp. 297–325, at p. 300.

10 Hélène Cixous, 'The Laugh of the Medusa', trans. Keith Cohen and Paula Cohen, *Signs* 1 (1976), pp. 875–93, at p. 885.

11 Adrienne Rich, 'When We Dead Awaken: Writing as Re-Vision', *College English* 34 (1972), pp. 18–30, at p. 18.

12 Luce Irigaray, 'The Forgotten Mystery of Female Ancestry', in *Thinking the Difference: For a Peaceful Revolution*. Trans. Karin Montin (New York: Routledge, 1994), pp. 91–113, at p. 100. Originally published as *Le temps de la différence: pour une révolution pacifique* (Paris: Librairie générale française, 1989).

13 Cook, 'Iphigeneia's Wedding', pp. 409–10.

14 Marilyn B. Arthur [later, Katz], 'Politics and Pomegranates: An Interpretation of the Homeric *Hymn to Demeter*', *Arethusa* 10 (1977), pp. 7–47, at p. 8. The essay was republished with a new preface in Helene P. Foley, *The Homeric Hymn to Demeter* (Princeton: Princeton University Press, 1994), pp. 214–42.

15 Arthur, 'Politics and Pomegranates', p. 8.

16 Ibid.

17 Ibid., pp. 30–1.

18 Helene P. Foley, 'Interpretive Essay on the Homeric *Hymn to Demeter*', in *The Homeric Hymn to Demeter*, pp. 77–177, esp. pp. 118–36.

19 Ibid., p. 133.

20 Marianne Hirsch, *The Mother/Daughter Plot: Narratives, Psychoanalysis, Feminism* (Bloomington: Indiana University Press, 1989), pp. 35–6.

21 Andrew Radford, *The Lost Girls: Demeter–Persephone and the Literary Imagination, 1850–1930* (Amsterdam: Rodopi, 2007), p. 27.

22 H. D., *Red Roses for Bronze* (London: Chatto & Windus, 1931).

23 Luisa Muraro, 'Female Genealogies', in Carolyn Burke, Naomi Schor and Margaret Whitford (eds.), *Engaging with Irigaray* (New York: Columbia University Press, 1994), pp. 317–33, at p. 331.

24 Irigaray, 'Body Against Body', p. 19.

25 Luce Irigaray, *Marine Lover of Friedrich Nietzsche*. Trans. Gillian C. Gill (New York: Columbia University Press, 1991), p. 115. Originally published as *Amante marine: de Friedrich Nietzsche* (Paris: Éditions de minuit, 1980).

26 Irigaray, 'The Forgotten Mystery', p. 109.

27 Ibid. (emphasis added).

28 Ibid., p. 110.

29 Cavarero, *In Spite of Plato*, p. 67.

30 Ibid., p. 80.

31 Lynn Meskell, 'Goddesses, Gimbutas and "New Age" Archaeology', *Antiquity* 69 (1995), pp. 74–86.

32 Lynn Meskell, 'Feminism, Paganism, Pluralism', in Amy Gazin-Schwartz and Cornelius Holtorf (eds.), *Archaeology and Folklore* (London: Routledge, 1999), pp. 83–9, at p. 85.

33 Lynn Meskell, 'Denaturalizing Gender in Prehistory', in Susan McKinnon and Sydel Silverman (eds.), *Complexities: Beyond Nature and Nurture* (Chicago: University of Chicago Press, 2005), pp. 157–75, at pp. 168–71.

34 Ibid., p. 162.

35 Angela Carter, quoted in Vanda Zajko, 'Women and Greek Myth', in Roger D. Woodard (ed.), *The Cambridge Companion to Greek Mythology* (Cambridge: Cambridge University Press, 2007), pp. 387–406, at p. 403.

36 Joyce, *Ancient Bodies, Ancient Lives*, p. 130.

37 Margaret Atwood, *The Penelopiad: The Myth of Penelope and Odysseus* (New York: Canongate, 2005), p. 165; Mary Beard, 'A New Spin on Homer', *The Guardian*, Saturday 29 October 2005, available at: http://www.guardian.co.uk/books/2005/oct/29/highereducation.classics (accessed 29–06–2011).

38 Eleni Varikas, 'Who Cares about the Greeks?: Uses and Misuses of Tradition in the Articulation of Difference and Plurality', in Athanasiou and Tzelepis, *Rewriting Difference*, pp. 231–46, at p. 239.

39 Tina Chanter, *Ethics of Eros: Irigaray's Rewriting of the Philosophers* (New York: Routledge, 1995), p. 126. See also Chanter's more recent essay 'Irigaray's Challenge to the Fetishistic Hegemony of the Platonic One and Many', in Athanasiou and Tzelepis, *Rewriting Difference*, pp. 217–29.

40 Maternal thinking: Jean Bethke Elshtain, 'Antigone's Daughters: Reflections on Female Identity and the State', *Democracy* 2 (1982), pp. 46–59. Reprinted in slightly revised form in Irene Diamond (ed.), *Families, Politics, and Public Policy: A Feminist Dialogue on Women and the State* (New York: Longman, 1983), pp. 300–311. Citations are from the reprint. Matrixial space: Bracha L. Ettinger, 'Antigone with(out) Jocaste', in S. E. Wilmer and Audronė Žukauskaitė (eds.), *Interrogating Antigone in Postmodern Philosophy and Criticism* (New York: Oxford University Press, 2010), pp. 212–28.

41 G. W. F. Hegel, *Aesthetics: Lectures on Fine Art*. Trans. T. M. Knox (Oxford: Clarendon Press, 1975), p. 464, p. 1218; *Lectures on the History of Philosophy*. Trans. E. S. Haldane (London: Kegan Paul, 1892), I.441.

42 George Steiner, *Antigones: How the Antigone Legend Has Endured in Western Literature, Art and Thought* (Oxford: Oxford University Press, 1986), p. 18.

43 Miriam Leonard, *Athens in Paris: Ancient Greece and the Political in Post-War French Thought* (Oxford: Oxford University Press, 2005), p. 148.

44 G. W. F. Hegel, *The Phenomenology of Mind*. Trans. Sir James Black Baillie, 2nd rev. ed. (New York: Macmillan, 1931), p. 257 (emphasis original).

45 Seyla Benhabib, *Situating the Self: Gender, Community and Postmodernism in Contemporary Ethics* (Cambridge: Polity Press, 1992), p. 247.

46 Hegel, *Phenomenology of Mind*, p. 262.

47 Ibid.

48 Ibid., p. 264.

50 Ibid.
51 Patricia J. Mills, 'Hegel's *Antigone*', *Owl of Minerva* 17 (1986), pp. 131–52, at p. 137.
52 Ibid., p. 141.
53 Ibid., pp. 146–7.
54 Jacques Lacan, *The Seminar of Jacques Lacan*, Vol. 7: *The Ethics of Psychoanalysis*. Trans. Dennis Porter (New York: W. W. Norton, 1992), pp. 243–87, at p. 249.
55 Ibid., p. 284.
56 Ibid., p. 247.
57 Ibid., pp. 278–9.
58 Ibid., p. 279.
59 Ibid.
60 Ibid., p. 283.
61 Slavoj Žižek, 'From Antigone to Joan of Arc', *Helios* 31 (2004), pp. 51–62, at p. 55.
62 Cecelia Sjöholm, *The Antigone Complex: Ethics and the Invention of Feminine Desire* (Stanford: Stanford University Press, 2004), pp. 107–8.
63 Ibid., pp. xiii-xiv.
64 Irigaray, *Speculum*, p. 225.
65 Ibid., pp. 217, 221.
66 Ibid., p. 223 (emphasis original).
67 Luce Irigaray, 'Between Myth and History: The Tragedy of Antigone', in Wilmer and Žukauskaitė, *Interrogating Antigone*, pp. 197–211, at p. 210.
68 Luce Irigaray, 'Civil Rights and Responsibilities for the Two Sexes', in *Thinking the Difference*, pp. 67–8. But Irigaray's relationship to Antigone is complex. She has also cast her as the 'anti-woman', who serves the state, trying to atone for the crimes of her brothers and to erase the stain of maternal filiation: see 'The Female Gender', in *Sexes and Genealogies*, pp. 110–11; *Ethics of Sexual Difference*, pp. 118–19.
69 Irigaray, 'Between Myth and History', p. 205.
70 Mills, 'Hegel's *Antigone*', p. 152.
71 Elshtain, 'Antigone's Daughters', p. 307.
72 Ibid.
73 Sara Ruddick, 'Maternal Thinking', in *Feminist Studies* 6 (1980), pp. 342–67, and *Maternal Thinking: Toward a Politics of Peace* (Boston: Beacon Press, 1989; reprinted 1995 with a new preface).
74 Mary G. Dietz, 'Citizenship with a Feminist Face: The Problem with Maternal Thinking', *Political Theory* 13 (1985), pp. 19–37, at p. 20.
75 Ibid., p. 29.
76 Jan Hartman, 'Cindy Sheehan: American Antigone', *CommonDreams.org*, 18 August 2005. Available at: http://www.commondreams.org/views05/0818-21.htm (accessed 10–08–2011).
77 Judith Butler, *Antigone's Claim: Kinship between Life and Death* (New York: Columbia University Press, 2000), p. 2.
78 Ibid., pp. 73–4.

79 Ibid., p. 72.
80 Ibid., p. 2 (emphasis original).
81 Ibid., p. 6.
82 Ibid., p. 65.
83 Ibid., p. 82.
84 These readings form the core of Honig's book *Antigone, Interrupted*, forthcoming from Cambridge University Press.
85 Bonnie Honig, 'Ismene's Forced Choice: Sacrifice and Sorority in Sophocles' *Antigone*', *Arethusa* 44 (2011), pp. 29–68, at pp. 62–4. For a different reading of Ismene, see Simon Goldhill, 'Antigone and the Politics of Sisterhood', in Zajko and Leonard, *Laughing with Medusa*, pp. 141–62.
86 Bonnie Honig, 'Antigone's Two Laws: Greek Tragedy and the Politics of Humanism', *New Literary History* 41 (2010), pp. 1–33. See also Bonnie Honig, 'Antigone's Laments, Creon's Grief: Mourning, Membership, and the Politics of Exception', *Political Theory* 37 (2009), pp. 5–43.
87 Honig, 'Antigone's Two Laws', p. 22.
88 See Mary Beth Mader, 'Antigone's Line', *Bulletin de la Société Américaine de Philosophie de Langue Française* 15 (2005), pp. 18–40, and 'Antigone and the Ethics of Kinship', in Tzelepis and Athanasiou, *Rewriting Difference*, pp. 93–104.
89 Tina Chanter, 'Antigone's Political Legacies: Abjection in Defiance of Mourning', in Wilmer and Žukauskaitė, *Interrogating Antigone*, pp. 19–47, at p. 45.
90 Ibid., p. 24.
91 Ibid., p. 45.
92 Peter Burian, 'Gender and the City: *Antigone* from Hegel to Butler and Back', in Karen Bassi and J. Peter Euben (eds.), *When Worlds Elide: Classics, Politics, Culture* (Lanham, Md.: Lexington Books, 2010), pp. 255–99, at p. 285.
93 Cynthia Eller, *The Myth of Matriarchal Prehistory: Why an Invented Past Won't Give Women a Future* (Boston: Beacon Press, 2000), p. 18.
94 Vanda Zajko, '"What Difference Was Made?": Feminist Models of Reception', in Lorna Hardwick and Christopher Stray (eds.), *A Companion to Classical Receptions* (Malden, Mass.: Blackwell, 2008), pp. 195–206, at p. 201.
95 Catherine A. Holland, 'After Antigone: Women, the Past, and the Future of Feminist Political Thought', *American Journal of Political Science* 42 (1998), pp. 1108–32, at p. 1115.
96 Mark Griffith, 'The Subject of Desire in Sophocles' *Antigone*', in Victoria Pedrick and Steven M. Oberhelman (eds.), *The Soul of Tragedy: Essays on Athenian Drama* (Chicago: University of Chicago, 2005), pp. 91–135. Revised and abridged version published as 'Psychoanalysing *Antigone*' in Wilmer and Žukauskaitė, *Interrogating Antigone*, pp. 110–34.

INDEX